TALES OF FORGOTTEN CHICAGO

RICHARD C. LINDBERG

TALES OF FORGOTTEN CHICAGO

Southern Illinois University Press

CARBONDALE

Southern Illinois University Press
www.siupress.com

23 22 21 20   4 3 2 1

Cover illustration: "Wabash Ave. [Avenue], Chicago, Ill.," (Detroit Publishing
Co., 1907; cropped and tinted). PRINTS AND PHOTOGRAPHS DIVISION,
LIBRARY OF CONGRESS ONLINE CATALOG.

Library of Congress Cataloging-in-Publication Data
Names: Lindberg, Richard, 1953– author.
Title: Tales of forgotten Chicago / Richard C. Lindberg.
Description: Carbondale : Southern Illinois University Press, [2020] |
    Includes bibliographical references and index. | Summary: "This
    entertaining collection of twenty-one stories of people and places in
    Chicago, from roughly the time of the Civil War to the1960s, is a potpourri
    of personalities, human foibles, heartbreak, and triumph." — Provided by
    publisher.
Identifiers: LCCN 2019047299 (print) | LCCN 2019047300 (ebook) |
    ISBN 9780809337811 (paperback) | ISBN 9780809337828 (ebook)
Subjects: LCSH: Chicago (Ill.)—History—1875- —Anecdotes. | Chicago
    (Ill.)—Biography—Anecdotes.
Classification: LCC F548.36 .L56 2020 (print) | LCC F548.36 (ebook) |
    DDC 977.3/11—dc23
LC record available at https://lccn.loc.gov/2019047299
LC ebook record available at https://lccn.loc.gov/2019047300

Printed on recycled paper ♻

This paper meets the requirements of ANSI/NISO Z39.48-1992 (Permanence
of Paper). ♾

I dedicate this book to my lifelong friend Jim Pistorio,
without whose kindness, support, and generosity of spirit
dating back to my earliest remembrance of our Northwest
Side Chicago childhoods, I would be truly lost.

CONTENTS

CONTENTS

Galleries of illustrations beginning on pages 83 and 151

TALES OF FORGOTTEN CHICAGO

TWENTY-ONE TALES
OF OLD CHICAGO

A city, in order for it to attain rightful grandeur among the capitals of the world, must first have a good story to tell. In its frantic pace to evolve from a desolate, marshy frontier town anchored by the wooden palisades of a military fort into a global rendezvous for international business, commerce, and the arts, Chicago has passed through many phases.

Echoing the words of Richard Wright who reminds us that "Chicago, it seems, has a way of leaving its imprint upon those who live in it," the city has inspired its historians, chroniclers, and storytellers to pass down, from one generation to the next, in an affectionate manner of course, its fondest memories, saddest tales, ironic anecdotes, and keenest observations of people, places, and things that have gone before.[1]

Chicago, a city bathed in shadows and light. Chicago—the glistening jewel of the American heartland. Chicago, always notorious, lusty—a gawky, overgrown adolescent city in its most formative years—today, an international city and a hub for global business. Visit Chicago and see the world as it so often has been said. It still holds true.

Chicago always shall remain a city of imagination, a city of high hopes, and a refuge and sanctuary from the storm of life for the displaced, the poor, and the tired masses, and regrettably for some, a city of heartbreak.

Presented in this volume are twenty-one tales drawn from the divergent worlds of politics, show business, invention and innovation, sports, and crime and punishment, with an ensemble cast of quintessential Chicago characters—famous and forgotten dreamers, society mavens, inventors, planners, politicians, schemers, actors and actresses, idealists, visionaries, philanthropists, social engineers, crooks, cons, gamblers, and work-a-day people, spanning the midpoint of the nineteenth century up through the second half of the twentieth.

Within the broader framework of familiar historical currents such as the Great Chicago Fire and the saga of the sprawling Union Stockyards, the reader will find lesser known vignettes from the lost corners of Chicago. For example, who *really* started the Chicago Fire? I think I have come up with the answer and it's *not* who you might think.

John Wilkes Booth spent some time in Chicago. So did Cardinal Mundelein, Lar Daly, Al Capone, Jane Addams, and history's bypassed young genius who invented the telephone. And his name is *not* Alexander Graham Bell.

I have deliberately left out Mr. Capone and Ms. Addams with all due respect to the latter, because their stories have been told and retold in countless books, articles, and electronic media. By design, I have chosen to sidestep the 1893 World's Fair in favor of the 1948–1949 Railroad Fair, because, after all, what more can possibly be said about Chicago's great "coming out party," the grand pageant of illumination and invention marking the earliest stirrings of globalization for Chicago. Yes, it is true that an inspired, awestruck L. Frank Baum fashioned the *Wizard of Oz* and his fabled, romanticized Emerald City from the spectacle of the White City in Jackson Park.

I submit, however, that the spirit of any great city is best captured not by a handful of isolated historical events, but rather through collective storytelling about its people. I therefore present in twenty-one chapters, Chicago—in the estimation of many, the most American of all American cities—in all its unvarnished glory.

THE BROTHERS BOOTH

oreshadowing the darkest tragedy in American history, a brilliant and greatly admired young thespian from a proud theatrical family graced the stage of McVicker's Theater in two lengthy, sold-out engagements with a resident stock company in January and June of 1862.

James McVicker, a man of sunny disposition, formed a strong bond with this young actor, a man remembered by the *Baltimore Sun* as "standing five-feet-ten inches in height and possessing a good figure, well-cut features, black waving hair and eyes large, dark and expressive with a peculiar ring about them which distinguished him from others . . . easily recognizable, and his manners easy and polished."[1]

McVicker's playhouse, opened November 3, 1857, on Madison Street between State and Dearborn adjoining the Chicago Tribune Building at a cost of $85,000. It had a seating capacity of twenty-five hundred and earned plaudits as one of the nation's premier theatrical venues. "For the first time since Chicago took rank as one of the great cities in the Union. She has a theater worthy of the hundreds of citizens who patronize the drama," the *Tribune* enthusiastically reported.[2]

The owner of the theater promised a first-class theatrical experience and regular appearances by the leading lights of the stage. On opening night, after a rendition of the "Star Spangled Banner," James McVicker and actress Alice Adams stood before the sold-out house to welcome patrons to a performance of *Rough Diamond* and *The Honeymoon*. Of these performances, the *Tribune* was not kind. "Of the performance itself we shall attempt no criticism. Most of the company are strangers to each other, and it would be unfair to judge them by a first performance which would readily embarrass any performer."[3]

To open this capacious palace of the arts required tremendous personal sacrifice, the expenditure of money he did not have in the bank, and a fearful debt load McVicker would be forced to carry. Other men might have shied away from the risky venture, but McVicker (a former journeyman printer who appeared on the stage for the first time in New Orleans in 1840 making his bones as a song and dance man before making his Chicago stage debut in *My Neighbor's Wife* at the Rice Theater, on May 4, 1848) believed that Chicago would support a first-class theater. The theater was never free from debt, however, and the Panic of 1857 and the hard times that followed resulted in foreclosure. The new owners of the theater did not know what to do with the building; they were not stage people and conceded as much by selling it back to McVicker not long after they had bought it on "the most liberal of terms."

As both theater proprietor and actor who took his place on the stage alongside members of the stock companies he personally hired, McVicker worked hard to retire his financial obligations and was able to do so by 1862. The owner introduced his twelve-year-old stepdaughter, Mary Runnion McVicker, to the stage in 1859, where she performed an aria from *Rigoletto* in the original Italian. The girl was an immediate sensation and McVicker permitted her to appear at the Boston Museum (theater) and in other large cities in the East, playing Little Eva in *Uncle Tom's Cabin* and in original plays written for her by the duo of Solomon Wilson and John Brougham.

In June 1867, twenty-year-old Mary played Juliet opposite the great Shakespeare tragedian Edwin Booth appearing as Romeo at her father's theater. A successful twelve-week run at Booth's theater in New York City followed in February 1869, and a romance quickly bloomed between the veteran actor and McVicker's daughter.

Booth, a widower prone to fits of depression and recurring bouts of alcoholism, wed Mary on June 7 at her father's second home in Long Branch, a New Jersey beachside town. Mary's flourishing career on the stage came to a sudden halt as she willingly surrendered fame for the routines of domestic life and the joys of anticipated motherhood. However, their baby lived only a few hours, lending credence to the growing suspicion that the Booth siblings had been born under a dark star.

After the death of her infant son, Mary's physical and mental health began to fail. In 1880, Edwin Booth sent his wife abroad to regain her strength in a sea voyage and a more favorable climate, but the rest cure failed. James McVicker brought his frail and sickly daughter back home but her condition only worsened and the thirty-two-year-old Mary expired at her parents' home on West 53rd Street in New York City on November 13, 1881—Edwin Booth's birthday.

Mary's body was brought back to Chicago for funeral services and internment in Rosehill Cemetery. The Reverend David Swing eulogized the deceased as a woman of noble calling before a large assembly of Chicago elites at St. Paul's Universalist Church on Michigan Avenue. "When Mrs. Edwin Booth was known to us as Mary McVicker she was an embodiment of mental acuteness and taste and vivacity. As a child she appeared upon the stage in some light pieces and this task and the excitement of the drama hurried her mind onward and intensified her natural forces and perhaps had kindled that zeal which too soon consumed the body. The harp became broken by its own music."[4]

The sorrowful James McVicker never recovered from his loss, a loss compounded by estrangement from his son-in-law Edwin, the gifted tragedian of a cursed family beset by alcoholism, the stormy and erratic behavior of the family patriarch Junius Brutus Booth Sr. who had abandoned his first wife, and the unmitigated horror inflicted upon the United States by Junius's third son John Wilkes Booth, stage player, Confederate sympathizer, and presidential assassin.[5]

The actor with the "well-cut features, black waving hair and eyes large, dark and expressive," made the first of his two Chicago appearances on Monday, January 20, 1862, commencing a two-week engagement at McVicker's, where he accepted an invitation to portray Richard III before one of the largest and most receptive audiences of the season. Desperately wanting to escape the shadow of both his father and brother to achieve acclaim on his own merit, Wilkes Booth at times performed like a man possessed.

"John Wilkes Booth gave promise of being the greatest of all those men of genius, even greater than his wonderful brother Edwin," declared former dramatist John Marion Barron in a published 1899 interview. "He would have been canonized in American dramatic history. All the faults of an erratic nature would have been lost in the blaze of glory created by his wonderful and magnetic genius. I realized that if he died a month before that cruel act of April 14, 1865, his name would be associated with all the leading stars of a most brilliant galaxy of stars than whom none more famous ever lived and dazzled America by their greatness."[6]

Wilkes Booth gained early notoriety during his theatrical apprenticeship in Southern theaters in the late antebellum period, the time when he sharpened his proslavery attitudes through the company he kept and a simmering resentment against fiery Northern abolitionists whom he viewed as oppressors seeking to destroy a culture and way of life he had come to deeply cherish and admire. He witnessed the execution of John Brown in Harpers Ferry with growing rage. The brazen raid on the arsenal by Brown and his men allayed whatever lingering respect and patriotic feeling he might have once held for the institutions of government above the Mason–Dixon line.

Yet, for all his angry denunciation of Northern politics, he refused to enlist in the rebel armies, asserting that he intended to honor the wishes of his sainted mother who pleaded with him to remain true to his professional calling and avoid the bloodshed of war.

Wilkes Booth, a son of Maryland, the border state torn in its loyalties between the Union and secession, found favor among Southern theatergoers, working with Southern actors, drinking in Southern saloons, and romancing a bevy of stock company actresses and fawning females who sought his company outside the stage door.

A ruggedly handsome man, Booth was a compulsive seducer cohabiting with prostitutes and young women of social status during his brief years of success, showering them with sentimental verse, expensive jewelry, and tender missives. Here was a man more in love with *the idea* of love, who enjoyed the pursuit of romance and the thrill of the chase much more than the outcome, for he never married. The night after committing the murder that would make him infamous, his Washington, DC, mistress attempted suicide by inhaling fumes of chloroform. A physician revived the woman, and upon returning to consciousness she exclaimed, "Oh why did you not let me die?"[7]

Booth's attainment of national prominence coincided with his first theatrical engagement in Chicago. As Richard III, he stunned the house with a dramatic show of expert swordsmanship in a staged duel with actor Edwin C. Prior, portraying Richmond. In a frenzy that left theatergoers gasping, Booth broke the stage sword used by Prior in the scene and appeared to be intent on killing his fellow actor for purely dramatic effect. "It is this very absorption of part and forgetfulness of self that rendered the elder Booth the man he was," the *Tribune* critic noted. "In this respect the son certainly follows the sire, yet he cannot be said to copy. J. Wilkes Booth is a very youthful actor, and as a consequence has hardly reached the point in which a full appreciation of his powers as a tragedian can be arrived at, but to judge from a single hearing, we would at once pronounce him a genius."[8]

Over the next few weeks he played Hamlet; Claude Melnotte in *The Lady of Lyons*; Duke Pescara in *The Apostate*; and acted in *Romeo and Juliet*, *Othello*, and *Macbeth*. He won over the critics and impressed James McVicker who bestowed upon the young actor his friendship and encouragement. Setting aside political differences, McVicker delivered numerous speeches throughout the Civil War urging the young men of Chicago to enlist in the Union army. Booth deeply admired and gave his respect to the older man.

During his Chicago stay, wealthy Chicago businessman John F. Stafford provided Booth with food and lodging at his commodious Michigan

Avenue and Adams Street mansion, which Booth happily accepted. The actor's late-night drinking escapades in the McVicker's basement saloon stirred comment—but no public censure.[9] Stafford described his guest as pleasant, agreeable, and full of heart.

In June 1862, Booth returned to Chicago for an eighteen-day engagement as Raphael the Sculptor in the melodramatic tragedy *The Marble Heart*; as Claude Melnotte in *The Lady of Lyons*, and as Shylock in *The Merchant of Venice*. He delivered his final Chicago performances in an engagement that began December 1 and left the city behind to continue his tour in the Eastern theaters. "No actor has ever gained a firmer hold upon a Chicago audience, and his return next season will be anxiously looked for," praised the *Tribune*.[10]

Despite his rising celebrity, Booth was not a wealthy man. After losing large sums in failed real estate ventures and an oil investment scheme late in the war he frequently turned to his family and associates for cash loans to cover his travel expenses and costuming. However, his December 1862 Chicago engagement netted him a sizeable honorarium, and in a boastful letter to Edwin Keach of the Boston Museum, he bragged: "My goose does indeed hang high!"[11]

James McVicker invited Booth back the following June to appear as Charles De Moore in Friedrich Schiller's tragedy *The Robbers*, playing opposite McVicker and Jennie Hight, a dancer. According to biographer Terry Alford, Booth confided his innermost thoughts to McVicker during a rehearsal: "What a glorious opportunity there is for [a] man to immortalize himself by killing Lincoln!" Booth exclaimed. "What good would that do?" McVicker replied, to which Booth answered with a quote from Herostratus, a real or imagined figure from Greece who, in 356 B.C. burned down the temple of Diana at Ephesus, one of the seven wonders of the ancient world. "The ambitious youth who fired the Ephesian dome—outlives in fame the pious fool who raised it!" McVicker, puzzled by the response, asked: "Who was that ambitious youth, what was his name?" Booth frowned. "That I know not, but the fancy of a man's deeds live after his bones have decayed to dust and even his name is forgotten." Arguing the point, McVicker replied: "If that be the fame you covet I prefer to live a quiet life and die without it; for in my opinion such notoriety would be infamy!"[12]

Catching up with McVicker in Cleveland not long after, Booth clarified his earlier statement, which should have left little room for doubt in James McVicker's mind that the actor posed an imminent threat to the president: "The man who killed Lincoln would occupy a higher niche of fame than George Washington!"[13]

After his last Chicago appearance in 1863, Booth refused further offers to perform at McVicker's and never returned to the city. Then, in 1864, eight months before the assassination of the president and plagued by a lingering bronchial infection, Booth abandoned the stage to plot his diabolical intrigues while cultivating secessionist sympathizers as he moved easily through Washington, DC, social circles. Actor Charles Pope recalled that "he was a great favorite in Washington society; his talent as an actor, beauty of person and engaging manners made him a welcome guest in any company. The men were charmed and the women fascinated."[14]

The emotional and high-strung actor's greatest theatrical fame lasted all of three years, from 1861 to 1864. In Washington, DC, on the evening of November 9, 1863, Booth performed one of his signature roles in *The Marble Heart*, a popular melodramatic tragedy at Ford's Theater, as Abraham Lincoln, a devoted theater patron, occupied the presidential box.

According to the published recollections of Mary B. Clay, daughter of the Kentucky abolitionist Cassius Clay in attendance at the playhouse that night, "Twice Booth in uttering disagreeable threats in the play came very near and put his finger close to Mr. Lincoln's face; when he came a third time I was impressed by it, and said, 'Mr. Lincoln, he looks as if he meant that for you.' 'Well,' he said, 'he does look pretty sharp at me, doesn't he?'"[15] While the story may well be an exaggeration on the part of an elderly woman, it nonetheless illustrates the depth of Booth's mounting hatred for the president. By 1864, the celebrated dramatist had all but abandoned his budding stage career in order to devote his energies and dwindling finances to the Southern cause by formulating a fiendish plot to abduct Lincoln.

Booth and a small band of no-account operatives planned to abduct the president on the afternoon of March 17, 1865, as Lincoln traveled several miles north of the White House unguarded to visit wounded soldiers at the Campbell General Hospital. In his disordered state of mind, Booth imagined that by kidnapping the president and dispatching him to what was left of the rebel government in Richmond, the Confederacy would be able to regroup and secure the release of thousands of Southern prisoners of war held captive in the North as a way of prolonging the military campaigns in exchange for Lincoln's safe return. Found among Booth's possessions at the National Hotel in Washington where he was staying were two pairs of handcuffs, two boxes of cartridges, and a packet of letters, one dated from Hookstown, Maryland, urging Booth to proceed to Richmond to ascertain the views of the authorities, presumably concerning the plot to kidnap the president.

According to conspirator John Surratt, "With an hour's notice, the gang raced out [and] waited until they saw a carriage approach. Riding alongside, they saw the man in the vehicle was not Lincoln. It may have been Salmon P. Chase, the chief justice of the Supreme Court, who did attend the show [a performance of the play *Still Waters Run Deep*]."[16] With Lincoln still in the city, the scheme unraveled, and Booth turned his attention to murder.

Booth's infamy as the assassin of Abraham Lincoln, a crime he likened to the murder of Julius Caesar by Brutus in his final diary entry written shortly before Sergeant Boston Corbett of the 16th New York Cavalry shot him down inside a burning barn in the Caroline County, Virginia, wilderness on April 26, 1865, will endure for an eternity.[17]

In New York City several years after the assassination, Edwin requested that all of the costumes worn by his ill-famed brother through the years be returned to his custody at the Booth Theater, the playhouse he opened in 1869 at 6th Avenue and 23rd Street.[18] Late one night, long after the performers and the stage hands went home Booth opened the trunks and removed John's costuming. In the flicker of the gaslight lamp in the basement, Edwin Booth, his life torn asunder and his reputation forever stained, pitched each garment into the blazing furnace in an attempt to ease his conscience and erase the memory of his brother's insane action. Their sister, Asia Booth Clarke, the poet and writer in the family, moved to England with her husband and eight children and rarely discussed John's crime again.

Within days of the assassination, Chicago theater owners and members of the acting fraternity gathered inside the Sherman House hotel to collectively renounce Booth for his terrible deed that cast the entire profession into a dark light and jeopardized future box office profits. McVicker, with his son Horace at his side, spoke dispassionately of Booth's better qualities of mind and heart, but with sadness, he agreed to sign the resolution of censure presented to the Chicago City Council.

Despairing of the business, James McVicker, a long-time resident of the Tremont House, retreated to his home in Long Branch, New Jersey, leaving the day-to-day management of the theater to his brother-in-law Samuel Meyers. Unwilling to let go of it entirely, McVicker retained ownership of the house and invested heavily in a lavish interior renovation costing him upward of $90,000. The theater triumphantly reopened August 29, 1871, with McVicker as a guest star in the drama *Extremes*. Within six weeks of that memorable opening night, however, the Great Chicago Fire reduced the playhouse to a pile of charred brick and cinder, ruining his plans for a comfortable retirement back East.

Undiscouraged by the setbacks in his personal and professional life, the veteran actor and manager rebuilt the house on the same site and reopened in August 1872. In the years to come the greatest stars of the age—Blanche

De Bar, Edwin Booth, Edwin Forrest (arguably the nineteenth century's most esteemed male dramatic actor whom Edwin Booth was named after), Lotta Crabtree, Charlotte Cushman, Charles Kean, the internationally renowned Sarah Bernhardt, John Barrymore, Joseph Jefferson, the Polish actress Helena Modjeska who played opposite Edwin Booth as Ophelia, Maggie Mitchell the star of *Jane Eyre*, Laura Keene, the ill-fated comedienne starring in *Our American Cousin* at Ford's Theater the night Lincoln was shot, and comedian John Dillon—graced the McVicker's stage. It was an era of Victorian grandeur.[19]

Edwin Booth never forgot the evening of April 23, 1879, when, in the third scene of the fifth act of *Richard II* inside his father-in-law's theater, Mark Gray Lyon, a spectator seated in the gallery arose from his seat and fired three bullets at Booth just as he recited the famous soliloquy,

> I have been studying how I may compare
> This prison where I live unto the world.[20]

The bullets missed their mark and after the third shot, Booth calmly approached the stage footlights, pointed out the gunman to the gendarmes, and continued on with his performance.

Adjudged mentally incompetent and an alcoholic by a grand jury who patiently listened to his nonsensical and rambling discourse in which he asserted, among other things, that Edwin Booth was his father, Lyon was ordered confined to the Insane Asylum in Elgin, Illinois. A darkly humorous side note to this near tragedy: after paying a visit to the shooter in his jail cell, Edwin Booth, a lenient man who rarely spoke a harsh word to anyone, extracted one of the bullets embedded in a wooden beam on the stage and hired a Chicago jeweler to mount it on a gold cartridge case bearing the inscription "From Mark Gray Lyon to Edwin Booth."

A third ruinous fire struck the theater on August 26, 1890. The flames severely damaged the second McVicker's theater, but once again the phoenix rose from the ashes. This time, fireproof materials were used to build a larger house. Following James McVicker's death on February 10, 1896, at his Michigan Avenue residence, his cherished theater passed from the hands of the family to Jacob Litt, the former lessee of the Board of Education (the original owner of the land upon which the building stood). In 1912, Aaron J. Jones Jr. acquired the building with the intention of making it the most famous "dollar-high" theater in the world, promoting continuous vaudeville acts until twenty-four-hour vaudeville, with its crazy pie-in-the-face baggy pants comedians, lavish choral dance routines, orchestrations, and otherwise frenetic tempo waned in popularity.

Owners Jones, Linick, and Schaefer rebuilt and opened in the fall of 1922, adding an ornate Greek-columned façade, two first-floor shops, offices, and additional seating.[21] Under their direction, the first talking motion picture presented in Chicago, *Lights of New York*, directed by Eddie Foy's son Bryan, debuted at McVicker's on August 3, 1928. "We will demand again the peace and relaxation of the dim and silent movie house, which we have learned to regard as sanctuary from a jangling world," groused a *Tribune* critic writing under the clever *nom de plume* "Mae Tinee."

The Royal Russian Ballet Company kindled memories of the former glory years of the McVicker's theater with their month-long dance program in November 1937, but the return to "legitimate" live performance of serious stage productions proved only temporary. The venerable downtown show spot premiered dozens of Hollywood blockbusters over the years as public taste and popular culture evolved. By 1971, B-grade films and X-rated porn appeared on the marquee. A glorious era approached an inglorious and pitiful end as Chicago building inspectors closed the place down in 1971 for code violations.

The First Federal Savings and Loan Association of Chicago (forerunner of Citicorp) acquired the dilapidated property in 1979. Following an engineer's report that the building had become structurally unsound, McVicker's closed its doors in the summer of 1984. The old landmark fell to the wrecker's ball in October of that year, and with it the memories of the Booths, Barrymore, and Bernhardt; and the forgotten prelude to the greatest American tragedy of them all that occurred on April 14, 1865, faded forever.

THE FAMILY O'LEARY AND THE REST OF THE STORY

A mid the cinders, ash, and charred remnants of a thousand humble worker cottages laid to waste by the firestorm of October 8, 1871, in the poor Irish settlement of Conley's Patch, rival reporters from the *Chicago Times* and the *Chicago Journal* sent out by their respective editors to identify the source of the fire paid a call on Catherine and Patrick O'Leary.

The purpose of their inquiry was to confirm a rumor and ascertain the facts surrounding the origins of the Great Chicago Fire, a calamity that swept across the city south to north in one harrowing night, leaving three hundred dead and ninety thousand homeless. Sadly, the true origin of the Great Chicago Fire is obscured, by rumor and conflicting testimony, although the O'Learys were hastily convicted in the court of public opinion and the blame for the citywide devastation fell squarely on Catherine O'Leary's tired shoulders.

In an overheated and exaggerated newspaper account filed within ten days of the disaster, the *Times* reporter found Cate O'Leary, mournful and broken, seated on the front steps of her home that had miraculously survived the blaze. She told him that on Sunday, October 8, at nine thirty in the evening, she had gone out to check on the cow, intending to feed her a portion of salt and milk her. In the cramped and poorly illuminated space, the woman had been accused of carelessly placing a kerosene lamp near the cow's hind leg. The animal allegedly flinched, kicking the lantern to the ground and thus igniting the combustible hay pile, or so it has been retold and handed down through the generations ever since, with fragments of truth intertwined with myth and conflicting first-person versions.

James Haymie of the *Times* described Cate as "an old woman who had for many years been a pensioner on the county. It was her weekly custom to apply to the county agent for relief which in all cases was freely granted her. Her very appearance indicated poverty. She was apparently about seventy-years of age and bent almost double with the weight of many years of toil and trouble and privation. Her dress corresponded with her demands—being ragged and dirty in the extreme. 'My poor cow! My poor cow! She is gone and I have nothing left in the world.'"[1] In point-of-fact Mrs. O'Leary was not seventy years old. She was only thirty-five, and her living circumstances, while modest, did not suggest that the family were paupers solely dependent on the public dole.

Offering a more rational and balanced assessment of the origins of the fire on October 21, the *Chicago Evening Journal* declared that "even if it were an absurd rumor, forty miles wide of the truth, it would be useless to attempt to alter the verdict of history. Mrs. O'Leary has made a sworn statement in refutation of the charge and it's backed by other affidavits but to little purpose. She is in for it and no mistake. Fame has seized her and appropriated her name, barn, cows and all. She has won, in spite of herself what the Ephesian youth panted after." (Note: that is, fame.) Cate O'Leary informed the *Journal* reporter that five cows and a horse occupied the barn. "We all knocked out our living out of those five blessed cows and I never had a dint [sic] from the parish in all my life and the dirty Times had no business to say it! There is not a word of truth in the whole story. I always milked my cows by daylight and never had a lamp or any kind of a candle about the barn. It must have been set afire. Two neighbors at the far end of the alley saw a strange man come up about half-past nine in the evening. He asked them was the alley straight through. They told him it was and he went through. It wasn't five minutes until they saw the barn on fire. Before we had time to get out, the horse cows, it was all gone and the fire was running in every direction. I hope to die if this isn't every word of it true. If you was [sic] a priest, I wouldn't tell it any different!"[2] The *Journal* concluded that "whether fired by an incendiary or kerosene lamp kicked over by an irate cow, [the fire origin] must remain an open question."

"Mrs. O'Leary testified that she milked the cow at five o'clock and went to bed herself at 8:30," author Henry Raymond Hamilton reported in 1910. "There was no lighted lamp in the stable, unless the cow lighted it after Mrs. O'Leary finished milking. The name of the man who started the cow story has been lost to posterity."[3] Or has it?

The entire city from DeKoven Street north to Lincoln Park burned down in the path of the horrific, fast-moving flames. In the rush to judgment, another *Times* account stated that it was no accident, but an act of revenge. "The old hag swore she would be revenged on a city that would deny her a bit of wood or a pound of bacon," alleging that the county agent had cut off her fuel and food supply.[4] This wasn't the only conspiracy theory Wilbur Storey, the reckless *Times* publisher simmering over the destruction of his building in the wall of flames, advanced. He charged a dangerous cabal of subversive radicals from the Internationale Society with hatching a plot to burn down Chicago. The *Journal* called this wild yarn "a mess of nonsense" and the editor "a notorious liar."[5]

The city, parched by draught, burned for two nights and a day, and the ruins of once majestic buildings in the central business district smoldered for weeks. Who was to blame? The public demanded fast answers and the press was more than delighted to deliver to them a convenient scapegoat in the person of a downtrodden Irish immigrant woman, or a communist conspiracy.

In 1871, institutional anti-Irish and anti-Catholic prejudice, a throwback to the bigotry of the nativist Know Nothings of the 1850s toward the newly arriving Potato Famine refugees, had not yet dissipated in northern cities despite an ever-increasing number of office holders of Irish extraction holding elected positions in city government or employed in police and fire departments. Nativist sentiment must be taken into account in attempting to understand why the media saddled the O'Learys with such bigoted and unfair censure.

In a sworn affidavit given to Michael McDermott, Chicago city surveyor on duty October 15, the O'Learys asserted that the entire family was in bed by eight, having completed all of the day's necessary chores and had settled in, oblivious to the imminent danger, until Denis "Peg Leg" Sullivan, the one-legged drayman from across the street (112 DeKoven Street) knocked on the O'Learys' door around nine fifteen to notify them that their barn was ablaze and the animals were in grave peril.

The public and the press believed what they wanted to and accepted the superficial reports of the *Times* at face value. "It was [*Times* reporter] Jim Haymie I think who faked the story about the cow kicking over the lamp," recounted Michael Ahern, a writer for the *Chicago Morning Republican* in a 1915 interview. "No newspaper was printed the morning of October 9, but when the papers were able to get out extras, the cow and the lamp story was given as the cause of the holocaust."[6] (Ahern is wrong here. The *Journal* managed to publish a one-page extra the morning of October 9 while the conflagration was still in progress.)

It is the events occurring in the hour immediately *before* the eruption of the fire that leave us with the greatest mystery. However, overlooked eyewitness statements given after 1900 may finally fill in some critical missing details.

The O'Leary clan struggled against long odds to live quietly and prosper in the harsh and unrelenting landscape of Chicago. It was a family beset by much personal tragedy. Patrick O'Leary, clan patriarch, whose name is inseparable from the events of that awful night, was a County Kerry man, born in 1819 and raised in the southwest corner of Ireland. He is remembered as a common laborer—a stevedore—a large, burly man with a quiet and kindly disposition who mostly kept to himself. He married Catherine, his lifelong companion, in County Cork and immigrated to America not long after the birth of the couple's first child. Patrick served in the Union Army, after enlisting in Harrisburg, Pennsylvania, where the growing family, soon to number five children—Cornelius ("Con"), James, Cate, Patrick Jr., and Mary—had established their home after arriving on US shores.

Six years after the war ended, the O'Learys moved to Chicago, settling into a four-room home at 137 DeKoven Street in "The Patch." The house was one of two cheaply built wood-frame, single-story dwellings occupying the same lot. In the rear of the two properties stood a hay barn, large enough to shelter five milking cows and a horse belonging to Catherine who had established a small business supplying milk to the neighborhood. There were very few grocers to serve the needs of residents in the Patch in those days. Retail grocery establishments were widely scattered and not always within easy walking distance.

On the sixty-second anniversary of the fire in 1933, Cate and Patrick's last surviving offspring, Catherine O'Leary-Ledwell, broke the family's long vow of silence and discussed at length her recollections from that long-ago night with the media. "I am the true sole survivor," she said. "It was a Sunday night. Mother had put me to bed with the other four children at 8:00. She went to bed too and father followed a half-hour later. It was a hot night and the sun had been blistering for weeks."[7]

Ledwell remembered that her father Patrick had rented the cottage in front of his own home to Patrick McLaughlin, an immigrant musician whose fiddle tunes evoked pleasing memories of the *auld sod* to the transplanted West Side Irish population. McLaughlin's services were much in demand at local gatherings, christenings, weddings, and anniversary parties that summer.

That evening, as the O'Learys tried to sleep in the stifling heat and high humidity, there was much merriment—dancing and singing and commotion—going on inside the Patrick McLaughlin quarters where neighbors celebrated the arrival of Denny Connors, a cousin of McLaughlin's wife from the old country who had landed in Chicago only a few days prior.

"It was one of a dozen little parties the boys and girls held in the home of Mrs. Pat McLaughlin, jigging and waltzing to the time of the old man's fiddle—and he was one of the best that ever crossed the water," said Mary Callahan in 1901. Mary was a teenaged girl from the neighborhood in the company of her friends when the trouble started" ("Centennial Eve Reveals," *Chicago Tribune*, September 26, 1903).

"There were eight of us in the party besides the old people, their children and grandchildren," Mary continued. "We were all in the habit of going over to the McLaughlins on Sunday evenings and singing and dancing and merry making after the week's work." Pat McLaughlin mounted the coal stove, resting his feet on a wood box and began his fiddling. Mary never forgot the lively songs he played, "Mrs. McLeod's Reel," "The Blackbird," and other traditional Irish folk tunes to entertain and amuse the young people. It was shaping up to be a memorable evening in every way until Mrs. McLaughlin volunteered to brew up some tea, and milk punch—a rum concoction sprinkled with nutmeg—but she suddenly noticed that the milk pitcher was nearly empty.

The O'Learys could sell them some milk of course if they dared to knock on their door, but "folks worked hard in those days and went to bed and got up early and we didn't want to roust the poor woman," Mary said. "We knew the cows were in the shed in the rear but never gave it a thought until Denny Connors was the wild *omadhaun* [foolish, nonsensical person] said to come with him and we'd get milk in the pitcher. There were no locks on the sheds or the houses either in those days and taking the lamp from Mrs. O'Laughlin's kitchen we started for the milking cow stable" ("Centennial Eve Reveals").

Mary carried the lantern. Denny Connors, Alice Reilly, and Johnny Finnan trailed close behind with the tin pail. Not wanting to create a stir and awaken the slumbering O'Leary family, they remained quiet and approached the hay barn with stealth.

"Denny Connors—the Lord ha' mercy on his soul—he's dead now . . ." Mary recalled, her voice fading. "Denny said he would milk the cow munching away in the corner. Sure any of us girls could have drawn the milk in a minute but there must have been few cows in the part of Ireland where poor Denny came from. The lamp had been put down on an old milking stool and we were standing by laughing at Denny trying to grip the cow which kept moving away from the strange hands and awkward movements" ("Centennial Eve Reveals").

"In the dim light I'll never know whether the cow kicked or Denny fell over the stool in his wild stumbling, but the lamp went over, sure it did and Alice and myself screamed and ran for the house" ("Centennial Eve Reveals"). It seems rather curious in retrospect that the panicked girls would dash back into the party and pretend that nothing had happened unless they were confident in the belief that Denny Connors had managed to extinguish the blaze.

What happened in the next few moments was telling. Johnny Finnan rushed into the McLaughlin house and whispered to Mary and Alice that Denny was not hurt, and the fire would be put out in a minute. He was wrong of course and may have simply lied. With fear of the consequences for what they had just done registering in his eyes, Denny warned, "Don't say anything!" and Mary nodded.

Across the street, Denis "Peg Leg" Sullivan lounged on the plank side-walk, his back resting against the fence as he enjoyed the warm night and the musical airs of Pat McLaughlin, when he first spotted flames shooting out from the hay barn.

"We thought nothing more of it and were waltzing with the boys when Connors and a man named Denny Sullivan, who lived across the street came running in and shouted that the house was all afire," Mary added. "We ran to the rear and sure enough the barn was blazing and the fire now reached the O'Leary house" ("Centennial Eve Reveals").

Cate O'Leary-Ledwell later confirmed this version of events, saying that it was Sullivan that sounded the alarm that saved them all. "At 9:15 there was a pounding and bellowing at the back door and we were all dragged from bed. And he had hearty lungs and dashed for the barn to save the horse and cows. His peg leg caught in the loose planking and he was lucky to make his way out safely with a burned calf."[8]

"Peg Leg" Sullivan, a person without means who could neither read nor write, may in fact have been the forgotten hero instead of history's scapegoat. Recent scholarship concerning the origin of the fire has transferred blame from Mrs. O'Leary to the local drayman, Sullivan. It is further alleged that Sullivan vanished from Chicago within twenty-four hours of the calamity. However, city surveyor McDermott took a statement from Sullivan on October 15. Sullivan signed his name with his customary X and swore to the following, which McDermott recorded in the ledger:

"Denis Sullivan being duly sworn before me testifies that he was at Patrick O'Leary's house No. 137 DeKoven Street on Sunday night the 8th from about 8:30 to 9:00 at night during which time Mr. O'Leary and wife were in bed; that he went a few blocks east of O'Leary's on the opposite side of DeKoven Street until about half-past nine, when he saw the fire. He went across the street and cried "fire," and went into O'Leary's barn where he found the hay in the loft on fire. He then attempted to cut loose the cows and horse but failed to save anything but a half-burned calf. He then came to O'Leary's and found them out of bed. Denis Ryan alarmed them during the time in the bar. Subscribed and sworn to before me this 15th day of October 1871.

"Denis "X" Sullivan (mark)"[9]

In his dotage, Cate's youngest son, James Patrick O'Leary, advanced the notion that spontaneous combustion caused the fire. He was just two years old at the time but seemed to remember the event. "The day before the fire—it was a Saturday—I helped the 'old gent' (his father) put in some timothy hay in the loft above the cow shed," said O'Leary. "My part of the job was to stamp it down in the mow. I thought it was great sport. They say that when green hay sweats it causes spontaneous combustion, and that I heard the old gent say, was the cause of the fire."[10]

Roused to action by Sullivan's clarion cry, the neighbors formed a bucket brigade, but it was of little use. From his perch in the belfry atop the courthouse at Randolph and Clark Streets, fire department watchman Mathias Schaefer sounded the first alarm and ordered that Box 342 be struck—a mile southwest of the O'Leary home.

A day earlier, a devastating fire had exhausted the resources of the city fire department of 216 men, 15 engines and 54 hose carts. "Some of the men said the firemen were drunk from the free whiskey and liquor passed out at the big fire the night before but I believe the poor men were tired out and not able to do the work they might have done otherwise," Ledwell later said.[11]

John Sollitt, one of the city's old settlers and a failed aldermanic candidate in 1852, sharply criticized the fire brigades for their inattention to duty in an 1881 interview. "In my opinion there was no necessity for the fire to spread as it did, and it would not have done so if the firemen had not been intoxicated," Sollitt recounted. "They all got drunk at the Saturday night fire and I saw lots of them drunk on Sunday and at 10:00 on Sunday night. Instead of being at work on the fire they were engaged in looting the saloons on Jefferson Street and getting drunk again. But for this the city would have never burned."[12]

The wind was high and it blew steadily from the Southwest. The skies were hazy and the smoke from the earlier fire still blanketed the West Side and impaired Schaefer's vision and judgment. He struck the wrong alarm box.

And so with the sounding of the alarm and a chorus of bells chiming from churches across the city, the first engine companies, the "America" hose cart and the "Little Giant" were deployed as first responders, although they were not the closest company in proximity to DeKoven Street, and took a circuitous route. Engine No. 9, with a pumping capacity of 500 gallons per minute arrived at the closest hydrant located at Forquer and DeKoven Streets. The loss of time and the prevailing strong wind gusts accelerated the flames as the fire jumped from one building to the next, and eventually across the Chicago River.

"Although we intended no harm, we couldn't tell what might be done to us," Mary Callahan confided, "and when we heard that they were giving away free tickets to get out of town we went. I got a ticket for Sheboygan the next day and I started up for the home of relatives and didn't come back to Chicago until most of the burned homes had been rebuilt. Denny Connors left the city too, and a little later went to Ireland where he died a few years ago. There was an investigation afterwards I heard and the McLaughlins were questioned about the party in their home but sure the old folks knew nothing of the prank of ourselves and weren't able to tell them anything. Mrs. O'Leary did not know until years afterward."[13]

The fact that Callahan maintained a wall of silence for all those years disputes the notion set forth by some historians that she was a shameless "publicity seeker" looking to capitalize on the notoriety or had spun a yarn based on distorted memories and misconstrued facts. Rather, her guilt, fear of social ostracism and possible criminal penalties factored into her decision to keep quiet about the matter for as long as she did.

Mrs. Mary Dawson told the delegates at a Chicago Historical Society symposium held on October 9, 1928, that there was no doubt in her mind of the story's veracity. "I was only a school girl, but I remember the version told was authentic in our neighborhood which was only a block from De-Koven Street where the fire started. A young Irishman named Connors said he would milk the cow, so he got a lamp at McLaughlin's. Whether the cow kicked or the party that milked the cow jumped, I don't know. The fire started there but it was a little paint shop nearby that really spread the fire."[14]

Callahan explained her reasoning for breaking her long period of silence. "Now that it's past and gone, I can see they never would have harmed us for something that was entirely an accident, but I was younger then. Now it can do no harm to tell it."[15]

If the events of October 8, 1871, played out exactly as Mary Callahan described, the greater harm, apart from the terrible destruction of property, the death of innocents, and the suffering of the homeless, were the years of shame, humiliation, and sorrow foisted upon the O'Learys, their children, and their descendants.

Nellie Mahoney Hayes, who lived with her parents, Mr. and Mrs. John Mahoney, at 214 West Taylor Street at the time of the fire, shed new light on the chaotic aftermath and the fate of the O'Learys. According to her 1927 statement, neighborhood vigilantes, believing Patrick O'Leary to be responsible for the calamity that had left them all homeless, formed a mob and set out to track him down.

"People were hunting for O'Leary," Hayes remembered. "They thought he had started the fire by going into the barn at night with a lamp. 'Where is O'Leary? Lynch him,' men cried. A great hunt commenced and the district was patrolled and put under martial law. I knew where O'Leary and his family were. They were hiding in our house with a family of roomers named McCarthy. They stayed there a week, and my father who was one of the deputies and knew the password, helped them get away. O'Leary went out of our yard dressed as a woman."[16]

The family's livestock (with the exception of the one calf) was destroyed by the fire, and the family cottage was besieged by an unrelenting army of reporters, curiosity seekers, and vengeful neighbors. Catherine and her husband knew they could never return to the old place. After fleeing the Mahoney home, they took refuge south of the stockyards and moved into a small frame home on Wallace Street in the parish of Visitation. It wasn't much, and for the next few years the family lived a dirt-poor existence, barely managing to scrape by.

While the move represented a modest step up in a better neighborhood, mostly, their new surroundings provided a deeper degree of anonymity that was not possible at the frame cottage on DeKoven Street, that by 1874 had been torn down and replaced by a two-story gray stone house with a mansard attic. On the ten-year anniversary of the fire, the Chicago Historical Society placed a commemorative stone marker on the exterior wall.

Within the next two decades the Irish Conley's Patch settlement dispersed, giving way to an influx of newly arrived Italians and Eastern European Jews who had immigrated to this impoverished section of Chicago. The area would remain poor for years to come.

In her new home, Catherine drew increasingly inward, refusing to speak to anyone outside of the immediate family circle about the ordeal of October 8–9, 1871. There is no surviving photographic image of Mrs. O'Leary, because she resolutely refused to allow her picture to be taken. Reporters who managed to catch up with her were promptly shooed away—their ears ringing from a harsh rebuke, as they retreated from the front door of her home, embarrassed and red-faced from the scolding. One day, agents of the famous showman P. T. Barnum showed up at her door to see if she would be willing to tour with Barnum's famous circus in return for a handsome salary. Catherine grabbed her broom and drove them off.

The woman's troubles did not end there. A different kind of tragedy befell Catherine and Patrick in August of 1885 when their eldest son, twenty-three-year-old Cornelius "Con" O'Leary, a querulous barroom brawler, committed a double murder out on the open prairie.

Con O'Leary, also known to the hail-and-well-met fellows in the saloons and in the Yards (as the stockyards were called) as "Puggy," had been drinking in a tavern on Emerald Avenue with the boys. They consumed as much beer as their budget would permit. Then, with his pockets emptied, Con left the gathering and walked southward to what is now Forty-Ninth Street and Halsted. In 1885, this was the edge of civilization. Beyond it lay an expanse of open prairie. Groves of trees, wild grass, and scattered houses dotted the landscape looking south.

Two versions of the fateful encounter were given to police. Out on the prairie, Con met his sister Mary and her friend Kate Campbell clad in a calico dress with a gingham apron. Boisterous and in his cups, Con suggested to the women that they should "rush the can"—a nineteenth-century euphemism for filling a pitcher or bucket with beer. Because beer was not commonly available from grocers, people would carry a tin pail to the saloon to be filled by the proprietor with rich, frothy lager. Kate Campbell agreed and went off to fetch the beer while O'Leary's sister scolded Con for bad habits. Heavy-set and loosely built, Con was an excitable man and his temper riled up from his afternoon joust with his friends over on Emerald Avenue.

Kate Campbell, who had recently lost her husband in a Kansas City bar room fight, returned with the beer and presented the bill. "Give me a half a dollar Mary," Con said, turning to his sister.

"No I won't! You can't get a half a case from me the way you are now."

"And you won't give it to me?" O'Leary snapped, his voice rising. "Wait here!"

The man stormed off, returning about fifteen minutes later to find his sister and the Campbell woman enjoying the beer he perceived to belong to him. He repeated the command to his sister. "Mary, give me a half a dollar!"

"You're drunk Con and don't need it," came the reply. Kate Campbell echoed her friend's sentiment and by doing so, she wrote her death warrant, at least according to what the police were able to surmise.[17]

O'Leary produced a pistol from his pocket and shot the woman in the stomach. Con and Campbell were not on the best of terms. A moment later he discharged a second shot, striking his sister in the neck, then raced off. Aroused by the sound of distant shots, Halsted Street residents came running. Police and a wagon from the morgue were summoned. Kate Campbell's corpse was placed on ice and driven away. Clinging to life, Mary was transported to the County Hospital where police pressed her for the identity of the shooter.

Mary admitted to detectives that her brother did not care much for Campbell. Con had said that she had a "reputation," but Mary stopped short of identifying him as Kate's shooter. Police told Mary that Kate's chances of survival were slim, so it would be to everyone's benefit if she gave up Con to the police. She refused. And then she died.

Under questioning, Edward Kelly, a friend of O'Leary's, confessed to providing him with the murder weapon. Meanwhile, Con O'Leary did not linger in Chicago. He hopped a Chicago and Alton freight train bound for Kansas City, where he soon found work in a Wyandotte packing house using the alias "Quinn." In the packing house a floor manager recognized O'Leary from his Chicago days and sent word to the town of Lake police. Six weeks after the murder of his sister and her friend he was arrested and extradited back to Chicago to stand trial.

In his confession to the police, Con O'Leary spun an entirely different, but much more plausible version than the tale told by Mary Scully as she lay dying on her bed. O'Leary said that he had found his sister sitting on a sidewalk on Fiftieth Street drinking in the company of three idlers, identified as James Horn, William Gross, and David Cushing. Three gallons of beer had already been consumed and he didn't care for the company his sister was keeping.

He said he ordered his sister to go home, but Mary's friend Kate Campbell, using vulgar epithets, defied him and told Mary to pay her drunken brother no mind. Then someone threw beer in O'Leary's face. The young man, a stocky, clean-shaven, two-hundred-pound fighter became enraged. It was at that moment that he produced the revolver and shot both women dead. Mary received her wound quite by accident. She had thrown herself between Con and Kate and the second bullet caught her in the throat.

Gross, Horn, and Cushing corroborated the story, and Con O'Leary was arraigned and put on trial before Judge Henry Shepard. When asked how he would plead, O'Leary replied, "Guilty." In the presence of his sister, his little brother James, and his father who sat at a respectful distance in stone-cold silence, Con was sentenced by Judge Shepard: "While the absence of pre-meditation does away with the necessity of the death penalty, the case is so brutal that a long term of imprisonment is deserved." Con O'Leary received forty years in the Joliet Penitentiary.[18]

Stoic and accepting of his fate, O'Leary said that he was a young man and expected to "pull through on the two-thirds rule." Having lost a daughter in a senseless act of violence and a son to the Illinois penal system, and their good name tarnished by an unfortunate occurrence in a hay barn years earlier, Catherine and Patrick lived out their remaining days retreating from the world, each struggling with the infirmities of old age.

Afflicted by heart disease, the seventy-five-year-old family patriarch collapsed on the front stairs of his second Southwest Side home, a three-story brownstone at 5133 S. Halsted Street, on September 16, 1894. Without much fanfare Patrick was buried in Mount Olivet Cemetery, with a modest marker placed above his grave.

Catherine's troubled journey through life ended less than a year later, on July 3, 1895, when news of her death hit the press. Four days earlier she had contracted a cold that quickly developed into a fatal pneumonia. Though her life had been scarred by shame and denial, this mark of Cain was lifted in the 1990s when Alderman Ed Burke and the Chicago City Council passed a resolution absolving her of blame for the great fire.

An amusing footnote to the story of the fire and the cow concerns the plight of the O'Leary livestock. The *Tribune* reported on September 13, 1899, that "Dudley, reputed in the neighborhood to be a sister of Mrs. O'Leary's cow of '71 fame, lies dead in Patrick Sexton's yard in the rear of his house at 28 Waller Street. Paddy Sexton, as the children call him, is a bricklayer, and as a public-spirited citizen took pride in the animal and its history. A sorrowful procession followed him when he went to the police station to notify the authorities of the death of the cow and make suitable arrangements for the disposal of the body."

In September 1946, B. George Kleker told how his father, Hynek Kleker, a butcher, bought the carcass of a cow and a calf from Mrs. O'Leary after the fire. The cow hides were allegedly hung on the wall of the elder Kleker's shop and remained there for many years until they were finally taken down, stored, and then lost.

"Big Jim" O'Leary grew to manhood working in the stockyards with his older brother Con. The hard and demanding labor made him tough, resilient, and unafraid, but observing the habits of the rollicking, spendthrift drovers, cowboys, and stockmen who came to town to gamble away all they had earned, O'Leary understood that through the green-cloth trade there was a far easier path to the attainment of riches than butchering cattle and hogs.

Gambling became his life's calling, and his famous saloon replete with a Turkish bath, billiard parlor, barber shop, bowling alley, card room, and restaurant at 4183 S. Halsted Street stood opposite the main gate of the Yards on Exchange Avenue. It was a grand show spot in Chicago from the 1890s until 1934, featuring a maze of secret rooms concealing roulette wheels, tote boards, Western Union telegraph lines to import racing results from all across the country and dice and card tables. To his clientele Jim guaranteed that his fortress of pleasure and relaxation had been made fireproof, lightning-proof, bomb-proof, burglar-proof, and police-proof.

O'Leary, a man full of sardonic humor, remembered by many as a legendary sportsman and unrepentant gambler who would bet on anything, against anyone, and at any time, even if the odds were stacked heavily against him. Just twenty-three years of age in 1892, Jim drew early attention to himself as an up-and-comer in the sporting world by picking "Gentleman Jim" Corbett, a bank teller and amateur actor from San Francisco to defeat the mighty John L. Sullivan in a battle for the heavyweight championship of the world inside the Olympic Club in New Orleans on September 7. O'Leary laid four-to-one odds on the underdog Corbett who delivered a stunning knockout in the twenty-first round. Thereafter Chicago's sporting fraternity took a long look at O'Leary as he cashed in their markers.

Jim's most famous wagers—the outrageous bets that old-time reporters recounted to younger ones inside the City Room of the big downtown newspapers long after O'Leary had died—often involved Pat O'Malley.

O'Malley, a crusty, old-school saloonkeeper and First Ward Democratic boss during the horse and buggy era, came to Chicago in 1889 from Ballyagran, Limerick, and was often called the "king of the handbooks" by the local sports. He owned a sagging, "down in the dumps" saloon at 742 South Dearborn Street, near where First Ward alderman Michael "Hinky Dink" Kenna ran his "Workingman's Exchange" at Van Buren and LaSalle. A lifelong bachelor, O'Malley lived above his bar.

At the famous First Ward Ball in 1908, O'Malley and O'Leary occupied adjoining boxes. An obliging porter placed a case of expensive, vintage champagne near their tables. "You'd be a long time in Ireland, Pat, before you'd drink any of this stuff," chuckled O'Leary.[19]

"Oh, I don't know," drawled O'Malley. "I often drank champagne in Ireland. I'll bet you a thousand that I can be in my father's home inside of a week with a bottle of this grape juice in front of me."[20]

"You're on!" O'Leary grinned. It was a sucker's bet, or so it seemed to Big Jim. At two thirty that morning, O'Malley staggered out of the Coliseum and climbed into a hack, ordering the driver to deliver him to the LaSalle Street Station—fast! He caught the late-night mail express bound for New York and arrived there just in time to book a cabin on the HMS *Lusitania* bound for Liverpool and Queenstown. According to John Kelley, the veteran reporter, O'Malley met up with a friend who conveyed him to Ballyagran in a fast-moving motor car. They arrived in less than two hours, traversing rough, unpaved cow paths to get there. O'Malley made it to his father's home and popped open the "grape juice" with one hour to spare. He sent a cable to O'Leary containing just two happy words: "You lose!"

In 1918 O'Malley was certain he had his old friend on the hook for a cool grand after he wandered into his Halsted Street resort to unwind following a funeral at Mount Olivet Cemetery. The saloon talk that afternoon concerned

Milo H. Piper, an accused killer and bigamist incarcerated in a Muskegon, Michigan, jail for murdering Frieda Welchman on a grassy knoll near the railroad tracks outside of town in September 1916.

Milo Piper had seduced a bevy of women, including the murder victim, Ms. Welchman of Chicago. He sent the young woman a raft of love-sick, ludicrous poetic verse. "For when a girl can look at me; I will change from beer to tea. I mean when a girl can change a man, I think it time to shake her hand; Now Welchy when you read this line, you will know you are on my mind; and I hope you will believe me too, when I say I love you."

The story was sensational for the time and the trial progressed.[21]

"I'll make a book he'll never hang," O'Leary said.

"What odds?" O'Malley wanted to know.

"Two to one."

"I'll lay a hundred at that price." O'Malley peeled off a century note from a thick wad of bills and laid it on the bar. "You think you're a pretty wise guy," O'Leary said, smugly satisfied. "You hooked me once for a thousand on that race to Ireland, but I've got you forty ways this time. There is no capital punishment in Michigan! What do you think of that? They can't hang Piper even if he is found guilty. This is a sure thing bet—a million to one shot that I cop! Sorry for you, Pat!"[22]

The midnight hour approached. A newsboy rushed into O'Malley's saloon with a copy of the late edition reporting a stunning development in the Michigan trial. O'Malley glimpsed the headline and roared with laughter. Milo Piper, the bigamist insurance agent, hanged himself inside of his jail cell on December 21, 1918. O'Malley raced over to O'Leary's saloon in a taxi-cab and dropped the newspaper on the bar in front of his friend. O'Leary read the story without offering comment. He sighed, then opened the safe and carefully counted out the money he owed, slamming it down in front of O'Malley.

"Hinky Dink" Kenna later paid O'Leary the supreme gambler's compliment by saying, "He was a square shooter. 'Big Jim' never welshed on a bet. He was a good loser and his patrons had confidence in him that he would always pay if he lost."[23]

As he gained prominence in betting circles, Jim ran his games with a simple philosophy uppermost in his mind: "There are three classes of people in the world, gamblers, burglars and beggars. Nearly everybody gambles," he often said. "Sometimes it's with money, sometimes it's with time, sometimes it's with jobs. Nearly every fellow is willing to take a chance. Other folks are burglars. They make their living by stealing. The second-story man, the safe-cracker and the dip are not the only burglars. You'll find a lot of others in offices in the Loop. A fellow who won't gamble or steal is a beggar."[24]

Across the United States gambling patrons adapted the "Sport of Kings" as their national pastime beginning in the mid-to-late 1880s. Within a few short years betting on the ponies became a craze, bordering on obsession, and it spelled the doom of the old crooked faro banks and "dinner pail" resorts for the workingmen lining Clark Street from Randolph south to Harrison Street.

The parlors (situated along what was then known as "Gambler's Row" were operated by tin horns and a gang of card cheats answering to gambler boss and political overseer Michael Cassius McDonald) slowly vanished as real estate speculators bought up the land for the development of future commercial office buildings. McDonald, seeking legitimacy through the buying and selling of real estate, moved deeper into the threshold of city politics as the treasurer of the Cook County Democratic Party and as a behind-the-scenes "kingmaker."

This left a growing vacuum in the evolving "sporting world" for a new generation of gambler focused on clocking bets on the fly as "handbook" operators. The only tools of the trade necessary to take a bet on a local or out-of-town horse race were a notebook and pencil. The mobility of these gamblers made it difficult for police to pinpoint an exact location of the home base or clearing house. The traveling handbook operator eliminated the need to operate a resort with costly overhead and the ever-present danger of police raids.

The *Tribune* reported on August 26, 1900, that "Blind" John Condon, a former business partner of McDonald, had laid the groundwork for a unified consortium to be known as the "Gambler's Trust." "The combination of gambling magnates will be known as the 'Big Four.' Inasmuch as the quartet of interests which have controlled pool selling will now be amalgamated. Competition has been so bitter that some of the bookmakers have laid the raiding of their places to the instigation of their rivals," the paper reported.

O'Leary, having successfully cultivated the friendship and cooperation of the stockyards police, enjoyed some limited immunity from arrest and prosecution and thereby refused to join the trust. Instead he fought against them by notifying the gambling detail of rival handbook operations. Or if he chose to do so, O'Leary personally directed the constables to the saloons, poolrooms, and the Washington Park, Hawthorne, and Harlem tracks in the outlying areas where he knew a competitor handbook operated by the Smith-Perry Trust was known to operate.

Sly old trickster that he was, O'Leary thwarted police by sprinkling blinding red pepper into the keyholes and in between the cracks in the floorboards after he had been tipped off about an impending raid against his stronghold on July 11, 1906. A police squad under the command of Sergeant O'Malley of the stockyards station fled the premises choking and wheezing from the roseate mist that filled the air once the first sledgehammer hit the oaken door. Red pepper saved the day.

Police inspector Bill Clancy was one of the Yards' oldest settlers. He operated three newspapers in the district before becoming a police officer, and during his years of service, he had withstood many accusations of perpetuating graft and allowing O'Leary a free hand to do as he pleased. While it was true that the two men had an amicable "understanding," the friendship went only as far as personal family matters.

Uproar ensued after the press got wind of the elopement of Clancy's daughter Gertrude with O'Leary's son James junior on January 10, 1910. Friendship between a denizen of the gambling underworld and a police inspector with jurisdiction over much of the South Side had its limitations, and the sudden marriage of Gertrude and James Jr. did not go over well in either household. "My private affairs are none of the public's business!" thundered Clancy to a swarm of reporters awaiting him outside his door. "People can say what they please. If they injure me or mine they will have to settle with me."[25]

The $100,000 palatial brownstone mansion O'Leary had built for his family at 726 West Garfield Boulevard was similarly besieged. "Big Jim" was incensed by the intrusion of the press and with James Jr. His impetuous 22-year-old son had been studying civil engineering at Notre Dame up until the moment he became enamored with Gertrude Clancy, a student teacher in Chicago. When the couple returned home after a whirlwind honeymoon, James Jr. found himself locked out of his father's home and without income. The young man went to work in a South Chicago steel mill to support his wife. There was no annulment forced upon them and life went on.

With the coming of Prohibition and a new and violent criminal order laying claim to the holdings of the old-time gentlemen gamblers who never resorted to gunplay in their disputes, Jim O'Leary looked to the future and eventual retirement. "I've got enough to take a trip around the world when I sell my shop," he remarked. "Then I'm going to settle down in some live little town."[26]

In his twilight years, Jim kept the saloon and the betting action going, but he branched out into the commission brokerage business—a different type of gambling racket he found very appealing. Late in life, he paid homage to his parents by erecting a fifteen-foot obelisk above their gravesite. He had never forgotten their sufferings.

After battling a year-long illness, Jim expired on January 22, 1925, inside his Garfield Boulevard mansion. Hundreds turned out to pay their respects to James O'Leary as his funeral train rumbled past rows of worker cottages in the Back of the Yards neighborhood inseparable from his family name and his legendary presence.

O'Leary never could part ways with the Halsted Street resort after telling everyone about his longing for a "live little town" to settle down in. After Jim passed, control of the saloon went to Tommy Tuitt, who spent the remaining years of Prohibition fending off take-over attempts by Joe Saltis, Frankie McErlane, "Spike" O'Donnell, and other Southwest Side Prohibition-era gangster-hoodlums eyeing the gambling action.

Where there once stood a friendly, welcoming saloon bearing a brightly lit sign–"O'Leary"—now only an empty, rubble-strewn lot remains. The greatest irony of all, the saloon, like much of Chicago in 1871, had been constructed almost entirely of wood and it burned down in the Great Stock-yards Fire of 1934.

FOUR BUTCHERS TRYING TO GO TO HEAVEN

A tall, broad-shouldered man, distinctive in his long frock coat and knee-high boots, named John B. Sherman, emerged from his residence in the South Loop (at a time when there were still private homes in the commercial district), to mount his horse and travel southward through acres of cabbage patch fields, uneven dirt roads, and swampy marshes en route to the rural hinterland at Forty-First Street and Halsted—the remote countryside of Chicago. On this bright, sunlit morning in June 1865, the man on horseback would close the deal on a speculative business venture that would alter the course of history, and inspire Carl Sandburg to redefine Chicago as the "hog butcher to the world."

When he was barely thirty years old, Sherman, a former gold prospector and commission man had, in 1848, converted a vacant lot adjacent to the old Bull's Head Tavern at the junction of Madison Street and Ogden Avenue into a "stockyard." The purpose of the enclosure was to expedite the sale of a few hundred sheep, hogs, and cattle escorted by cowboys and "drovers" for direct sale to Chicago butchers.

In the days of the Bull's Head Tavern and the Willard Myrick Yards at Cottage Grove and Thirty-First Street (leased and opened by Sherman), swaggering, rough-housing men on horseback accompanied their herds to Chicago from distances of a hundred miles or more. Through the dust of the trail, lake-effect shoreline squalls, and by means of whip and a dog these hearty "drovers" directed the animals into the "butcher's corral" in the half-dozen stockyards scattered across Chicago. The farmers of the Illinois, Indiana, Wisconsin, and southwest Michigan hinterland sold directly to the butcher, and the butcher to the consumer without a middle man.

A third stockyard opened on the future location of the Chicago Opera House at Wacker and Madison drawing livestock dangerously close to Chicago's central business district. Escaping, panicked steers often broke free from the pens in a mad bolt for freedom. They charged headlong into throngs of downtown pedestrians, resulting in chaos, pandemonium, and frightful injuries. Time was money, and money was lost chasing after the stock and transferring them from one yard to the next.

Animal slaughter conducted along the banks of the Chicago River presented a disturbing and grisly image. In 1835 Archibald Clybourn, an old Chicago settler, butchered a bear in plain sight, hours before serving the animal as the evening's fare during a gala banquet welcoming Senator Daniel Webster of Massachusetts to Chicago.[1] The spectacle sickened the children and jarred the sensibilities of the faint-hearted observing the proceeding. Meat was a staple of their diet, but these early Chicagoans did not care to witness the process by which supper arrived at their tables.

In this growing city where manufacturing and transportation repositioned a sleepy frontier military garrison (Fort Dearborn) into a new and emerging metropolis of the midcontinent, the livestock and meatpacking industry required sound business practices, organization, and discipline to bring it under control.

Amid the lowing of cattle and the squeal of pigs as dollars and herds changed hands weekly, John Sherman, the enterprising and ambitious, albeit mostly forgotten man in Chicago history, urged consolidation of the independent yards into a remote location, somewhere out on the prairie beyond the line that would *never* be reached by the expanding city.

Sherman shrewdly recognized that the convergence of railroads— including the Michigan Central, the Burlington, the Michigan Southern, the Chicago and Northwestern, the Pittsburgh Fort Wayne and Chicago, the Chicago and Danville, the Rock Island, Chicago and Alton, and the Illinois Central in Chicago—was key to the plan. He sensed that the railroad moguls would line up for the privilege of becoming chief contributors in building this livestock colossus where the lambs went to slaughter in a city marching to global prominence. There is much that can be said about John B. Sherman, but mainly he was a brilliant and intuitive promoter who glimpsed the future. On the first of June 1865, investors broke ground on the Union Stock Yards and Transit Company, a venture that had been incorporated by the Illinois state legislature four months earlier on February 13, 1865.

As he surveyed the scene at Forty-First and Halsted on that long ago afternoon, Sherman observed crews of workmen laying ties and rail at a feverish pace. These special tracks connected with every railroad line in Chicago. Contracts were signed. Handshakes and cigars followed. Samuel Waters Allerton, pioneering meat packer, farmer, and financier, who arrived in Chicago as a cattle buyer in 1856 and cornered the local hog market four years later to earn his first million, clapped his associate, John Sherman, on the back. Allerton, a behind-the-scenes operative had written a series of persuasive letters imploring the leading money men in Chicago to merge the three stock receiving yards into a central location under the supervision of his erstwhile business partner, John Sherman.[2]

Within days, a thousand former Civil War veterans home from the southern battlefields, were on the job building the largest open air "hotel" for meat animals the world had ever seen. For 106 years—from 1865 to 1971—the "frontier supply post of the nation," as one commentator adroitly described it in 1904, fed the nation in war and peace, depression and prosperity.[3]

The obliging railroad titans spared John Sherman out-of-pocket costs in their quest to become "kings of the Chicago yards." They happily put up a million dollars in stock to acquire 120 acres of soggy marshland owned by Chicago's colorful and loquacious former mayor and wealthiest landowner, "Long John" Wentworth, to construct the holding pens, the packing houses and the terminals, a brick hotel, the Union Stock Yards National Bank, and the scale houses. In return the nine railroads counted on the untold fortunes awaiting them from what can accurately be described as a shared monopoly that within a few years would be worth millions to them.

The relentless push of the westward rails (notably the Kansas Pacific— later the Union Pacific—and the Atchison, Topeka, and Santa Fe) made it possible for the farmers and ranchers from as far south as the Rio Grande to ship in herds of a thousand or more from the sprawling pasturage of Texas northward via the Chisholm Trail to the lawless cow town of Abilene, an important transit point for cowboys and their herds. Within a few years of the founding of Abilene, the trade route spread into Hays City, Newton, Ellsworth, and Dodge City, Kansas.

Joseph G. McCoy, a cattleman from Sangamon County, Illinois, literally "bought" the rough and ready Abilene for the express purpose of establishing a railhead for livestock and built it up along the adjoining Union Pacific line. McCoy encouraged Texas ranchers to drive their massive herds of longhorn through "the first guide meridian west from the sixth principal meridian," the trade route officially sanctioned by the state of Kansas. The first Chicago-bound shipment steamed out of Abilene on September 5, 1867. Before the end of the year, thirty-five thousand head of cattle were shipped east to the great abattoir of Chicago where they fetched thirty to forty dollars a head. A year later, the number doubled, and the grateful citizens of Abilene elected McCoy mayor, although few among them could possibly have anticipated the scourge of crime, prostitution, drunkenness, and bloody gunfights that would paralyze the town in the years to come. McCoy often referred to himself as "the Real McCoy."[4]

Christmas-time temperatures in Chicago in 1865 hovered near zero. It was a bitterly cold winter that year as war-weary Chicagoans celebrated the return of peace after surviving four long years of conflict, the loss of loved ones, and searing memories of the bloody skirmishes on southern battlefields. But now the joyous prewar times had returned. The Wabash Avenue Skating Rink advertised "beautiful ice" and all-day skating on that long-ago Christmas Day. At Washington Park, the "Great Union Band" entertained skaters with lively patriotic renditions and a promise that "The Great Attraction in the Evening Will Be the Calcium Light—The Same as Used to Light Central Park, New York!" Crosby's Opera House, a gleaming palace of the arts until it was reduced to cinders and ash during the Great Chicago Fire, advertised a performance of *La Dame Blanche*. Chicago in 1865: the emerging city of stockyards and Giuseppe Verdi.

The next day, a Tuesday, Sherman's plan to transform nineteenth-century Chicago into the greatest livestock market in the world commenced, but press coverage was scant. The city's contribution to the advancement of Western Civilization through its eating habits earned barely two inches of coverage in the morning *Tribune*. The newspaper laconically noted on December 27, that "yesterday the roads and avenues leading to the yards were lined with people going to and fro. A host of 800 persons were present yesterday morning at the opening of business. The first load of livestock was purchased by Colonel John Hancock, and Worcester, Hough, and Company turned the first load of hogs into the road to the packing town."

After an inauspicious beginning—Sherman's vision of empire unfolded. The "Big Four," a consortium of rich and powerful men with New England roots, took over packing town while Sherman ambled through the yards on horseback each morning inspecting the chutes and pens and barking orders.

Heinrich Schliemann, the German archeologist who discovered ancient Troy, also uncovered the wonders of the Sherman stockyards on his own during his 1867 Chicago tour. "The Superintendent, Mr. John B. Sherman, gave us leave to visit the whole establishment, which covers 345 acres of land and cost $1,700,432. There is an immense hotel, a large bank, and 120 acres planked and covered with pens and yards laid off in blocks; the planked roads are thirty to forty feet broad. There is an artesian well 1,100 feet deep which delivers 40,000 gallons of water daily. The establishment is extremely grand. It is west of the city and there is no doubt that the city will reach this point in a few years."[5]

The skillful Big Four monopolists reaped a whirlwind on the backs of hogs, steers, cattle, and sheep pouring into Chicago from Texas, Iowa,

Nebraska, Kansas, Colorado, Wyoming, New Mexico, Missouri, and down-state Illinois to become the titans of Packing Town.

Phillip Danforth Armour of Stockbridge, Madison County, New York, a stout man of regular habits, made his first fortune in the California gold fields by founding Armour and Company in 1867. This resolute and devoutly pious New England Yankee introduced a fleet of refrigerated train cars to ship packaged meat long distances without spoilage. His Armour Refrigerator Line, established in 1883, revolutionized the industry and became the largest private car fleet in the nation.

Before this innovation packers shipped barrels of salt pork, the staple product of the Yards and the safest animal product resistant to spoilage, to remote markets. In 1857, the first consignment of dressed beef left Chicago in railroad cars filled with ice. However, the process was costly and ineffective. Ice would melt away. Unless the beef had been properly cured before shipment it would rot. In the warm summer months before refrigeration, operations in Packing Town ceased. For four months each year previously, the workers were idled.

Despite advances in refrigeration, accusations flew that cattle and dressed beef that shipped out of the Union Stockyards to eastern markets were diseased and unfit for consumption. It struck a raw nerve with the fiercely loyal Sherman. "For many years, the Health Department of the City of Chicago has maintained at these yards a rigid inspection of livestock and livestock products," he fired back in a letter dated October 14, 1886. "For many years also, these yards have been patrolled by an officer of the State, charged with the duty of enforcing good care, sufficient feeding, and humane treatment of our livestock. I know our cattle were never healthier than they are now and have been throughout the season. The only cattle that are allowed to enter these yards are those that come from rail from the country. I believe it is practically impossible to ship diseased cattle or dressed beef from these yards!"[6]

Complaints about the unfitness of Armour meat products reached Washington in March 1899, when a presidential court of inquiry heard testimony from service veterans of the Spanish-American War that the canned beef sent to the troops in Cuba from Armour and its subsidiaries sickened the troops and caused dysentery, scurvy, and other illnesses despite assurances of proper refrigeration and handling.

Drawn to the company defense for this and many other health-related concerns, Sherman bristled when confronted about the muck and mire of Bubbly Creek, the 1.2-mile-long sewage outlet of the South Branch of the Chicago River utilized by Packing Town workers to wantonly discard animal entrails, carcasses, offal, and blood into the river. Over five hundred thousand gallons of water were drawn from Bubbly Creek every day and processed through a filtration plant, which the packing house titans refused to allow inspectors to tour. "We contribute to the wealth, the importance and the greatness of Chicago," Sherman angrily told an aldermanic delegation investigating conditions in January1890. "We will not be behind in contributing to Chicago's good sanitary conditions. It is true we have been sewering [*sic*] into the South Fork. But all Bridgeport has been doing the same thing. The Town of Lake has been sewering into the South Fork. Are we then to be held responsible for the whole?"[7]

In its worst and most vile period, the water bubbled methane and hydrogen sulfide, the result of blood and animal decomposition. It created an appalling stench. Murderers, armed robbers, and criminal thugs of every stripe frequently tossed victims of their foul play into the muck below from atop the Ashland Avenue Bridge. One notorious example occurred on May 20, 1911, when three hold-up men tossed the unconscious Joseph Mischelot over the rail of the bridge. A solid bed of grease provided a buoyant cushion that prevented Mischelot from sinking to the bottom and drowning. Five hours after his fall, Mischelot awoke in stark terror. Too weak to cry out for help, and fearing he might sink to the bottom at any moment, the victim of this crime later recounted that pedestrians crossing the bridge overhead spotted him in the creek but kept walking with no offer of assistance. After all that time in the water, Mischelot finally managed to wiggle his way to the bank, covered in ooze and deathly sick.

After considerable effort, and however delirious, he made his way home where family members helped clean him up. An ambulance from the Stockyards Police Station answered the family's call for emergency help and dispatched him to the Cook County Hospital where the poor man expired from the ravages of pneumonia three days later.

In our modern age, neighborhood residents living nearby occasionally spot bubbles percolating to the surface in the summertime. Until Wallace G. Clark, trustee of the Chicago Sanitary District demanded that the powerful packing house magnates dredge this "most pestilent spot in the city, the region remained a plague spot on the city map."[8] Upton Sinclair, the outspoken novelist and muckraking journalist of the Progressive Era, called Bubbly Creek a great "open sewer"; "like a bed of lava; chickens walk about on it!"[9] And sometimes people. It is estimated that the disease-bearing spillage from Bubbly Creek claimed eight thousand lives in 1914. For decades the Sanitary District of Chicago prodded and badgered the meatpacking industry titans to invest in a cleanup. "It is absolutely unthinkable that the packing industry should continue the cesspool because it costs a few dollars to abate the nuisance," complained Wallace Clark in 1915 during a meeting of concerned residents.[10] That year, the district agreed to pay two-fifths of the cost of sanitizing the settling tanks. The cleanup began September 8, 1920, when Charles G. Wacker, members of the Chicago Plan Commission, and Wallace Clark turned the first spade of dirt commencing a steam shovel project to remove the sludge and fill in portions of the river, although pollution stretched well north of Thirty-Ninth Street.

On August 3, 1959, the US House of Representatives, by a voice vote, authorized the closing of Bubbly Creek with the construction of a bulkhead to prevent fill materials from washing out into the main channel of the river. The bill passed through Congress and went to the president for his signature. Even these draconian measures failed to put a permanent end to the public nuisance. In 2015, the Army Corps of Engineers halted a $2.65 million cleanup and restoration of the waterway when it was revealed that a private firm had been hired to remove contaminants in a remediation project at several former industrial gas plants nearby once associated with the Yards. An oil spill from an unknown source occurring near Ashland Avenue in October 2017 spread west to Pulaski Avenue killing wildlife, and further complicating the efforts of the Environmental Protection Agency and the Water Reclamation District of Greater Chicago to restore this body of water for public use.

"I am just a butcher trying to go to Heaven," sermonized the abstemious Armour amid harsh criticism over sanitary conditions and the plight of labor struggling mightily for union recognition. "Through the wages I dispense and the provisions I supply, I give more people food than any man alive!"[11] In his public philanthropies, Phillip Danforth Armour garnered praise as a worldly-wise, God-fearing benefactor and friend of the poor whose largesse funded the Armour Mission, Armour Flats (company housing near the Yards) and the Armour Institute of Technology (now the Illinois Institute of Technology [IIT]).

"Most men talk too much!" sayeth Armour. "Most of my success has been due to keeping my mouth shut! I have no other interest in life but my business. I do not want any more money. What I do love is the getting of it. God did not overlook me. I don't go to theaters or clubs, and the mild enjoyment of home does not wear me out. What other interest can you suggest to me? I do not read. I do not take any part in politics. What can I do?"[12]

In a sermon given at St. James Methodist Church following his death on Chicago on January 6, 1901, the Reverend Dr. Robert McIntyre eulogized, "We have not many artists, musicians and authors, but we have plenty of splendid businessmen. I have visited many of his [Armour's] establishments in various cities. All of his benefactions are not written here below but are inscribed upon the golden book in the other world."[13]

Gustavus Swift, a tall, angular butcher and breeder from Cape Cod, Massachusetts, moved his packaging business from Milwaukee to Chicago in 1875, becoming Armour's most formidable competitor, while sharing a similar outlook on life. Swift entered the packing business at age sixteen with twenty dollars borrowed from his father that he invested in a meat wagon he drove up and down Cape Cod. In his lifetime, Swift made every penny count, and was the first to conceive the idea of slaughtering the animals in Chicago and shipping the dressed meat to the Eastern seaboard.

"The secret of all good things," Swift observed, "is hard work and self-reliance. Chicago is the finest city in the world for the moderate, natural average man of affairs in which to live. The New Yorker who says Chicago is a city of no luxuries is probably one of that constantly growing number who are insatiable in their greed for the softer things of life. I do not go in for luxuries."[14]

Swift raised six sons, all of them involved in some degree with their father's meatpacking empire. In later years, Edward Foster Swift, the second son, served as chairman of the board of the company. He fell to his death from the eighth floor of his luxurious Gold Coast apartment at 1150 North State Parkway on May 28, 1932. No one could say with any certainty if his untimely death was an accident or suicide.

Nelson Morris, the largest exporter of live cattle in America, was another meatpacker with little taste for travel and the extravagance of maintaining social position. He enjoyed the simple pleasures afforded him by whittling. When Morris sat down to talk with a colleague or client, the first thing he did to relax was pull out a knife, test the sharpness of the blade with his thumb, then reduce the wood or a sheet of paper to shavings. Testifying before a congressional committee in Washington, DC, inquiring about dressed beef in the summer of 1890, he drew out his trusty knife and whittled a sheaf of notepaper during questioning.

Morris was cursed with a high squeaky voice but blessed with a shrewd business sense. He took a job as a shoeshine boy in the vicinity of the Yards before accepting a night job from John Sherman in the hog pens of the Myrick Yards.[15] After learning the ropes, he hired himself out to cattle buyers as a drover and with money in hand he opened a small butcher shop and slaughterhouse. Sensing an opportunity, he bought up herds of broken-down and diseased cattle and sold the manufactured animal byproducts. He was a recognized expert judge of meats, inspiring oft-told tales and legends.

"If Nels Morris ate a piece of beefsteak, he could tell you from what part of the country came the steer from which it was cut. He knew the stock raisers as no other man," a Yards stockman confided to a *Tribune* reporter on August 27, 1907, following Morris's passing at age sixty-nine. The Morris Company boasted annual sales of $11 million by 1873 and $100 million by the time of his death.

Milwaukeean John Cudahy, the fourth wheel of the blood-soaked meat-packing engine, founded the company town of Cudahy, Wisconsin. He was an early investor in a fledgling football team Chicago Bears fans love to hate—the Green Bay Packers.[16]

The Chicago Union Stockyards and Packing Town directly west of the holding pens laid out in rectangular streets is where the industrial age unfolded. This free-wheeling example of American capitalism and ingenuity at its finest inspired Henry Ford to invent the automotive assembly line at his River Rouge plant in Dearborn, Michigan, after studying the great disassembly of animals through the speed of Armour's massive conveyor chain operation.

Ford stood in awe as the carcasses passed from one man to the next in amazing precision, each performing a simple task during the butchering and packaging of animals. Nothing went to waste, except the lowing of a cow and the pig's oink and squeal. In 1894, the bemused French critic Paul Bourget described an efficient, albeit frightening process. "A pig that went to the abattoir at Chicago came out fifteen minutes later in the form of ham, sausages, hair, hair brushes, hair oil, glue, gelatin, insulin, fertilizer, pepsin, canned fruit, cosmetics, margarine, and binding for Bibles."[17] A factory located at Forty-Fourth Street and Ashland processed animal hair into saleable items.

The meat business and its retail product formed the mainstay of Yards operations and reached consumers in pickled, salted, frozen, cured, or processed forms. Dairy and poultry products distributed to grocery stores, and bales of processed manure collected from the city streets and the animal pens sold to rural farmers as fertilizer formed the nexus of a kindred trade that accounted for the second highest revenue stream inside the world's largest open-air "waiting room" for animals.

Slaughterhouse operations manufactured and delivered an estimated 2,500 to 3,000 by-products to consumers during its 106 years of existence. Meatpacking houses, lard refineries, cooling plants, fertilizer and glue factories, railroad car repair sheds, chemistry labs, fertilizer shops, and related businesses spanned fourteen acres adjacent to the Yards and employed more people—upward of seventy-five thousand during its peak years—than any other Chicago industry. Packing Town had its own newspaper, the *Drover's Journal*, a "Whiskey Row" for habitual imbibers, an elevated rapid transit line connecting the adjoining neighborhoods to the workplace, a hotel, and tourist office.

By 1931, three hundred thousand visitors including schoolchildren escorted by their teachers during class outings, passed through the gates of Packing Town to marvel at (or be sickened by) the spectacle. Arthur Meeker, Prairie Avenue author, sophisticate, and the son of Arthur Meeker Sr., general manager of Armour and Company, recalled the powerful allure of the place. "Crowned heads and presidents, political leaders, famous authors, stars of the stage and musical worlds seemed to have an irresistible urge to investigate what went on in slaughter houses and canning factories. Father told me that Sarah Bernhardt watched the pig sticking for an hour; not content with that, she forced the shrieking members of her troupe down to the last tearful ingénue, to do likewise. '*Quelle technique!*' she declared. '*C'est terrible, mais c'est superbe!*' Miss [Mary] Garden, fresh from her triumphs with [Oscar] Hammerstein in New York, then in her first season as a feted prima donna in Chicago's newly formed opera company decided to join the rush."[18]

High-stakes gambler "Big Jim" O'Leary provided entertaining diversions for the *hoi polloi*, relieving the cowboys and packers of their hard-earned wages inside his plush saloon at 4183 S. Halsted. Crooked games of chance—faro, euchre, and poker—a hot Turkish bath, bowling, and female companionship awaited. Big Jim boasted: "I've been raided a thousand times, but I ain't ever had a real raid!" Why? Inspector Clancy of the Stockyards Police Station was an accommodating and cooperative ally.[19]

The Union Stockyards and Transit Company functioned as a service organization and vast public market where farmers and cattlemen from across the nation sold their animals on a competitive basis to commission men representing the meatpacking firms, Eastern shippers, local butchers, and other stockyards from around the country. The Chicago market set rural farm pricing rates every day of trading. The price of livestock in the Yards reflected the costs of feed lots and auction barns across the nation. It was not a simple business.

Commission men and buyers in this open-air market relied on judgment, brains, and experience to assess and price the fourteen classifications of cattle, ranging in quality from fancy and choice cattle to common-to-choice bulls, northern range steers, Texas steers, poor-to-medium cows, veal calves, and milk cows. The Yards provided unloading docks adjacent to the railways; pens, feed, water, and counting and weighing devices for the drover accompanying the herds. The company did not own, buy, sell, or enter into livestock transactions. Prices were determined by the law of supply and demand, and the hours of operation extended from 8:00 A.M.

until 2:00 P.M. Stockyard cowboys were a familiar sight to the Back of the Yards neighbors. As a young man in search of life's calling, native son Richard J. Daley rode his mount in hot pursuit of escaping steers. As mayor of Chicago from 1955 to 1976, he maintained tight control over a corral of a far different nature in city hall.

A sense of excitement hung in the air, comingled with the noxious odors wafting across the greater South Side on lazy, hot summer nights. Packing Town and the Yards linger in memory as a metaphor of hardship, unsanitary working conditions, rising desperation when the paycheck failed to cover the rent and groceries, ruthless labor practices, and two horrific fires—the one that claimed the life of fire chief James J. Horan on December 22, 1910, and the big one occurring in the scorching heat of May 19, 1934. It took the efforts of sixteen hundred firefighters to spare the city a second Great Chicago Fire.

The 1934 blaze, the second worst conflagration in city history, might have engulfed the entire city if not for the prevailing winds blowing northward. Although Big Jim O'Leary departed the world in 1921, his gloriously festooned saloon burned to the ground.

The decentralization of this billion-dollar industry that fed standing armies, explorers, and "littered the deserts, the morasses, and the tenantless mountains of the world with their meat cans," in the words of writer Jonas Howard in 1904, spelled the end of a way of life beginning in the late 1940s.[20] Advances in interstate trucking made it possible for breeders to sell to the packers directly and conduct the slaughter of animals where they were raised, eliminating the need for costly rail shipment to Chicago and an army of middle men. Armour, Wilson, and Swift vacated their plants in the 1950s, and by 1955, the Omaha Union Stockyards overtook Chicago as the largest livestock market and packing town in the nation.

As the years passed, the cattle business and meatpacking industries migrated from the Midwestern Corn Belt to the Great Plains. One by one the famous old stockyards of Chicago, Kansas City, Kansas, and Sioux City, Iowa, closed the gates. In Omaha, a 116-year-old operation ended its run in 1999. Meatpacking giants led by IBP (formerly Iowa Beef Processors), built their own slaughterhouses closer to the sources of supply and decentralized the entire industry. Ironically, Dodge City, Kansas, one of the focal points of the Western cattle drives of the 1870s, remains an important center of meatpacking in the United States. With this major demographic shift, there was no further reason for farmers to bundle their livestock into city-bound freight trains and over-the-road trucks.

Hog trading in Chicago concluded in May 1970. On the last full day of operations, August 15, 1971, scavengers tore through the empty animal pens in search of souvenirs—rusted latches from the wooden gates mostly. In the Stockyards Industrial Park, a collection of third-party logistics (3-PL) warehouses now line paved streets and neatly manicured park lawns. They bear no resemblance to the clamor and hustle of the old Yards. On most days it is eerily quiet. That commercial stretch of Halsted Street fronting the park from Forty-First down to Forty-Seventh is today a ghost town.

John B. Sherman, the Duchess County, New York, middleman and overseer of the pens served as an officer and president of the Chicago Union Stock Yard and Transit Company for thirty-four years. It was his vision, inspiration, and creation, but rarely is he mentioned in the company of Armour, Morris, Swift, and Cudahy, the packing town bravos dispensing the wages, beating back the unions, and inspiring Upton Sinclair to expose the squalor and filth in his 1906 novel *The Jungle*.[21]

Sherman, as history's forgotten man, retired as president of the Union Stock Yards and Transit Company on January 17, 1900, informing the trustees that at age seventy-five, he was old and tired and in need of rest. He said he would be dividing his time between his Prairie Avenue mansion on Chicago's sequestered "millionaire's row" east of Indiana Avenue and a summer home in Nantucket, Rhode Island.

"I think it's about time that I get out of the way and give young blood a chance. I will throw off my business harness entirely when my resignation is formally received. I am an old man and I think I better begin looking for recreation."[22]

He passed away inside his mansion on February 25, 1902, from the grippe, what we now call influenza. In October 1905, over a thousand residents turned out for dedication ceremonies marking the opening of John B. Sherman Park on the Southwest Side. The new field house and green space inaugurated the city's fledgling Outer Belt Project, a strategy aimed at establishing smaller public recreational parks for the benefit of children living in densely packed inner-city neighborhoods and slum sections of Chicago.

The last surviving iconography celebrating the man, the Yards, and the era, peers forlornly down on Exchange Avenue a block west of Halsted, the eastern exposure.[23] A bust of a bull's head commemorating John B. Sherman's prized animal "Sherman" is embedded in the ceremonial limestone arch designed by architects Daniel Hudson Burnham and John Wellborn Root in 1879. Burnham conceived the bust as a lasting homage to his old friend and father-in-law, John B. Sherman, whose ornate Ruskinian Gothic-styled mansion at 2100 S. Prairie he personally designed.[24] Sherman's only daughter, Margaret, married Daniel Burnham.

ELISHA GRAY AND THE INVENTION OF THE TELEPHONE

eturning from a brief but productive excursion to the Continent where he had displayed a remarkable new device that transmitted sounds from one end of a telegraph wire to another to the captains of industry, Elisha Gray, superintendent of the Western Electric Manufacturing Company of Chicago, stood nervously before a private gathering of a dozen curious Chicago industrialists.

Anson Stager, the cold and mechanical retired military general who figured so prominently in the doomed nuptials of Mr. and Mrs. Leslie Carter, hosted this impromptu demonstration of Gray's odd-looking little machine inside his office in the Union Building, at the corner of Washington and LaSalle Streets.

Gray's stated purpose, this cold morning of January 5, 1875, was to impress upon these important gentlemen the practical value of his newest and grandest invention following years of trial and error inside his Highland Park laboratory on Chicago's once remote North Shore. Elisha Gray called his creation the "telephone." An invited reporter from the *Chicago Tribune* peppered the inventor with questions.

Q—What is the practical application of your invention?
A—The practical feature of the invention lies in the fact, that with my instrument, I can transmit all the common chords of a seventeen octave piano along a single wire at the same time, and in the further fact that these harmonic sounds can be analyzed at the receiving end on instruments, each of which selects its own peculiar note and rejects all others. Thus one wire can easily be employed by twenty-two different sending and twenty-two different receiving operators.
Q—Does the length of line make any difference?
A—Of course the longer the wire, the larger the battery required, but the sound is carried over any length of wire which is

electrified from a sufficiently strong battery. In England I made experiments on what they called there an artificial cable, representing the conditions of the actual ocean cable. The experiments were . . . thoroughly successful.

Q—What did the Continental scientists think of your invention? A—I had it in London at the Royal Institution for one week where it was exhibited by Professor [John] Tyndall to quite a number of leading scientific gentlemen whose names I forgot.[1] I think that a couple hundred people in all must have seen the working of my apparatus in London, and they were all very much astonished. One gentleman told me that when he first heard the idea he set it down as a Yankee humbug but after seeing it, he acknowledged his opinion had to undergo a radical change.[2]

Emboldened by the favorable response of the British scientists, Elisha Gray, the forty-year-old facile genius who had worked his way through Oberlin College in Ohio for want of funds, summoned forth Chicago's leading business lights to the Union Building at the behest of General Stager, his wealthy benefactor. A mile distant, at a Kinzie Street address just east of State Street, the transmitting operator controlled the sound-producing instrument. Engaging the device, the operator, not coincidentally an accomplished violinist, provided the musical accompaniment, playing "Auld Lang Syne," "Coming through the Rye," "Yankee Doodle," and "Robin Adair" directly into the device.

In the Union Building office, Gray positioned a wooden "sounding box" measuring sixteen inches in length and four inches high with an electric magnet placed on the top surface. "The sound was produced at the other end of the line by an instrument fitted with keys, which under the action of the electric current, underwent a certain number of vibrations of the higher keys, being of course, much greater than the lower," the newspaper scribe reported, although he was not quite sure if his scientific description was 100 percent accurate, of course.

Sound had been transmitted by force of an electric current. "I have made an experiment which satisfies me that a musical sound can be transmitted four thousand miles without losing correctness of the tone!" beamed the excited inventor. "The quality of the tone at the receiving end is determined by the nature of the receiving apparatus, the time, the tune, by the musician who plays the electrical instrument at the transmitting end of the wire."[3]

Professor David Swing, pastor of the Fourth Presbyterian Church and an eminent theologian until he had to answer to twenty-two counts of heresy in 1874, observed the proceedings with a critical detachment. At the end of the demonstration, his face unexpectedly brightened. "By Heavens Gray, I think you have come up with the invention that will change the lot of all mankind!" gushed Dr. Swing. "It is a miracle of the age!"

Stephen Francis Gale, one of the city's oldest settlers and the half owner of the Illinois Stone Quarry in Lemont—a manufacturing concern supplying the "Athens" limestone that built so many of Chicago's notable public buildings of the Gilded Age—nodded his assent. "It remains to be seen how far all of this will go."[4]

Six months passed. On July 27, 1875, Elisha Gray obtained a patent for his successful invention that made it possible to transmit musical values (electro-harmonic telegraphy). The next step, the toughest challenge of all lay ahead: the transmission of vocal sound.

A Scotch-Irish Quaker whose gift of scientific genius was only exceeded by his poor financial acumen and propensity for making millionaires out of his competitors, imitators, and business rivals, Gray was born into rural poverty at Barnesville in Belmont County, Ohio, on August 2, 1835, to David and Christiana Gray. The boy was apprenticed to the village blacksmith at age twelve, after his father's sudden death and his mother's marriage to a Quaker farmer in East Bethlehem Township, Pennsylvania. The physical demands of blacksmithing proved too much of a strain on his body, forcing Elisha to give it up and try his hand as an apprentice carpenter and steamboat builder the Carver and Wood planing mill in Brownsville, Fayette County, Pennsylvania. In this drab industrial mill town where the manufacture of flatboats and petroleum coke kept an immigrant population working, through the sweat of his brow, Gray helped build and launch the steamship *Monongahela* in 1860.

Oberlin College, the oldest co-educational liberal arts college in the United States, admitted African American students and young men and women of reduced financial circumstances in the nineteenth century, thus becoming the first institution of higher learning in the United States to liberalize admission standards with the intention of making higher education universal to all people. Elisha Gray submitted his credentials to the registrar.

Gray entered college in February 1856 at age twenty-one and worked his way through Oberlin, graduating at the head of his class after five years of diligent and disciplined study. The young man, burdened by poverty, managed to finance his education through earnings received at the carpenter's bench. He was betrothed to his landlady's daughter, Delia Minerva Sheppard, an Oberlin girl, upon graduation. Gray tried his hand at farming but was unsuccessful in the endeavor and abandoned the whole idea of it by the advent of Reconstruction in 1865.

At age thirty, Gray, a tall man with steel gray eyes, had turned his attention to the study of electricity, fascinated as he was by its properties and its research potential. He was instilled with an ambition to invent and create everyday miracles he believed would benefit mankind. In so doing, Gray developed an automatic, self-adjusting telegraph relay and obtained his first patent—the first of forty he would hold in his lifetime—in 1867. It was the first of his many creations that set in motion a remarkable chain of events that ultimately introduced the telephone to modern American life.

General Stager, a telegraph expert whose skills were put to good use by the Union Army during the Civil War, recognized Gray's genius and invited him to the telegraph office of Western Union in Cleveland to conduct further experiments. Warmly received by Stager in Northeast Ohio, Gray was given a free hand to work with an array of electrical gadgets.

With working capital of $2,000, Elisha Gray organized a company in 1869—Gray and Barton—manufacturer, seller, and dealer of burglary alarms, telegraph equipment, and electrical supplies. Gray and Enos M. Barton pooled their savings and purchased a building with the help of a $500 note endorsed by General Stager. The partners operated the business from inside a small storefront at 162 South Water Street, Chicago's commercial, wholesale, and produce market adjoining the river.[5]

The Chicago Fire of October 8, 1871, missed their building by two blocks; a fortuitous turn of events for the charred and stricken city. During the reconstruction of the central business district in the postfire period, Gray and Barton supervised the repair of telegraph facilities and electrical installations.

Over the next few years Gray perfected a telegraphic switch, a needle annunciator for hotels and elevators, a telegraphic repeater, and a private telegraph line printer (in widespread use before the telephone). None of these long-forgotten creations changed the world nearly so dramatically or impactful as the telephone, of course, but Gray's gadgets helped to establish the *terra firma* of his long and useful career as an inventor. It gave him a measure of national acclaim he so desperately coveted and a place in the history of communications, although one ultimately and unjustly diminished by bad luck, poor business decisions, and cruel fate.

In 1872, after J. P. Morgan acquired one-third of Gray and Barton Company and with Gray's acquiescence, he renamed the entire operation the Western Electric Manufacturing Company of Chicago. Gray moved his family of five into a white Victorian Highland Park home at 460 Hazel Street, tucked away in several acres of lush forested land.[6] At the time, the Elisha Gray residence was one of only four residential dwellings in this stagecoach whistle-stop twenty-seven miles north of the Union Building where the inventor would unveil and demonstrate his invention to Chicago's most important people three years later. An adjoining barn functioned as Gray's laboratory and research room.

One afternoon, as Gray observed his nephew playing with coils and wires attached to a zinc-lined bathtub in the house, the inventor was struck by a sudden inspiration—electroharmonic telegraphy, the theoretical transmission of sound through wire. "My nephew was playing with a small induction coil taking shocks for the amusement of the younger children," he explained. "He had connected one end of the secondary coil to the zinc lining of the bathtub which was dry. Holding the other end of the coil in his left hand, he touched the lining of the tub with the right. In making contact, his hand would glide along the side for a short distance. At these times, I noticed that a sound was proceeding from under his hand at the point of contact, having the same pitch and quality as the vibrating *electrome*. I immediately took the electrome in my hand and repeating the operation, I found to my astonishment, that by rubbing hard and rapidly, I could make a much louder sound than the interrupter or the electrome. I then changed the pitch of the vibrator and found that the pitch of the sound under my hand was also changed, agreeing with that of the vibrator."[7]

After brainstorming the possibilities, Gray tested and refined the telephone instrument, succeeding in sending nine different messages over a wire five hundred miles long at the same moment. Elisha Gray demonstrated his musical telegraph wire before a private gathering of friends, neighbors, and fellow parishioners at the Highland Park Presbyterian Church, organized a year before the Grays moved west from Cleveland.

Immersed in his private world of research and a growing obsession with sending the spoken word over the wires, Gray borrowed heavily from the downtown money men to finance his scientific ventures, while often forgetting to pay the grocer. A $50,000 windfall from the sale of a patent financed a lavish European junket and the purchase of expensive art treasures on the Continent to decorate the Hazel Street home, earning Gray a reputation as a spendthrift. Elisha and Delia squandered the $50,000 leaving the inventor short of cash and forcing him to sell nearly all of his forty patents to raise money for further research and development. It was said that Gray lived like a man in a perpetual dream, and the financial titans of Chicago and New York instinctively knew when the time was right for them to purloin one of his patents for far less than it would have otherwise cost them when the inventor was flush.

"The time to deal with Gray is when he is dreadfully hard up," observed the head of a telegraph company to a *Los Angeles Times* reporter on March

4, 1901. "It is never good business to make him an offer when he has money. He wants a big price for the idea, which is practical working order. His figures are way up. The thing to do is wait until his bills get way up. He will then sell for a song."

Pressured by his financial backers and the certain knowledge that other men (among them Scottish-born Alexander Graham Bell), were competing against him for preeminence in the race to perfect the speaking telephone for person-to-person communication, Gray continued his experiments inside the Highland Park lab and brought the project to a resounding and successful completion in early 1876.

Early in the morning on February 14, Gray paid ten dollars and filed his "caveat"—a confidential report of an invention not yet fully perfected—with the US Patent Office in Washington, DC, for his electrical water transmitter. His principal rival, Alexander Graham Bell of Brantford, Ontario, *allegedly* submitted his application through his lawyer a few hours *ahead* of Gray. However, Mr. Bell, who experimented with a single pole magnet telephone as a means of communicating with his deaf mother, was in Boston on the fourteenth and did not arrive in Washington until February 26.[8] Based on the time stamp and the verification of the attorney's credentials, the examiners granted Bell two letters of patent numbered 174,465 on March 7, 1876, and 186,787 on January 30, 1877.

A bitter, decade-long patent infringement battle followed as the Bell Company ran roughshod over Gray and other scientists and inventors in their quest to establish the framework of a potent telephone monopoly to choke off competition. The Western Union Company telegraph division acquired patents held by both Gray and Thomas Edison and manufactured telephone equipment while the Bell Trust controlled service distribution. Litigants filed nearly six hundred lawsuits and counter lawsuits, including an action in the Southern District of Ohio to void the issuance of the two Bell patents.

With justification, Elisha Gray indignantly rejected Bell's narrative, disputing the legitimacy of his patent based on reliable reports of subterfuge and corruption within the US Patent office and a damning affidavit filed by one Zenas Fisk Wilber, principal examiner in charge of patents related to electrical inventions in the years 1875–1877. Wilber's startling confession that he had interceded on Bell's behalf for financial remuneration surfaced during a congressional hearing convened by the telephone committee on Capitol Hill, May 21, 1886. In his own words, Wilber revealed that he was a former alcoholic, and was personally indebted to one of Bell's patent attorneys.

"It will be impossible for the courts of the country to mete out exact justice without a knowledge of the influence brought to bear upon me while examiner in the patent office in 1875, 1876, and 1877 which caused me to show Professor Elisha Gray's caveat then under my charge and control, as by law provided and which caused me to favor Bell in various ways in acting on several applications for patents made by him. One of the affidavits [executed between July 30, 1885, and October 21, 1885], given at the request of the Bell Company by Mr. Swan of its counsel was given with and suffering from alcoholism and was obtained from me. I was vilified and attacked before the commission referred to. I could not reason in my condition the effect or scope of the affidavit, the data for which were supplied by Mr. Swan, who paid me $100 thereafter for the Bell Company. In this instance and at this time I am entirely and absolutely free from any alcohol whatever. I am perfectly sober and conscious master of myself, mentally and physically. I am convinced that by my action while examiner of patents Elisha Gray was deprived of proper opportunity to establish his right to the invention of the telephone and I now propose to tell how it was done. Upon my appointment to the patent office in 1870 our old acquaintance [with Washington patent attorney Major (Marcellus) Bailey representing Bell] was renewed. I had several times borrowed money from Major Bailey.[9] I was consequently in debt to Major Bailey at the time the application of Bell was filed in the office. In addition I was under obligation to him for a present to my wife—a very handsome and expensive gold hunting-case lady's watch. As I recollect, I borrowed $100 from him about the time Bell's application was filed. Feeling thus in his power from the obligations noted, surrounded by such environments, I was called upon officially upon the application of Alexander Graham Bell. . . . I was anxious to please Major Bailey and was hence desirous of finding that the Bell application was the earlier filed and I did not make as thorough an examination as I should have done, so when I found in the cash blotter the entry of the receipt of Gray's fee, I closed the examination and determined that Bell was the earlier, whereas I should have called for proof from Bell and Gray and have investigated in other directions instead of being controlled by the entities alluded to and the statements of Major Bailey to me. The effect of this was to throw Gray out of court without his having the opportunity to be heard or of having his rights protected, and the issuance of the patent, hurriedly and in advance of its turn to Bell."

Continuing with his testimony, Wilber confessed that he had "showed him [Bell] the original drawing of Gray's caveat and fully explained Gray's method of transmitting and receiving. Bell presented me with a $100 bill. Gray's caveat was a secret, confidential document under the law and I should not have been influenced to divulge the same; but I did so as hereinbefore related. The caveat for some was for some weeks in a file box on my desk. I stand ready and shall always be ready and willing to verify this statement before any court or proper tribunal in the land."[10]

The *Baltimore Sun* and the *Washington Post* reprinted the complete transcript of Wilber's testimony before Congress on May 22, 1886. Seen through the lens of history, and taking Zenas Wilber at his word, Elisha Gray appears to be the victim of a grave injustice and Bell a poseur, guilty of the crime of bribery.

Bell, of course, flatly denied Wilber's accusation of collusion that the two had met for the purpose of exchanging money in return for a glimpse of Gray's caveat and drawings. Several days passed, allowing Bell the opportunity to file his own affidavit disavowing any "corrupt practices." Bell conveniently produced an earlier communique written by Wilber and dated October 31, 1885.

The document, Bell asserted, had been circulated within the offices of the secretary of the interior, and the following statement written by Wilber was in fact true and verifiable: "In the conduct of such application there was no fraud of any kind whatever, nor anything, any transaction, any communication, oral or written, which would support any such allegation in the least manner whatsoever, either on the part of Professor Bell, his attorney, myself or any other person whatsoever."[11]

Professor Bell stated that he had met up with examiner Wilber only two or three times in his life, including a chance encounter on a New York street. "I did not recognize him and he introduced himself as Mr. Wilber. Even then I did not know who he was and then he said that he was a patent examiner when our patent came out. I then said I was glad to see him. But as far as the statement that I ever paid him a cent or offered to pay him anything, at any time is not true. I knew at the time the Bell patent was issued, I would have been glad to have $100 in my possession."[12]

Whether Wilber had been coerced into making this startling written declaration by Bell's lawyers under the pain of prosecution only to suffer remorse and guilt over perjuring himself, cannot be ascertained. The second affidavit, in support of Gray, "has been denied, affirmed and withdrawn until little credence is attached to it, but it is reported that on his deathbed Wilber again stood by his extraordinary story," the *Baltimore Sun* noted on January 22, 1901.

Zenas Wilber's credibility was assailed, and his reputation as a drunken patronage employee with a yarn to spin dissuaded the US Supreme Court from ruling in Gray's favor in its final decision rendered on March 19, 1888, after the preliminary hearings in January-February 1887. The justices of the Morrison Waite court came within one vote of overturning the Bell patent.[13]

There is a vast difference between a caveat and a patent, as the unhappy Gray soon learned.

All that Elisha Gray gained from the numerous court cases was the right to collect royalty payments on certain design aspects. Appalled and disillusioned by the outcome, the Highland Park inventor continued to assert his claim and never backed down from speaking against Alexander Graham Bell and his monopoly through the remainder of his days.

"Oh, I have always been on good terms with Bell," he said half-apologetically on September 1, 1882, six years before the unfortunate Supreme Court rendering. "I met him frequently during the controversy. I am indebted to him for no little notoriety. He made photo-lithographs of my private correspondence with him and published them all over the world when trying to establish priority of the invention for himself. He wasn't willing to concede any point in his own favor. His father-in-law, Gardiner Hubbard, managed the newspapers for him and worked up a body of literature on Professor Bell's side. I was never given that sort of notoriety, [but] let matters arrange themselves in their own time. The Paris Exhibition put a quietus on his modus operandi and works published since have given me all the justice necessary."[14]

By 1882, 220,000 telephones were in use across the United States. From his Highland Park workshop Gray continued to experiment and conceive new electrical components including the "*telautograph*"—the first facsimile machine capable of reproducing a written message, letter, or drawing at the other end of the wire. Gray received patents for the telautograph in 1888 and 1891 and demonstrated its practical value before a gathering of visiting scientists at the 1893 World's Fair in Chicago. The same year, Gray chaired the first International Electrical Congress held in Chicago and began experimenting with underwater sound transmission for ships at sea.

That Gray never abandoned his work—despite disappointment and bitterness and having been marginalized by history—is remarkable. Suffering from heart disease, Gray took up residence at 82 Huntington Avenue in Boston in 1898. Through sheer will and force of mind, Gray continued his experiments with Arthur J. Mundy in the development of effective underwater communication and submarine signaling designed to prevent nautical collisions until the moment of his death on January 21, 1901, in Newtonville, Massachusetts, a suburb of Boston. In his lifetime, he was one of only two Americans to be awarded the Grand Cross of the Legion of Honor of France by the president of the French Republic. The groundbreaking work and example set by Elisha Gray, Anton Stager, and Enos Barton inspired and paved the way for succeeding generations of Chicago-based pioneering industrialists to move forward: Eugene F. McDonald of Zenith Corporation; Paul V. Galvin of Motorola; Ross D. Siragusa of Admiral; and George A. Hughes, founder of Hughes Electric.[15]

Elisha Gray held the chair in Dynamic Electricity in two colleges, Oberlin and Ripon, and his powerful, albeit forgotten legacy inspired a small but loyal group of admirers to launch the Elisha Gray Historical Society decades after his death. The home of the man whose brush with immorality is measured in lost hours stands in quiet repose in the historic district of Highland Park. The families who lived there have come and gone. Ghostly sightings have been reported inside the old dwelling from time to time—but they must be considered benign—for this was a well-intentioned man, a genius among his peers but tragically ignored in our wireless, digital age.

"The history of the telephone," Gray lamented in his declining years, "will never fully be written. It is partly hidden away in twenty or thirty thousand pages of testimony and partly lying on the hearts and consciences of a few whose lips are sealed—some in death and others by a golden clasp whose grip is even tighter."[16]

CRIME AND PUNISHMENT AND THE FIRST POLICEWOMAN

n the worst years of sweatshops, unregulated factories, child labor, and rat-infested living quarters where, more often than not, one or both parents were incorrigible drunkards, it was the children who were made to suffer. Homeless boys peddling newspapers and blacking boots, referred to in the parlance of the day as "Street Arabs," hustled for pennies and slept on the floor of the Newsboys Home each night, enjoying sumptuous food only twice a year, Thanksgiving and Christmas Day, when the beau monde came calling with turkeys, pudding, and candies in hand.

The debased poverty and squalor of inner-city neighborhoods of the late Gilded Age, searing episodes of society's abandonment of its "throw-away" children played out. In an 1888 case, a callous, unfeeling father fled to New York City following the death of his wife to marry another woman. His fifteen-year-old daughter, whose name was Annie Quarter, was left to care for a two-year-old infant and the two younger boys who were driven into the streets to peddle newspapers on street corners to help pay for the upkeep of the flat. From inside the airless wooden tenement, reeking of old food smells and the funk of the unpaved alley adjoining 169 Barber Street, Annie found that she could no longer cope.

The girl summoned the Humane Society of Illinois, a charitable and even-handed organization that, in 1880, not only combatted animal abuse, but rescued truant, delinquent, and dependent children of the slums from neglectful and abusive parents. "If you want to quote all the cases of cruelty to children which necessitated the interference of the Humane Society you will have to fill two pages of the newspaper!" declared secretary H. W. Clarke. "It illustrates the dark sides of life in a large city and gives an adequate idea of the work our society is doing."[1]

The Humane Society attempted to contact the runaway father. Failing in their attempt, the Society ordered Annie and her siblings to be removed from the flat and placed in the care of the Home for the Friendless near the

South Side elevated line at Wabash Avenue and 20th Street. It was one of a dozen "social welfare" agencies and "homes" not unlike the workhouses of London's East End slums that had gained terrible notoriety during the Victorian Era.

The Home for the Friendless opened its doors in 1857 in an old, deserted hotel on the West Side. The Wabash Avenue building, donated by one Jonathan Burr, served the needs of the abandoned until becoming hopelessly overcrowded. The institution relocated to a brighter, more hospitable location at 51st Street and Vincennes in the Washington Park neighborhood on the South Side in August 1897. Some of Chicago's leading financiers, John V. Farwell, George M. Pullman, Norman B. Judd, and W. W. Kimball donated furnishings to outfit the sprawling English-Gothic structure.

The Uhilen Orphan Home; the Foundlings Home on Wood Street; St. Joseph's Orphan Asylum on Crawford Avenue; the Polish Orphan Asylum; St. Anthony's Orphanage; the Home for Destitute Crippled Children; the Nursery and Half-Orphan Asylum on Burling Street; the Newsboy's and Bootblack's Home at Quincy Street and 5th Avenue (now Wells Street); the Protestant Orphan Asylum at Michigan Avenue and 22nd Street; and the House of the Good Shepherd were among many other institutions receiving homeless and abandoned street urchins at this time. Such places were often plague spots for scarlet fever and diphtheria.

Truants and youngsters caught up in the criminal justice system before attaining the age of majority faced certain exile to the dangerously over-crowded John Worthy School, an extension of the County Bridewell where delinquent boys co-mingled with adult criminals in adjoining cell blocks after their school day ended; or the Illinois School of Agriculture and Manual Training at Glenwood organized by an agent of the Humane Society on February 5, 1887; or the Chicago Industrial Training School for Girls, or the St. Mary's Training School at Feehanville.[2]

Children under the age of fifteen toiled in hazardous surroundings performing dangerous work for employers flaunting unenforceable statutes until the Chicago City Council passed an ordinance on February 14, 1888, banning the employment of boys and girls under the age of fifteen. The newly enacted Compulsory Education Act mandated that "every person having control or charge of any child or children between the ages of eight and fourteen years shall send such children to a public or private school for a period of not less than twelve weeks of each school year." Teenagers between the ages of fourteen and sixteen were required by law to obtain a working certificate, but the rules were weak and often unenforceable.

The statute limited the hours of daily employment to eight, and children were required to be able to read and write. By 1904, under the direction of Edgar T. Davies, chief factory inspector for the city of Chicago in charge of eighteen other inspectors, necessary reforms were enacted and the number of successful prosecutions against companies and parents in violation of the strengthened statutes swelled to seven hundred. In a *Tribune* article dated October 10, 1904, writer W. L. Bodine asserted that "an army of child savers" were out in force to curb abuses and "the child labor law has brought about a complete change in the conditions of working children, and with the enforcement of the compulsory education law has stopped the former practice of filling the factories of Chicago with children of premature age who should have been in school." However, a countervailing report published on August 15, 1906, stated: "There was a time when the educational conditions in Illinois were equal or superior to those of any other state. The public schools of Chicago, as of the surrounding cities and states, took care of the children admirably and it was rare to find any child who had been in this country ten years who could not read or write. These conditions have changed and Illinois is going downhill. There is a distinct gain in illiteracy of children between the ages of ten and fourteen years in this state."[3]

Under prevailing Illinois law, however, licensed notary publics were empowered to grant affidavits exempting parents from the ruling if they merely *stated* to an inspector that their son or daughter satisfied the legal requirement. Impoverished mothers and fathers desperate to receive their children's meager earnings from the hours of manual labor they performed were taken at their word and given the benefit of the doubt.

If state and municipal ordinances were properly enforced the worst examples of child labor characterizing the late nineteenth century industrial age might have been mitigated and the damage to families lessened. "The ordinary citizen does not trouble himself about them," a *Tribune* editorialist bitterly complained. In this angry diatribe clearly aimed at Chicago's poor immigrant colonies, the newspaper assailed, "the factory inspectors appointed under the city ordinance who were nearly all labor agitators of various degrees of radicalism at some time or other hardly make complaint of its neglect and violation. The cruel and greedy employers are permitted to keep children under ten in shop and factory just as long as it suits their convenience at such hours as they deem proper without objection. And the lazy, shiftless, drunken parents are freely permitted to send their offspring to such employment at tender ages. The factory inspectors hardly ever prosecute a case under the ordinance."[4]

A brutal killing on February 27, 1888, thirteen days after passage of the city council ordinance designed to protect children from ruthless exploitation, drew the factory system and the objectionable plight of Chicago's underage workforce into sharper focus. The John E. Green factory at 1319 State Street, a manufacturer of boot and shoe heels, employed numerous underage kids of mixed races and ethnicities ranging in age from thirteen to seventeen. Their work day commenced at seven o'clock in the morning and extended until five in the afternoon. Their job was to cut leather heels.

Fifteen-year-old Maggie Gaughan quit school in order to earn some money in the Green factory to help her parents, Owen Gaughan, a teamster, and his wife, Mary—who were barely making ends meet in their squalid flat at 233 Twentieth Street.[5] Maggie had promised her father that she would return to the Harrison School after St. Patrick's Day—a vow tragically broken.

Maggie arrived early and was admitted into the building by Zephyr Davis, the seventeen-year-old shop foreman entrusted by Green to keep the employees busy during the times of his absence. That morning, with no one else present, the emboldened Davis sexually assaulted Maggie, although in his confession given to police, he denied raping the girl. He blamed Maggie for refusing a direct order to go work and for defiantly "sassing" him. He hurled a small hatchet in her direction as the terrified girl fled into a closet concealed underneath a stairway. Davis chased after her, forcing his way into the tiny closet.

Fiercely resisting his advances, she kicked and clawed at his face. Davis, standing five-foot-nine inches tall and heavily tattooed on his left and right arms, choked the life out of the girl and smashed her face multiple times with the hatchet. Davis pushed the bloodied remains into the corner of the closet, concealing the body with several large bags filled with leather findings. At the end of the workday after the workers had left the building, he planned to remove the remains under the cloak of darkness and bury her in an open field nearby.

"All day long he was absent-minded and nervous," the *Chicago Times* reported. Throughout the morning Davis furtively eyed the stairway closet. His suspicious behavior, duly noted by Green and the factory workforce, seemed puzzling. Later that afternoon Green ordered Davis to run an errand to The Fair, a large downtown department store to purchase a seventy-five-cent stovepipe. With reluctance, he complied.

While Davis completed his purchase, John Green directed little Eddie Dwyer, another underage worker, to remove the five sacks of leather from the closet. The horror-stricken boy shined a light into the space and spied the corpse and a large pool of blood splattered against the wall. He noted the butchered and hideous extremities of the girl and her stained and disheveled clothing. Detectives dispatched from the Harrison Street Armory arrived fifteen minutes later. Jarred by the singular brutality of the crime, the men removed the body from the closet and located the bloodied hatchet lying on the floor.

By now Zephyr Davis had completed his assigned task and was on his way back to the factory—but stopped short after spying the police wagon parked in front of the plant and a crowd of people hovering outside the door. The youth panicked and made a desperate run for it. The suspicious proprietor of a boarding house down the street told detectives that the young man had knocked on her door early that morning asking for a pail of water to wash away blood stains from an accidental wound to his hand. After news of the murder spread up and down State Street the woman informed police.

Captain H. H. Henshaw dispatched most wanted flyers to the heads of all rail lines and section bosses for trains leading out of Chicago. A few minutes after midnight telegraph operator O. F. Clark of the Wabash Railroad in Forrest, Livingston County, Illinois, sent word back to Chicago that a man matching Davis's description had been spotted alighting from a train.[6] Early the following morning, the same suspicious man, seated in the waiting room, asked John Meyers, the station porter, for the arrival time of the next train to Kansas City. Meyers alerted Clark, and the information was passed on to the town constable, William J. Martin.

As the Chicago–St. Louis Express rumbled into the station, Davis spotted the porter and the station master and two other men huddled at the edge of the platform looking in his direction. Alarmed, the fugitive jumped from the platform and sped down the track in the direction of Chicago. Martin, leading a six-man posse, chased Davis for three miles for a little over a half hour before catching up to him in the middle of a field thick with standing corn.

With harsh words cutting through the chilled winter air, Martin ordered Davis to surrender. Presented with a warrant for his arrest and a pistol aimed at his heart, Davis meekly complied. Martin affixed handcuffs and with the posse trailing behind, he led the prisoner back to the railroad depot, placing Zephyr inside the operator's room, careful to lock the door after him. News of the capture spread quickly across the hinterland and within a short time a sullen crowd of a hundred ominous-looking men assembled outside the station—one of them threateningly brandishing a rope.

Fearing the worst, the armed posse doubled. Martin and Clark hustled the prisoner out the back door and onto the train seconds after the engineer opened the throttle. A newspaper man blithely reported that Davis opened the window and spat upon one of the crowd, "a big six-footer."[7] The farmer drew a wicked-looking knife and made a desperate lunge at the black man through the window. Davis drew back and Martin dropped the sash. It seems curious that Zephyr managed to pull open a passenger window while his hands were manacled.

The account, if not entirely factual, speaks to the prevailing bias of the press. Although the city of Chicago, up to this point in its history, could not be accurately described as a cauldron of racial hatred, at least not to the horrific extent of the Jim Crow South. Chicago's small, but steadily growing African American population coalesced west of State Street and south of Harrison in the postfire period.

"Why did you kill her?" queried Martin.

"Because I told her to go to work and she wouldn't. She sassed me and I hit her with the hatchet!" They asked Davis if he had "criminally assaulted" the girl, meaning did he rape her?

"No I didn't. If she was alive today, she'd say I never so much as laid my hands on her that way."[8]

Zephyr Davis's face appeared troubled and his gaze wandered off. He offered no reply when his interrogators asked him why Maggie's skirts had been raised above her waist and her undergarments rearranged. Captain Wheeler Bartram and his detectives removed Davis from the train at the Archer Avenue crossing on the South Side of Chicago. Bundled into a carriage, the prisoner was driven to the Central Station for another round of interrogation. He said he had turned seventeen the previous August, and by law (theoretically) Davis could not be condemned to death since he was still six months shy of his eighteenth birthday.

A coroner's jury emerged from the basement of the Cook County Hospital to return a verdict of murder in the manner of death, censoring John E. Green for his policy of employing underage children of mixed races that was found to be pernicious to public morals. Acting police chief George Washington Hubbard, whose hasty appointment to command a demoralized police force following considerable public uproar over the death of the seven officers killed in the Haymarket bomb explosion on May 4, 1886, and an ineffective departmental response, doubled the size of the detail assigned to protect Zephyr Davis. Extra armed patrols encircled the Harrison Street Armory station.

Chicagoans of the late 1880s sensed danger all about them. Paranoia of a looming anarchist threat in the post-Haymarket period set friends and neighbors against one another. Suspicion leveled against trade-union activists invited police surveillance and possible jail detention in the exaggerated belief that wild, foreign-born elements were fomenting a Red Revolution in the streets of Chicago. It was whispered that informants would turn you in if you were not careful. Bomb throwers were everywhere, the business-friendly press cautioned. Armed criminals, footpads, vice mongers, and second-story men lurked in the shadows. Pass by an alley in the dead of night and you were sure to be garroted. A climate of fear permeated the city.

Chicago had passed its period of innocence. The antebellum City in a Garden (Chicago's official slogan since 1837), remembered by the old settlers for its church steeples, white picket fences, and azure blue skies free of indus-trial pollution, yielded to the darker forces of urbanization, factories, child labor, and a widening gulf between rich and poor, laborer and management, and rising hostility between immigrant and native and white and black.

Although, in 1885, the city had outlawed racial segregation in public ac-commodations and had earned praise for its progressive legislation assuring African American rights, the slaying of Maggie Gaughan by Davis, the son of former slaves who had tilled the farmland of Pleasant Hill, Missouri, enflamed white Chicago and opened a racial wound that would intensify and fester into the second decade of the twentieth century. Between 1870 and 1890, the city's African American population had steadily grown from 4,000 to 15,000. In that same twenty-year span, the overall city population dramatically increased from 299,000 to 1.1 million. Chicago, at that time, was the fastest growing city in the world.

By 1920, following the period of resettlement from the southern cotton states known as the "Great Migration," the number increased to 109,000. Incarcerated in the same iniquitous Cook County jail cell no. 11 that had once housed Louis Lingg, the accused bomb maker, whose incendiary device killed the seven uniformed officers in the Haymarket, spewed hostility and rage.[9] "Put me in a dungeon if you want! I can stand it! It don't make any difference if I am to be the first black man ever hung in Chicago," he said, as he was led to his cell by Conrad Folz, for twenty-four years the jailer of Cook County. "I'll die like a man!"[10]

The pendulum of justice never swung between a scintilla of belief in his innocence or the slightest shred of doubt concerning his guilt. Attorney John J. Arney for the defense advised his client to plead insanity with the hope of saving Davis from the gallows. But with public interest running high and the sentiments of white Chicago firmly planted against the accused, conviction seemed inevitable. Each day, whites and blacks packed the galleries of the courtroom. Tension hung in the air. Despite the heinous nature of the crime, Chicago's African American community expressed its sympathies for the victim, its concerns for Davis, and questioned the fairness of the criminal courts and the scales of northern justice for the black man.

Judge Kirk Hawes of the superior court waived away defense counsel's request for a change of venue on the grounds that ill feeling against his client prejudiced the jury.[11] He dismissed medical testimony introduced into court attesting that Davis's mind was unsound and the murder committed in a moment of insanity. As expected, the jury returned a guilty verdict in less than an hour. After three ballots jurors came back into the courtroom unanimous for the imposition of the death penalty. As bailiffs led the prisoner out of the courtroom following sentencing, spectators elbowed their way forward for a chance to hold in their hands the blood-smeared hatchet and other items of criminal evidence.

"There seems to be a morbid fascination about handling the bloody relics of the dead," wrote a reporter, summing up his impressions of the trial. "The handkerchief that was around the girl's neck came in for a share of the attention."[12]

Few people questioned Zephyr's guilt or the rule of law that had been upheld to the satisfaction of the court and the Cook County state's attorney. Others were less sure. The factory owner Green, prosecuted by Clarence Darrow, an assistant corporation counsel at the time, resulted in conviction on a charge of violating the new child labor ordinance prohibiting children from working eight hours or more a day. John Green suffered only a small comeuppance: he paid a $200 fine and was released.

"Before Zeph came to Chicago a little over a year ago, he belonged to a church," explained his pastor, the Reverend Mr. Henderson, a black clergyman of resonant voice who attended to Davis and his mother Sophia from inside the jail. When asked where the father might be, Davis told the reverend that he had run off and "was driving a stage coach out in the Dakotas." "But after he [Zephyr] got here [to Chicago] he led a wild life. He now says that he has regained his old feeling of love and veneration for the Savior. And I believe he has."[13]

As the hour of execution drew near, throngs of spectators, many filled with vengeance, some expressing sympathy and remorse, joined with the morbidly curious outside of the Cook County Jail. Friends of Davis were admitted to the cell block for a private, final reunion. Each visitor received an autographed card—a souvenir, bearing the inscription: "From Cook County Jail: May 12, 1888, Zephyr Davis."

At five o'clock, the night before the execution, guards escorted Davis from Lingg's old cell into the Cook County Jail library—a curious Chicago penal custom afforded the condemned of death row with the hope they might find solace—and offer repentance—by reading scripture before their hour of doom. Provided with a cot to sleep on amid shelves of Bibles and books, Davis comforted his despairing mother and received the Reverend Mr. Henderson. In an aura of radiance, the minister had come to pray for the boy's soul and sing an old Negro spiritual:

> Jesus, keep me near the cross;
> There a precious fountain;
> Free to all, a healing stream;
> Flows from Calvary's mountain.

"Death lost its horror," the Tribune reported, "in the presence of such fortitude as this.[14] There were some in the crowd who had never seen a hanging and when at 11:07, Chief Deputy Gleason cried "Gentlemen, please remove your hats and quit smoking until—in short, until you leave the jail." The trapdoor opened and Davis dropped to his death. "If ever a man died game," said one observer, "it is the man who died here."[15]

A thousand people turned out at Oakwoods Cemetery on the South Side the next day hoping to glimpse the interment of the first black man to be executed in Cook County. Most were white. Many curious spectators were fashionably attired women, some carrying babies in their arms. "There were old gray-headed men and there were young girls and boys," a Times reporter noted. "The sight presented was that of a fourth of July excursion just starting out; in no way did it have the appearance of a funeral. The mourners numbered more than 100 black people."[16]

Davis's casket had been placed in a two-wheeled cart and pulled to the burial location by a cemetery employee. "They cut across lots, ran over graves, through shrubbery and over flower beds," in their haste to keep up with the cart, according to one eyewitness account. The grotesque proceeding strains the sensibilities of our contemporary world, but such grisly behavior was not so unusual in Victorian America. Executions stirred excitement.

All too often, the human dimension to these kinds of tragedies that leave a half-dozen ruined lives in their wake is lost or forgotten in the shifting currents of unfolding news events. The savage murder of Maggie Gaughan, however, continued to tug at the moral and political conscience of the city and hastened a renewed call for further reform of the child labor system by the leadership of Chicago's leading women's groups. A series of newspaper articles appearing in the Times under the headline banner "City Slave Girls" by Nell Nelson in July 1888 galvanized public opinion.

In a lifetime of social activism, Elizabeth Morgan, the wife of socialist labor leader Thomas P. Morgan, led a call to action to organize the Illinois Women's Alliance on October 6, 1888. Prominent during the Haymarket era, Thomas "Tommy" Morgan, took the bar exam and passed it in 1895 and in a failed bid, he ran on the Socialist Labor ticket for Cook County state's attorney.

As the organizational name implied, members of various coalitions joined to compel stronger enforcement of existing child labor laws, compulsory education for young people, and city council authorization to appoint and empower female factory inspectors under the auspices of the alliance—not the police or the politicians.

The alliance demanded the appointment of five women to the city of Chicago Health Department Sanitary Police to inspect factories, stores, small dress-making shops lacking mechanized sewing machines, tenements, and industrial outlets known to employ underage children. First Ward alderman William "Mockingbird" Whelan, a former altar boy and Madison Street barkeep in the guise of urban reformer with his self-interests more closely aligned with the gambling syndicates and wide-open town proponents, supported the women and introduced an ordinance on the floor of the council.

"I am credibly informed that there are factories where children and girls are obliged to work in water closets," Whelan curtly informed the city council.[17] Police superintendent Brennan, a vocal critic of the ordinance, objected, saying that "the law contemplated only police*men* and not police*women*."[18] Clarence Darrow filed the necessary legal brief stating there was nothing in the municipal codes that he could find that would bar women from becoming factory inspectors.

In a heated nighttime session of the Chicago City Council, "Foxy" Ed Cullerton the adroit politician, floor leader, and patriarch of a 145-year-old family political dynasty dating back to 1872, opposed placement of "irresponsible parties" being given "considerable authority to go into people's premises and making investigations."[19]

Cullerton and his colleagues sharing his oppositional stance were hastily voted down. Surprisingly, Cullerton, in a conciliatory gesture, proposed an amendment to compensate the inspectors with a fifty-dollar-a-month stipend. The resolution as amended passed, and the appointments of Anna Byford Leonard, a physician's daughter, Clara Doolittle, widow of prominent city attorney James Doolittle, former factory girl Mary Glennon, Ada Sullivan, Dr. Rachel Hickey, a volunteer emergency responder on the frontline of the catastrophic Johnstown, Pennsylvania, flood of May 31, 1889, and Marie Owens of Lower Town, Ottawa, Canada, followed. All were unmarried widows.

The alliance pushed for reform on many fronts, from demands to improve working conditions for saleswomen and seamstresses at the Siegel and Cooper Department Store to pressure to appoint a woman to head the county insane asylum at Dunning. They lobbied to extend the school term to twenty-four weeks, introduced mandatory kindergarten classes in the public schools, and promoted a ban on the sale of cigarettes to minors. Prominent social activists Ida B. Wells-Barnett and Lucy Flower were among their ranks.[20]

Elizabeth Morgan achieved a breakthrough during the Christmas season of 1891 by imploring incoming Republican mayor Hempstead Washburne to instruct commissioner of health John D. Ware to deputize a male or female factory inspector to accompany alliance members to stores and other places of employment where children under the age of fifteen were engaged in nighttime employment. "During the city administration preceding the present, unsuccessful efforts were made to have the municipal laws enforced which were enacted to protect women and children from the thoughtless or heartless cruelty of employers," the *Tribune* reported. "Impelled by a sense of duty and with the hope that you will recognize the justice of our appeal, join with us in our efforts to enforce the laws."[21] However, the legal authority enjoined the inspectors from entering private residences and tenement houses if the owner of the property refused them admittance. The needle trades often congealed inside dangerously overcrowded sweatshops.

Mayor Washburne endorsed the alliance proposal and empowered Ware to follow through with the directive that the child labor laws be vigorously enforced by deputizing them. Police superintendent Robert Wilson McLaughery, the former warden of the Joliet Penitentiary, stepped up the police response and rewarded Marie Connelly Owens for the diligence, zeal, and energy with which she investigated complaints to the health department involving working children with a promotion to the detective bureau as Sergeant 97 on December 16, 1891.

Qualified to make arrests when necessary, Marie Owens, a mother of five, donned the six-pointed star to become the first woman in the United States to be sworn in as a police officer. "She does her work in her own way," praised her supervisor, Lieutenant Andrew Rohan, "being directly responsible to no one as it is effectively performed, because she has long since performed her ability in this direction."[22] Marie entered factories, sweatshops, department stores, and places where children worked in plain clothes. She did not carry a service revolver, handcuffs, or a truncheon.

Illuminating the darkest corners of poverty and human suffering in Chicago, Owens adjudicated reported violations of the child labor laws with a stern warning and citation, gaining empathy from the shop girls, parents, and sympathetic employers. She investigated cases of wife desertion, tracking down deadbeat offenders to their known haunts, and conveyed the intelligence of their whereabouts to Captain Patrick D. O'Brien, chief of detectives at the central station for immediate arrest. "I see so much unhappiness, poverty, sickness and misery that could be relieved by a few dollars," this tall, striking woman in black confided to a reporter in 1904. "If I were only able to supply these dollars how happy I should be!"[23]

Sergeant Owens owned a two flat on Turner Avenue where she resided with three of her five children. She lived modestly, and always downplayed the importance of her mission. "My work is just a woman's work in my sixteen years of experience," she said in 1906. "It has kept me poor giving in little amounts to those in want. I have yet the time to come across a hungry family that they were not given food."[24]

Owens exercised personal discretion in the enforcement of the child labor laws. "If I found that the children were the bread winners of the widowed mothers and dependent families, I never interfered with their working, and right now many young men and women are holding high positions in the mercantile houses and big industries in Chicago because I did not disturb them."[25]

Marie Connelly Owens completed thirty-two years of public service on May 8, 1923, retiring on a police pension that paid her $83.33 a month. She moved to New York City that same year to take up residence with her daughter Gertrude and remained in the East up until the moment of death on June 10, 1927. Owens's remains were returned to Chicago. Her two surviving children interred Marie in Calvary Cemetery, the final resting place for thousands of Chicagoans of Irish descent. The stone bears a simple inscription: "Owens."

WHERE TIME BEGAN

efore 1883, there were eight thousand functioning time zones crisscrossing the United States. The confusing and mind-numbing exercise of trying to figure out the correct hour of the day when passing from one town and continuing to the next was based on the prevailing "local mean time" (or solar time) system. From the small hamlets of rural America to the big cities, people typically relied on the big clock perched atop city hall, a church, or a large commercial building overlooking the town square for the correct time or dropping a ball from a high tower at noon.

Chicagoans kept time from readings taken by the Western Electric Company from the Dearborn Astronomical Observatory located at Cottage Grove Avenue and Thirty-Fourth Street.[1] Chicago Board of Trade members relied on the striking of the Cook County Courthouse bell, controlled by an electronic signal from the observatory, for the opening and closing of markets.

Standard time was determined by the position of the sun at its highest peak—noontime, or midday. We were not a particularly mobile society up through the end of the early national period of American history. People rarely traveled long distances, and thus were seldom confused about time.

The expansion of the railroads in the 1850s changed everything. Train schedules, based on dozens of local times became impossible for passengers to reconcile, contributing to an incalculable waste of time, energy, and money. Crossing the country via rail from New York to Los Angeles required passengers to reset their watches a minimum of twenty times before reaching their final destination.

A traveler who set his time piece at 12:15 P.M. before boarding his train in Portland, Maine, would have to adjust the time to 12:00 in order to be consistent with the New York Central clock. In Buffalo the Lake Shore clock showed the local time as 11:25 A.M., and in Buffalo the city clock registered 11:40. A passenger had to be a mathematician to fully comprehend the bewildering train schedules.

Freight trains synchronized their schedules with those of factory owners, farmers, and logging camps and the availability of common tracks. Competition among the major carriers in the post-Civil War period resulted in bitterly fought price wars. Scheduling became a tool to undercut competitors. Not only did this drain profit margins, the eight thousand regional time zones contributed to deadly pedestrian and railway accidents.

The telegraph reduced the number of rail mishaps, but the comprehensive reforms advocated by the delegates to the Time Table Convention (meeting annually for the first time in 1872) to reduce the number of time zones and implement a simplified system everyone could agree upon remained elusive. The British government, in 1854, had legislated a Standard Railroad Time based on telegraph signals from their observatory at Greenwich. The United States Naval Observatory (formerly the National Observatory) in Washington, DC, adapted the British system in 1866. By this action it was clearly demonstrated to be much more efficient for timekeepers to reconcile to a single standard.

Dr. Charles Ferdinand Dowd, for twenty-five years the president of the Temple Grove Ladies Seminary (now Skidmore College), provided a practical, lasting solution. Dr. Dowd, a long-time resident of Saratoga Springs, New York, divided the United States into four even time zones, fifteen degrees each, based on the sun requiring an hour to move that far in the sky. Under Dowd's plan, conceived in 1863 and formally introduced to a committee of railroad superintendents in 1869, each successive time zone would be set one hour ahead.

For the next fourteen years, Dowd lobbied unsuccessfully for the nation's railroads to give his plan the proper attention it deserved. He asked for no financial reward or recompense, only the personal satisfaction of implementing a workable and orderly system to simplify matters for his fellow citizens. The powerful railroad titans, consumed by rivalry and self-interest, resisted the change.

Passengers, business leaders, commercial shippers, politicians, and the public grew impatient and clamored for reform. Meteorologist Cleveland Abbe, the director of the Cincinnati Observatory in Cincinnati, Ohio, submitted a white paper titled a "Report on Standard Time" in 1879.[2] In Canada, Scottish inventor and engineer Sir Sandford Fleming proposed a similar plan to his government that same year.[3] Separately, their proposals were presented to the Third International Geographical Congress in Venice in 1881, the European Geodetic Association in 1883, and the American Association for the Advancement of Science in 1881–1882.

The historical record suggests that Dr. Dowd, a mostly forgotten and over-looked figure in this story, is the rightful "father of standard time." The Dowd plan (it wasn't called that, officially), received backing from William F. Allen, editor of the *Traveler's Official Railway Guide* and secretary of the annual Railroad Time-Table Convention. Allen adjusted Dowd's map to fit four geographical divisions in the United States and one covering the maritime provinces of Canada. Allen presented it to the railroad managers and directors who gathered in Chicago's Grand Pacific Hotel to consider the matter during the plenary session of the General Time Convention, October 11–13, 1883.

Secretary Allen solicited the endorsement of director Edward Charles Pickering and the scientists and meteorologists at the Harvard College Observatory, a respected, major research institution. Pickering signaled his consent in a letter to Allen by specifying that the observatory would furnish telegraphic signals conforming to the minute and second of the proposed standards. The railroad lines emanating out of Boston made their acceptance conditional on the participation of the observatory. Most railroads fell into line and agreed to the plan to divide the nation into four time zones based on Greenwich Mean Time. The Michigan Central, the last of the large passenger carriers to accede to the mandate, adapted to the Central time zone although the state of Michigan delayed its compliance until 1885.

"Never before has so radical a reform as the establishment of the meridian time as the standard throughout the country been accomplished in so short a space of time," beamed the *Chicago Tribune* on November 26, 1883. "From the date agreed upon by the Railroad Time Table Convention that the new system should go into effect on the various railroad lines, it has taken just about one week not only to introduce the new system on all the railroads, but to have it accepted generally throughout the country."

On Monday, November 19, 1883, Mayor Carter Harrison I and the membership of the Chicago City Council unanimously approved standard time, and by resolution, directed the Dearborn Observatory, the board of education and the police and fire departments to comply.[4] School superintendent George Howland expressed support. "We must open and close the school by its [Central] time. If most of the railroads and a good many of the citizens adopt the new standard everyone will have to in order to secure uniformity. If parents don't do it the children will be tardy at first, but they would soon get used to the change. I am very decidedly in favor of the city adopting the new standard."[5]

The Standard Time Act (officially the Calder Act named after Senator William Calder of New York was enacted on March 19, 1918, and passed on

August 20, 1919, over President Woodrow Wilson's veto), authorized standard time and daylight savings time in the United States. The act directed the Interstate Commerce Commission to define nine time zones and it moved the borders to the rural areas of the nation.

The Grand Pacific Hotel, a Chicago landmark at Jackson Boulevard and LaSalle Street where modern time began, had a colorful and storied history of its own to tell. John B. Drake and his partners Sam Turner and Sam Parker opened the hotel in the aftermath of the Great Chicago Fire of 1871. Furnished with taste and magnificence, the palatial mass of brick and masonry quickly earned a national reputation as one of the nation's premier hostelries.[6]

President Chester Alan Arthur, an overnight guest in August 1883, was among a score of visiting statesmen and notables of the world including Lily Langtry, Edwin Booth, General William T. Sherman, James Whitcomb Riley, and the self-righteous New England clergyman and author Henry Ward Beecher to sample the well-appointed accommodations. Through its portals strolled David Belasco and Mrs. Leslie Carter to dine in the French room. Meatpacker Nelson Morris gave the hand of his daughter Gusta in marriage to A. M. Rothschild in the presence of six hundred guests (the cream of Chicago society) at the Grand Pacific on December 5, 1882. Lavish floral designs adorned a beautiful white arch. The bride's dress was swathed in diamonds.

Mark Twain gave the keynote address at a banquet at the Grand Pacific one memorable night, and at other times, two sitting presidents, Benjamin Harrison and William McKinley, checked in. In 1895, as its luster slowly dimmed following the addition of newer hotels into the Loop district, developers razed one half of the building. The wrecker's ball claimed the other half during the first week of June 1919.

Barely noticed by pedestrians hurrying by in the hustle and bustle of downtown, a small brass plaque affixed to the exterior wall of the Bank of America building at 231 S. LaSalle Street (on the north side of Jackson Boulevard) commemorates the former location of the Grand Pacific Hotel and the famous 1883 Railroad Time Table Convention.

Dr. Charles Dowd, the unsung and famously modest Presbyterian minister never received a dime of compensation for his effort to advance standard time. He perished in a freakish railroad accident underneath the wheels of a locomotive in Saratoga Springs on November 12, 1904. Dowd, seventy-nine years of age, might have escaped if only his watch had been in error and he missed the train.

THE SCARLET LETTER VERDICT

n air of quiet death hung over a sturdy Victorian mansion at 166 Cass Street (now Wabash Avenue). In the gloom of family tragedy, an emotionally distraught man—his brilliant intellect in eclipse following a failed suicide attempt in his bedroom five months earlier—lay dying.[1] Leslie Carter, lawyer, capitalist, and street railroad magnate gazed up unhappily at his younger sister, nearly prostrated by grief, and his attending physician. There was no hope for recovery, the doctor gently informed him. Every remedy known to the medical profession in 1908 had failed to restore Mr. Carter to robust health in the weeks and months following his rescue from the poisonous gas jets of the kitchen stove that had filtered into his bedroom and nearly asphyxiated him.

As the minutes turned to hours, Mr. Carter cried out for his son, Dudley Carter, and his ex-wife, the famed star of the Broadway footlights, the redoubtable Mrs. Leslie Dudley-Carter Payne.

Neither would give the physically ailing father the satisfaction of their company as the hour of death edged ever closer. All that Mr. Leslie Carter had hoped for was reconciliation with the boy who had meant the world to him, but now his hopes were dashed. The boy would not see him. Sensing an opportunity to write up a human-interest story certain to tear at the heart strings of the sentimental reader delighting in the maudlin tales of hearth, home, and broken vows, the gentlemen of the press traced the young man's movements to a flat owned by a State Street druggist. He had slipped into town unannounced. "I hope he will get well," spouted young Leslie when pressed for an explanation by the newspapers. "But I cannot go to see him. It is impossible. We have separated forever."[2]

The marital discord between Caroline Louise Dudley, "that shameless red-headed hussy of Chicago," as the judgmental society matrons whispered to one another during their afternoon kaffeeklatsches, and Mr. Leslie Carter, a church-going Yale man of moral rectitude, scandalized all of Chicago in the spring and early summer of 1889.

Never was there a less ideally suited couple preparing for a fashionable society marriage than Mr. Leslie Carter, a reserved and sensitive Scotsman who
amassed a fortune as an attorney and businessman serving as president of the
South Side Elevated Company, the Chicago Canal and Dock Company, and
related ventures, and Caroline Dudley, a vexatious beauty with red-golden
hair, green eyes, and a mercurial temperament. They had money, ambition,
and social position in common. Love, if it existed between them after their
honeymoon, had more to do with material gain and the intense physical
attraction that Leslie experienced with Caroline, eighteen years his junior.

Caroline "Carrie" Dudley came into this world in Cleveland, Ohio, on June
10, 1857.[3] She was the daughter of Orson Daniel Dudley, an English wholesale dry goods merchant later associated with the Standard Oil Company,
and his wife Catherine, an aristocratic southern woman of Scottish ancestry
who possessed status and wealth. For a time, the family resided comfortably
in Lexington, Kentucky, a city divided in its loyalties during the Civil War.
Later, the family moved to Dayton, Ohio, where Caroline spent most of her
childhood in the lap of luxury craving approval and seeking constant attention.
She was educated by private tutors and governesses and was indulged with
toys and fancy clothing until the sudden passing of her father. It was then left
to Catherine to bring up the girl alone, albeit in fairly reduced circumstances.

As Caroline matured, and her beauty became more noticeable to the
young swains of Dayton and Chicago with each passing social season,
Catherine contrived to place her in the company of socially prominent and
wealthy suitors whose fortunes they would place at her feet. This was mother's plan, and a golden opportunity arose quite by chance after Caroline
was introduced to Mr. Leslie Carter at the home of General Anson Stager,
wealthy Chicago socialite and vice president and general manager of the
Western Union Telegraph Company at his home at Eighteenth Street and
Michigan Avenue. General Stager had agreed to function as Caroline's legal
guardian following her father's passing.

Carter had called upon Stager about a business matter of some importance. The general introduced him to the pretty young maiden from Dayton
who had arrived for a visit with the Stager family. At first, neither of them
made much of an impression upon the other. Over the next eighteen months
they crossed paths in Chicago at social affairs with friends and society acquaintances they had in common.

Caroline's dealings with Mr. Carter were purely casual until August 1879
when they again met again at a resort in Waukesha, Wisconsin, west of Milwaukee. Caroline showered her attention on Leslie—who was now fully engaged
in a law partnership with Edwin Walker—and he became easily smitten. An

unlikely romance blossomed between these two polar opposites; Caroline, a pleasure-seeking spendthrift desirous of world travel, style, glamour, and a life filled with romantic adventures, and Leslie, a four-square, nose-to-the-grindstone achiever who shared her ambition for acquiring money and title, but lacked the desire to squander his fortune on hotel living and costly junkets to the Continent. For Mr. Leslie Carter, all the happiness he required could be found in the company of his ledger books, invoices, bills of lading, and the haze of cigar smoke that curled lazily toward the ceiling in the warm comforting glow of the gas lamps of his downtown office at 17 East Congress Street.

Superficially though, he was prepared to indulge Carrie's whims and flights of fancy in the belief that she would eventually settle into the rhythms and routines of motherhood, home, and hearth. The courtship ripened from warm regard to love—at least in his orderly, compartmentalized mind. In September 1879—just one month after their fateful reunion in Waukesha, Carrie accepted him as her beau and future husband. Although she lived in Ohio with her mother, it did not discourage Leslie from actively courting her. On Fridays, after putting his affairs in order, he would travel by train to Dayton to spend the weekend with her under the watchful reproach of her forty-seven-year-old mother, who bore a striking resemblance to Carrie.

The couple married in Dayton on May 26, 1880. They embarked on an East Coast wedding tour, taking in the attractions of Cincinnati and Baltimore, followed by a steam ship cruise to Norfolk, a train ride northward to Boston and on to Albany and a Catskills resort, and thence to New York City via a leisurely cruise down the Hudson River. Maybe it wasn't quite so exotic as a hegira to the capitols of the Old World that the eighteen-year-old Caroline might have imagined in her flights of fancy, but the older man and his bride remained content in each other's company and a spark of love that had kindled in Wisconsin a year earlier seemed to glow ever brighter.

Leslie Carter, remembered by his peers as a man of excellent manner, impeccable taste, and neat dress, soon discovered to his great dismay that Caroline was unsuited to the role of wife, mother, and society hostess—the proscribed role for the wives of Chicago millionaires in the rigid caste system of the late Gilded Age. She gave birth to their son Dudley, endured the unpleasant rigors of childrearing before relinquishing the tasks to the governess and household help. Becoming increasingly indifferent to Carter, but not to his tidy fortune, Caroline indulged in domestic and foreign travels, and found personal solace in the comfort of a rented summer cottage in Cooperstown, New York, the hometown of James Fenimore Cooper and Abner Doubleday, with picturesque views of Lake Otsego, and the pleasing company of the country squires living nearby. The cooler air of Cooperstown afforded her relief from the sweltering

Chicago heat. "Chicago frightens me to death in the summertime and I would much rather not stay there," she protested to her husband.[4]

Leslie accommodated his excitable and moody wife at every turn and exhibited remarkable patience as the pair continued to live apart for extended periods of time. She wrote to him frequently, showering endearments and calling him "her dear boy." She signed her letters "Kittie," the pet name Carter had given her.

From Dayton, Ohio, during a visit to her mother, Carrie wrote: "You will come to me soon, dearie, won't you and hold Kittie right close and make her happy!" In an earlier correspondence posted from "Jamestown, New York in June 1883, she writes: "Why is it that Satan gets into me and makes me so abominable? I make so many resolutions, good resolutions and break them all!"[5]

From the Magnolia Hotel in St. Augustine, Florida, in 1884, Caroline begged Leslie to pay for an expensive pair of new shoes she coveted, adding: "Lellie, Lellie [his pet name], "my dear, dear, dear husband. I have received your letters and they make me so happy. You have been so kind to me. I will be truer than I have seemed to be. Have faith in me, have faith and keep me close to you!"[6] Her erratic behavior and spiraling fits of sadness aroused Carter's sympathy. If her happiness required extended periods apart, he would go along with it and do what he could to make her happy with the hope of restoring her soundness of mind. Today, Caroline's condition would likely be diagnosed as bipolar disorder.

Leslie's money financed Caroline's lavish lifestyle and her zest for travel to the Continent and American resorts that seemed to bring some comfort to her. Meanwhile, back in Chicago, Carter fretted over his deteriorating finances after mortgaging personal property to pay for the growing debt she had incurred. He began to wonder what Caroline had *really* been up to during the long separations. Taking the "cure" at spas and villas was one thing. Had she remained faithful? That was the real question. He overheard troublesome whisperings about out-of-town suitors and romantic trysts. A man in Leslie Carter's station in life could ill afford gossip and scandal. He would soon have his suspicions confirmed.

In late October 1884, the Carters and their son embarked for New York City in order to consult with a medical specialist about young Dudley's weak ankles, an affliction that caused Caroline many sleepless nights. After a stopover in the Cooperstown rental home, they continued to Manhattan, booking a private suite of rooms at the luxurious Fifth Avenue Hotel.

In high spirits, Caroline arranged for a theater party one night and presented Leslie with the invitation list and asked if he would be a dear and invite an acquaintance, a young man she knew by the name of Charles C. Deming of New York, to join them on the evening in question. Deming signaled his acceptance by sending a messenger to hand deliver his favorable reply to Carter.

Later that day Leslie Carter searched the suite for an envelope to post a letter. He made the fateful mistake of opening Caroline's personal portfolio, and out tumbled three personal letters written to his wife by the same Charles Deming. They had been postmarked to Europe during Caroline's last sojourn abroad. "A glance showed me their true nature," he later remarked.[7] Although now knowing that he had been cuckolded, Leslie attended the evening's performance. He kept his chin up and the matter entirely to himself. He remained unusually quiet throughout the evening, a peculiarity noted by Caroline the following morning when they were alone in the suite.

"You were cold to me and to our guests!" she protested.[8] Leslie held up the letters in an accusatory manner and asked his wife to explain the meaning of the correspondence. His wife's face grew red and her voice cracked. "I cannot imagine why he would say such things to me as that," she stammered. Leslie read the letters aloud, at which point his agitated wife cast aside her embarrassment in the heat of rising anger. Seizing a pitcher of water, she emptied half the contents on Leslie and the other half on the bed. Then, according to published accounts, she reached for the letters that expressed Deming's undying love and affection and tore them in half. She deposited the torn pages in the "slop jar" (presumably a spittoon).

"After breakfast I was so disturbed in mind that I went back and got the pieces [of the letters] and put them in the envelope," Carter later told opposing counsel in divorce court.[9]

Following their initial showdown in the hotel, Mr. and Mrs. Leslie Carter reconciled . . . for the sake of Dudley, their social obligations, and the glint of romantic affection they held for each other. Caroline continued her pleasure travel. Leslie returned to Chicago, and Caroline showered him with maudlin Victorian era expressions of love, loneliness, and sentimental longing.

Caroline found sanctuary from the torment in her heart in Leslie's cozy rented cottage in Cooperstown, New York, where, in the midst of the summer holiday season in August 1883, a new romance began with New York state senator James Farnsworth Pierce, a fourth cousin twice removed of former US president Franklin Pierce. Married to Anna Maria Redington and raising six children in their Brooklyn home, Senator Pierce, according to historian Emmett Dedmon, "had sent Mrs. Carter erotic love poems and had been found seeking inspiration for his muse near the Cooper House at three o'clock in the morning."[10] They had attended parties and picnics together and Mrs. Carter went driving with Pierce and various other gentlemen. Leslie received the news of his wife's "flagrant behavior" stoically. Senator Pierce later testified that Caroline had the makings of a romantic poet and possessed a fine literary mind.

Craving romance and constant attention that the emotionally distant Leslie Carter seemed unwilling, or unable to shower upon his vain, insecure, spendthrift wife, Caroline fell into the arms of the middle-aged Pierce and several other men during those languid summer nights, including one Dudley S. Gregory. A hotel chambermaid caught them kissing behind a rose bush. William K. Constable, an elderly New York broker, was smitten by Caroline's radiance and demonstrated his willingness to invest heavily in her future happiness after a dalliance inside a Cooperstown beer garden.

Constable, with the approval of his wife, promised Caroline $45,000 as a gift to finance her next extended overseas vacation, scheduled for the fall and winter of 1885–1886. "It seemed extraordinary . . . that a married man should have made such a magnificent gift to another man's virtuous wife," chaffed a *Tribune* reporter on May 23, 1889. The funds were deposited in the London banking house of Buring Brothers and Company and were made payable to "Louise Carter." Attorneys for Mr. Carter later alleged that the money was given to her for improper purposes. Caroline testified that Constable and his wife were dear friends from St. Augustine, concerned about her well-being and the restoration of her good health.

Leslie Carter had cause for suspicion. Everywhere he turned a new gentleman appeared before him, seeking the favor of his wife. Standing dockside moments before the Cunard Line vessel admitted its trans-Atlantic passengers to their state rooms, Carter pulled Susan Peterson, Caroline's Norwegian maid to one side, and inquired, "Who is that?" Susan stammered that the young man was Howard Case, a member of the traveling party. "Now I want you to keep an eye on him during the voyage," Leslie exclaimed, sensing her moral failing, "and tell me how Mrs. Carter carries on with this young man and write me about it regularly."[11]

With Susan serving a dual role as Carter's spy and as the lady's chambermaid, Caroline gadded about the continent merrily, lavishing a fortune on hotel suites in London, Paris, Cannes, Vienna, Strasburg, Wiesbaden, Dresden, Basel, Nice, and Florence. She traveled under the invented alias "Louise Chamberlain," rented carriages, dined on oysters and champagne in Paris, and hired footmen over the strenuous objections of her husband, who, after several months had elapsed, lost his patience and pleaded for her immediate return to Chicago. She ignored his demands and lived in European hotels for nearly a year.

Upon returning to New York in September 1886 from Liverpool aboard the steamship *City of Rome*, Caroline rented rooms in two Manhattan hotels, the Colonnade and the Brunswick Hotel—the latter had been a place of assignation with another man, Dr. James G. Gilbert, two years earlier in April 1884. Caroline telegraphed Leslie of her arrival and bid him to make haste so they might enjoy a "cherished reunion of the heart."[12] Angered about William Constable's financing of his wife's lavish journey, Mr. Carter adamantly refused to come to New York. After much deliberation and soul searching, he had made the difficult decision to permanently separate his son Dudley from Caroline's care, in the belief that she was a wife in name only and an unfit mother. Caroline's mother, now permanently estranged from her son-in-law over the discord that tore the family asunder, confided the unhappy news to Caroline while in Europe.

In the following weeks, before sailing back to London on October 9, Caroline lavished her time and attention on her latest beau, the dapper English stage actor and future star of early silent films, Harold Kyrle Money Bellew, whom she met during the Atlantic crossing.

Bellew, an unhappily married man, charmed Caroline with exciting tales of the theater world as they dined on pheasant at Delmonico's—New York's most famous restaurant—where diners comingled with financiers, politicians, and the denizens of Tin Pan Alley.

The blonde-haired thespian, renowned for his dramatic roles in popular melodramas and Shakespearean tragedies and as an author and explorer, arranged to book room 101 at the Colonnade, adjacent to Caroline's suite, so that he might become better acquainted with Mrs. Carter, enjoy the pleasures of a romantic interlude (an accusation Bellew hotly denied), and spark her early interest in becoming a stage player.

Imagining herself prancing gracefully across the Broadway stage appealed to Caroline's vanity, and Bellew encouraged her dream of stardom by offering to give her drama lessons in the privacy of his hotel apartment—charging her the going rate of twenty-five dollars per hour.

"I can tell in five minutes whether a pupil will be successful on the stage or not," Bellew boasted on May 7, 1889. "My standing is such that I cannot afford to take pupils who will not be successful. I told Mrs. Carter that she would be successful in high comedy and I undertook to give her lessons."[13] Dignified and proud, Leslie Carter fought back. He named this "professor of the romantic art," as the press satirized Bellew, a correspondent in the subsequent divorce action.[14] To the surprise of nearly everyone in Chicago, it was not Mr. Carter who struck the first blow for liberation and a permanent separation but the missus.

Driven by the fear of losing her son, Caroline and her lawyers filed a petition for divorce in the superior court of Cook County on November 14,

1887, charging Leslie with mental and physical cruelty. The trouble began on their wedding night, she claimed, when Carter treated her in "an unspeakable fashion," demanding her participation in "unnatural" acts.[15] The startling accusations, unmentionable in polite company, were viewed as an affront to common decency by starchy Victorian society.

Appalled, the *Tribune*, on November 19, 1887, wrote that the "allegations in this bill [are] unspeakably base and will not be repeated here because there is reason to believe the plaintiff is demented." Mr. Carter's circle of friends and business associates shared this sentiment and rallied behind their old friend, as a half-dozen Chicago newspapers clamored for more salacious details in a nineteenth-century media feeding frenzy that would rival the 1994 murder trial of O. J. Simpson as a public spectacle.

Mr. Carter's brutality, Caroline asserted, undermined her health and drove her to seek refuge in the warmer Florida climate on the advice of a physician, but Carter followed her to the resort and renewed his cold, brutish behavior. Claiming that she was "without property and without income" because Mr. Carter was unwilling to finance her extended European forays, taken for the sole purpose of restoring her vigor, as she insisted, Caroline said that she had been forced against her will into the Oakwood Retreat in Geneva, Wisconsin—a sanitarium for the insane.[16] That Leslie Carter believed his wife to be insane upon her return from Europe in 1886, there is little doubt. Susan Peterson said that while in Vienna's Grand Hotel, Caroline's "mind was affected—she saw faces and she saw snakes" and was afraid that Susan had plotted to murder her.[17]

Leslie supplied a convincing response to Judge Egbert Jamieson by demonstrating that his net worth had dropped to under $75,000—far less than the $300,000 Mrs. Carter claimed title to. He said that he had been "obliged to sell some of his best income-producing property" in order to meet the household expenses that had become burdensome. He defended himself against the accusations of cruelty and neglect.[18]

While in Basel, Switzerland, Caroline had lived in a fashion that caused great scandal, Leslie testified.[19] At no time had he ever denied his wife the right to see her son, even in the final weeks leading up to their divorce action while she was institutionalized in Wisconsin. Hearing this, Judge Jamieson ordered Caroline to return Dudley to his father's custody within five days.

On advice of counsel, Mrs. Carter withdrew a number of her complaints listed in the original bill, including the charge of desertion and physical assault and adultery with the maid. In March 1888, she modified her complaint again. Weeks passed. Cast into a sympathetic light as a forthright, virtuous, and attentive father victimized by an extravagant, man-chasing flibbertigibbet, Leslie Carter maintained his composure and quiet dignity amid a storm of publicity as the famous divorce case finally went to trial on April 16, 1889. The plaintiff and defendant engaged legal minds of great sagacity. Caroline chose Sidney Smith, a retired Cook County Superior Court judge as her lead counsel. Luther Laflin Mills, a former Cook County state's attorney, and one of Chicago's most brilliant minds, represented Leslie Carter.

Over the next five weeks, the reading public, supplied with a profusion of courtroom detail by reporters, shared the couple's most intimate secrets in the publicity mill disguised as serious journalism. It was a Victorian media circus in the extreme. Caroline's daily coiffure, her facial expressions, and vivid (albeit sarcastic) wardrobe descriptions filled entire newspaper columns. "The gown of black lace may have come from a Chicago dry goods house, but the probabilities are it came from Felix or Worth," sniped the *Tribune* on the first day of the trial, April 18, 1889. "The gloves, the bonnet, the ostrich feather, everything was demurely black and yet on the cheeks under the veil there were suspicious rose tints that may on the one hand, have been born of youth and high spirit; or on the other hand may signify that when the trial is over, Mrs. Carter will turn an honest penny recommending face washes and complexion powders," the reporter added, with undisguised sarcasm.

Each morning, for five weeks the courtroom galleries filled with spectators straining to hear every scintillating detail of the calamitous Carter marriage. Men inched forward in their chairs and cupped their good listening ear with their hat as to not miss a word of testimony. As the witnesses and correspondents answered questions relating to sexual misbehavior, Judge Jamieson found it necessary to bar the doors to members of the public under the age of thirty-five, especially flashy young men known in common parlance as "dudes" and easily offended women. "We have no desire to take the place of the departed Gayety Burlesque Company," Judge Jamieson advised the court.[20]

Sidney Smith's characterization of Mr. Carter as "stingy and mean" and a "Jekyll and Hyde" villain who had subjected his wife to "damnable insults" and physical blows did not resonate or jibe with the known facts.[21] "Within six hours from this happy time [their wedding day] Mrs. Carter says that this young man treated her with the cruelty she described," Mills told jurors. "Can you, as thinking men, believe a story so horrible, so brutal, so on the face of it so abominable and improbable? If this young wife had suffered from the brutality of her husband wouldn't she have told someone?"[22]

Seated alongside his brother Ernest at the defense table, Leslie maintained his poise. He made his notations and comments on sheets of paper after affixing his gold-rimmed pince-nez to the bridge of his nose in order to see the paper more clearly. Unfortunately for Mrs. Carter, he was a careful and meticulous man. He had retained all of Caroline's letters in which she pledged undying love and affection, and directed Mills to read aloud the correspondence he believed would convince the jury that Leslie Carter was not the vile monster she had depicted him to be. If he had brutally battered Caroline, deprived his wife and son of financial support, and indulged in a sexual escapade with Susan Peterson as the plaintiff inferred, why hadn't any of these serious charges been mentioned in any of her private correspondence?

Attorney Mills hammered away at Caroline, accusing her of fabricating a wild tale. The look on Caroline's face was one of fiery anger as she narrowed her gaze upon Mills and listened intently to his denunciations. At the close of the proceedings, Mrs. Carter sat in her chair for a full five minutes, transfixed and unable to gather sufficient strength to rise following the blistering attack against her character and morals. By that time, the jury had retired to consider its verdict.

Jurors required twelve-and-a-half hours and six ballots to arrive at a decision. All through the night of May 21 and into the following morning the vote to acquit Carter on the amended bill wavered between 9–3 and 10–2. Three jurors expressed sympathy for Caroline. All agreed that Senator Pierce had kept company with her in Cooperstown, but he had not, as the defendant alleged, conducted himself improperly, nor had he violated his sacred vows of marriage.

During the trial, Kyrle Bellew, the New York actor who had arrived in town to portray Marc Antony in a performance of *Julius Caesar* at the McVicker Theater, had answered a summons and appeared as a witness for the plaintiff. In a deposition statement taken by Mills clearly designed to impugn his public and private reputation, Bellew admitted that he had sired a child out of wedlock with one Eva Sothern, a London woman he had earlier abandoned. The jury had a hard time believing the sincerity of this young man they had labeled a romancer and a cad.

As irrelevant to the Carter case as the Eva Sothern testimony might have been, it was allowed and thus, Bellew was narrowly viewed as an East Coast British dandy engaged in a shady profession by Chicago's faith-based moralists who had taken more than a passing interest in this case. As much as nineteenth-century folk enjoyed the dramatic arts, attending vaudeville performances, and laughing at the comedians in minstrel shows, they did not necessarily embrace theater people as virtuous upholders of common decency and moral rectitude. Stage players were frequently shunned and barred from social circles. Actresses and actors were seen as vagabonds, fops, tramps, and poseurs unless of course their names happened to be Booth, Barrymore, or Bernhardt.

The testimony of Kyrle Bellew effectively lost the case for Mrs. Carter who was judged and pronounced guilty of adultery, denied custody of her child, and publicly shamed in the court of public opinion. Sequestered in her suite at the Richelieu Hotel, Caroline refused requests to meet with reporters who stood outside her door awaiting comment. Over time, the appellate court and state Supreme Court upheld the verdict, however cold-hearted and cruel Caroline's admirers may have thought it.

Mr. Carter's vindication triggered a moment of sublime happiness, but his contentment was fleeting. Unbeknownst to the jubilant co-counsel Frank Loesch or to the implacable Leslie, millionaire developer, land speculator, and banker Nathaniel Kellogg Fairbank (the creator of Santa Claus Soap) met privately with the bedridden Caroline in her sumptuous Richelieu Hotel suite days after the trial verdict.[23]

Fairbank, a financial titan ranked high on the social register, had known Mrs. Carter since their first meeting at General Anson Stager's residence prior to the time of her formal introduction to Leslie. "N. K." as his circle of intimates knew him, served as president of the staid and decorous Chicago Club, and was the financial genius who put together the capital necessary to build Central Music Hall. For many years he was among the largest traders on the Chicago exchange. A much older man of wealth, power, and influence taking a personal interest in Caroline was by now a familiar refrain.

The very social and well-connected Fairbank advised the stage-struck Caroline to pursue her theatrical dream. He wrote a letter of introduction to Edward G. Gilmore, theatrical impresario at the Fifth Avenue Hotel in New York, that set in motion a remarkable chain of events.[24] "Mr. Fairbank offered to back me in the enterprise," Mrs. Carter later affirmed. "He said I had some dramatic talent. When I came to New York and saw Mr. Gilmore, he told me the best man to train me was Mr. David Belasco. When I returned to Chicago I told Fairbank, and he said we must get him. I came to New York and saw Mr. Belasco at the Academy of Music."[25]

N. K. Fairbank guaranteed Belasco, the author and producer of some 374 stage plays (by his own estimate), a hefty sum if he would agree to professionally train Caroline in the theatrical arts, and upon completion of her lessons, cast her in one of his productions. At first, Belasco balked. He said he had worked hard to build his reputation and could not get involved. Furthermore, he wanted nothing to do with backers.

From experience Belasco knew that upon the first sign of trouble the wealthy backer so often turns and runs, leaving the theatrical company stranded. "There is money in this!" Gilmore reminded him. "This is a great enterprise and you ought to buy into it!"[26] The playwright ignored his better judgment and finally agreed.

David Belasco recognized that Caroline possessed the raw talent to make a go of it on the stage—but she desperately needed training in proper stage deportment, voice culture, etiquette, and facial expression. "All the time as I listened to her," Belasco told his biographer William Winter, "I kept saying to myself over and over that the woman might be an actress if she could only act!"[27]

He abandoned all other projects and traveled to Europe in search of new plays before casting her in *The Ugly Duckling*, an original comedy-drama written by Paul Potter and A. D. Gordon in anticipation of a national tour to showcase this rising new talent. East Coast critics were surprised and delighted by Caroline's stage presence in her debut at the Broadway Theater in New York on November 11, 1890, as the impulsive, self-sacrificing heroine. On January 21, 1891, the *Baltimore Sun* called her acting "really astonishing. Considering nothing and making no allowances, Mrs. Carter's work can still claim decided merit and evidence of natural talent. Mrs. Carter will no doubt go on improving in her art for she takes as naturally to the stage as if she were a life-long daughter of the profession."

In a mean-spirited gesture of contempt, she adopted as her official stage name "Mrs. Leslie Carter" in order to publicly humiliate and spite her ex-husband. Caroline appeared before a Chicago audience for the first time on Valentine's Day, 1891, at the Grand Opera House in *The Ugly Duckling* after the indignant proprietor of Hooley's Theater informed Belasco that "Mrs. Carter is not wanted here."[28]

From her hotel suite in the stately Richelieu on Michigan Avenue, the temperamental and indiscreet actress sent out word that her ex-husband "hatched a conspiracy" to injure her professionally and personally by depriving her of the right to see her son, now nine years of age. Frank Loesch replied to the press that the charge was baseless in that Caroline had allowed months to pass before expressing the slightest interest in visiting the boy.[29]

A looming disaster instead became a moment of triumph for Caroline. Perhaps out of pity or respect for the lamented Mr. Carter, the local critics of her performance were less than generous in their praise. "Thus far one can see in her only a mediocre talent which would make her a desirable member of a stock company, but would not distinguish her as the star of an organization," wrote *Tribune* critic Edward J. McPhelim.[30] The *Inter-Ocean* of February 15 gave muted praise. "A miracle! She can act!"

There is no evidence to establish the presence of Leslie inside the theater that long ago winter evening, nor is there any way of knowing what his state of mind might have been had he been there. Newspaper accounts in the *Chicago Mail* of that day suggest that he had quietly slipped out of town with Dudley rather than confront an expected barrage of unwanted publicity.

Carter never overcame his bitterness and hurt. He instructed the domestic help not to mention his ex-wife's name in his presence, and ordered the removal of all pictures of her from the walls of his home. He directed employees of the South Side Elevated Railroad Company to ensure that no theatrical posters advertising her performances in Chicago theaters be affixed to billboards and buildings adjoining the route. Leslie Carter, a forlorn, increasingly desperate man was torn asunder. The divorce and its aftermath deeply affected his mental and physical health.

The unpredictable rise to fame of Caroline Dudley Carter and the fall of Leslie Carter evoke the grim storyline of *Sister Carrie*, Theodore Dreiser's richly textured and evocative 1900 novel about the rise of a feckless young actress through her romantic affairs with two prominent older paramours and the eventual suicide of George Hurstwood, the second man in the drama who died a penniless vagrant in the New York Bowery.

While the tide of bad fortune that doomed the fictional Hurstwood who had lost his family, his fortune, and his self-respect to an ill-fated romance was not as immediate or devastating for Leslie Carter, but it was certainly not without emotional cost.

Caroline Dudley Carter became a great theatrical star, likened to Sarah Bernhardt, Faye Templeton, Ethel Barrymore, Lillian Russell, and the immortal Maud Adams. They were the Broadway royalty of their generation. Blessed with the special gift of formidable acting ability, she accomplished all this with a fierce motivation to avenge the man who assailed her good name and sullied her reputation. On the perilous road to fame, she was a force of nature and at the center of several courtroom controversies that kept her prominent in public life outside of the weekly newspaper theater gossip.

David Belasco produced a series of plays written especially for his protégé. *The Heart of Maryland*, a Civil War drama co-starring Maurice Barrymore (the father of the famed siblings Lionel, Ethel, and John), and *Zaza* and *Madame DuBarry* were among Caroline's greatest successes. In large measure her life as a celebrity was mostly due to Belasco's genius and encouragement. However, as Leslie Carter, Kyrle Bellew, and other men in her life learned the hard way through close association with Caroline, financial setbacks, embarrassment, and scandal were certain to follow.

In the fifteen months of training and personal service designed to make Mrs. Carter a star, N. K. Fairbank paid Belasco the paltry sum of $300. Fairbank had promised an abundant reward but defaulted. Belasco was a patient man, but when no further payments were forthcoming, his patience ran thin. In May 1896, he sued Fairbank for $65,000 of unpaid acting lessons, travel expenses, and lost business opportunities. Inside the New York Supreme Court, the stone-faced financier denied that David Belasco had ever worked for him, before finally admitting that to the best of his recollection he had in fact agreed to pay Belasco—but only $10,000. Then Fairbank countersued Belasco for $53,000 for repayment of what he claimed to be an unpaid loan.

In a sharp legal skirmish marked by frequent and bitter attacks, David Belasco, his complexion deathly pale, told a packed courtroom, "That miserable old man sat there like an iceberg, like an icicle while [his lawyers] looked on with a sneer on their face!" Pointing an accusatory finger at Fairbank, he exclaimed, "I knew how he would turn out—that he was one of those backers who make promises and then sneak out!"[31]

Calling Mrs. Carter the "Titian-haired lady," Belasco's attorney read aloud her letters to Fairbank pleading for additional funding.[32] The issue was always about money with Carrie, or a lack thereof. After nearly three weeks of verbal sparring, the jury awarded Belasco $16,000 after a compromise had been worked out between the two warring parties.

David Belasco's long and mostly fruitful business relationship with Mrs. Carter came to an abrupt and sour ending on July 13, 1906, after news reached him that his prized pupil had secretly eloped with William Louis Payne, a little-known actor eighteen years her junior.

Furious by what he perceived to be a serious betrayal of their personal and professional dealings, the flabbergasted Belasco exclaimed, "Mrs. Carter married! It's like seeing the devil with Holy water!"[33] He had warned her to never marry below her station, especially to an impoverished actor. To her side rushed Charles Bancroft Dillingham, a forty-year-old producer and former theater critic for the *Chicago Times-Herald* who took a chance on representing Caroline Carter, but the venture was short-lived.[34]

Caroline, her ambition twined with increasing desperation, had larger worries to contend with than snoopy society reporters sniggering over her choice of a husband. Under her own management, and tasked with raising the necessary funding for traveling road productions now that Belasco and Dillingham were out of the picture, the headstrong Mrs. Carter struggled mightily in a succession of disastrous tours. In July 1908, she testified before a bankruptcy commissioner that she was without funds. Her present difficulties, she explained, dated back to November 1898 when she filed for her first bankruptcy, claiming at the time that her wardrobe was her only asset. Ticket sales fell below expectations and the actors limped home, broke and out of luck. The press dubbed her, quite appropriately, "The Queen of Bankruptcies."

Back home in Chicago, Leslie Carter suffered his son's loss of affection. Dudley, now a young man taking stock of his family situation, renounced his father and moved to New York to comfort his mother. Relations between father and son became increasingly strained. At the time of Caroline's marriage to Lou Payne, Dudley met up with his father inside the sample room of a posh New York hotel. Blows were exchanged. Dudley thrashed his father and kicked him to the street curb in the same vicious manner the down-and-out Hurstwood had endured a beating by New York thugs in *Sister Carrie*.

Leslie's tragic estrangement from his son and the perfidy of his ex-wife cost him the desire and willpower to live. He failed in a November 9, 1907, suicide following a stroke. He was declared mentally incapable of attending to his estate and a conservator was named to oversee his business affairs on July 25, 1908. In his final months he drifted in and out of consciousness, and was kept alive by artificial feeding and the care of his physician and two full-time nurses. The end came on September 25. Only his sister, Helen Leslie Carter was present at the moment of death. On the day of the funeral, the *Tribune* editorial of September 28, 1908, eulogized the fallen industrialist. "There will be buried today the body of as good a man as has lived in Chicago. He did his full duty as he saw it. In spite of almost appalling obstacles, calumny, and suffering, which might have made a man of less stiff courage give up life's struggle, he worked to the end."

Neither Caroline nor her disinherited son, were present. The tireless efforts of Caroline and Dudley to overturn the will continued into 1910 when mother and son exhausted their appeals and dropped the matter. Earlier, Dudley had shocked and horrified his mother by announcing his engagement to wealthy publishing heiress Norma Munro—Caroline's closest friend, boon companion, and source of vital financial support for nearly five years.

It was seen by Caroline as a betrayal and a dastardly act of revenge and shame thrust upon her by a friend she had trusted and loved. In a dramatic flourish, Mrs. Carter and Lou Payne sailed to Europe to live as expatriates for the next nine years. Caroline announced that "I am sick and tired and ready to die!"[35] She changed her mind, as she was known to do, before returning to New York to revive her career in the two-a-day Vaudeville circuit and purchase a new home in Los Angeles, where the childless couple adopted a daughter they named Mary.

"Just a few years ago they were saying that I was going to retire, just go someplace and die. But when I started playing in the *Shanghai Gesture* I got a new thrill out of life," she said of her celebrated return to the footlights.[36] But of course her word was never entirely her bond. Caroline abandoned the grind of vaudeville to return to the American stage. Recalling her earlier infamy and the choice of roles assigned to her by Belasco, the *Los Angeles Times* nostalgically recalled how "people went to see her in 'Zaza' to shiver deliciously and hope the neighbors would not know they had been."[37] Calling the fading actress "a remarkable old dear," the bemused *Times* critic described her latest appearance and a terrible loss that failed to sap her energy or check her unending ambition for audience approval.

"She still wears her hair a violent red, and pretty well lives in saucy pajamas. She was thus attired when she went down for rehearsal. And much conflict of emotion beset her—for this play is a calculated antidote to the tragedy of the death of her beloved son last month. That boy Dudley and her art have been the two great ruling passions of her life."[38]

Leslie Dudley Carter, just fifty-three years of age and betrothed to his second wife, Frances Gere, expired in his Chicago apartment house, a drab, five-unit, brown brick structure at 7630 N. Marshfield Avenue in the Rogers Park neighborhood on July 28, 1934. There were no footmen, servants, or chambermaids to receive his orders or captains of industry turning up at his door at the time of death to curry one last favor. Dudley Carter, by now ignored and forgotten, earned his living as a stocks and bonds salesman. His domestic and professional life was quite different from that of his late father.

The "American Sarah Bernhardt" withdrew from the profession in 1935 to quietly live out the rest of her days with Lou Payne and their adopted daughter Mary. The end came for the seventy-five-year-old actress on November 13, 1937, in Santa Monica, California. A heart ailment, aggravated by pneumonia, ended the life of a terribly complicated and occasionally disingenuous woman who had overcome a diagnosis of insanity, a term of confinement in a Wisconsin mental institution, and four declared bankruptcies to become an acclaimed international star of stage and screen.

Three years after her death, the Warner Brothers Studio cast Miriam Hopkins in the role of Mrs. Leslie Carter, Claude Rains as David Belasco, and Richard Ainley as Lou Payne in *The Lady with Red Hair*, the sentimental retelling of Caroline's stormy stage career. Moviegoers and critics praised Claude Rains's performance ("I'm David Belasco! I can make a telegraph pole look good!" Rains chortles in one memorable, albeit exaggerated scene) but were mostly lukewarm to this cinematic yarn. Director Curtis Bernhardt and the writing team ignored Mr. Leslie Carter in the screenplay. It was a not so surprising epitaph to the aggrieved husband's sad life and tragic end.

Mary Runnion McVicker (*right*), daughter of James McVicker, with her husband, the great Shakespeare tragedian Edwin Booth. Booth's daughter Edwina stands at left. COURTESY OF FOLGER SHAKESPEARE LIBRARY.

The home of Patrick and Catherine O'Leary, 137 DeKoven Street, survived the Great Chicago Fire. COURTESY OF THE UNIVERSITY OF ILLINOIS.

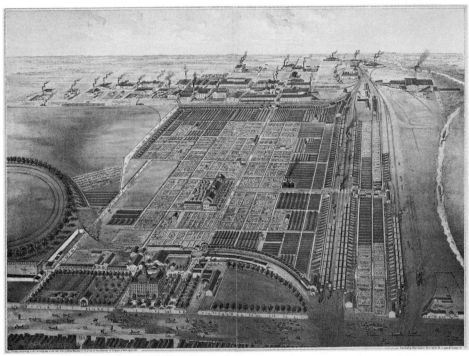

Map of the Union Stock Yard and Transit Company at the time of its grand opening, the day after Christmas 1865. COURTESY OF THE LIBRARY OF CONGRESS, PRINTS AND PHOTOGRAPHS DIVISION.

Electrical engineer Elisha Gray (1835–1901), cofounder of Western Electric Manufacturing Company, is believed by many to be the rightful inventor of the telephone. COURTESY OF THE LIBRARY OF CONGRESS, PRINTS AND PHOTOGRAPHS DIVISION.

Intolerable working conditions: child labor in a
Chicago packinghouse. COURTESY OF THE LIBRARY OF
CONGRESS, PRINTS AND PHOTOGRAPHS DIVISION.

Charles F. Dowd (1825–1904)
was the first to propose multiple
time zones in the United States,
which were formally adopted
at the Grand Pacific Hotel in
Chicago on October 11–13, 1883.
COURTESY OF THE LIBRARY
OF CONGRESS, PRINTS AND
PHOTOGRAPHS DIVISION.

LESLIE CARTER

Famed actress and free spirit Mrs. Leslie Carter (1857–1937) scandalized Chicago during her lurid 1888–89 divorce action against millionaire industrialist and husband, Leslie Carter. COURTESY OF THE LIBRARY OF CONGRESS, PRINTS AND PHOTOGRAPHS DIVISION, ALFRED BENDINER MEMORIAL COLLECTION.

Aaron Montgomery Ward (1844–1913) built the firm's steel-frame headquarters "Tower" building on Michigan Avenue at Madison Street in 1899 while leading the campaign to keep Grant Park free, open, and clear. COURTESY OF THE LIBRARY OF CONGRESS, PRINTS AND PHOTOGRAPHS DIVISION, DETROIT PUBLISHING COMPANY COLLECTION.

Chicago's most elegant mansion of the Civil War period, the Peter Schuttler home at Adams Street and Aberdeen on the Near West Side, fell into decay and ruin during the late Gilded Age and was reputed to be haunted by spectral entities, drawing throngs of tourists and curiosity seekers to the location. *PICTURESQUE CHICAGO* (CHICAGO: CHICAGO ENGRAVING CO., 1880).

Wallace de Groot Rice, author, essayist, and designer of the official flags for the State of Illinois and the City of Chicago. WALLACE RICE PAPERS, THE NEWBERRY LIBRARY, CHICAGO.

Pioneering automotive designer Charles Duryea won the race and claimed the top prize using only three and a half gallons of drugstore-purchased fuel in his "buggyaut" to complete the journey. COURTESY OF THE LIBRARY OF CONGRESS, PRINTS AND PHOTOGRAPHS DIVISION.

The tragic *Rouse Simmons*, the Christmas Tree Ship, braved the dangerous
waters of Lake Michigan every November to deliver Christmas trees
to the people of Chicago. Here the crew of the USCGC *Mackinaw*
honors the memory of the *Rouse Simmons* by transporting freshly cut
Christmas trees across the same lake. U.S. COAST GUARD PHOTO BY
PETTY OFFICER THIRD CLASS JOHN FILIPPONE; WIKIMEDIA COMMONS.

THE LAKEFRONT FOREVER OPEN, CLEAR, AND FREE

earing the end of a long and productive life, the exhausted and world-weary Aaron Montgomery Ward looked back on his greatest achievement with a mix of self-pity and underlying sadness. His attitude was quite understandable given Ward's many courtroom struggles against uncaring, powerful adversaries looking to deprive the city of Chicago of its verdant front yard.

Speaking to a reporter on October 26, 1909, in one of his rare public interviews, Ward, speaking in a tone of quiet, self-reflective calm, said: "It's been an uphill fight but the victory is sweet. Had I known in 1890 how long it would take me to preserve a park for the people against their will I would not have undertaken it. I think there is not another man in Chicago who would have spent the money I have spent in this fight with certainty that gratitude would be denied as interest. I have lived here since 1865 and have watched and assisted the city's development, but this is one of the best things I did for Chicago. I have nothing at stake in this fight but the good of the people now and for future generations. Perhaps I may yet see the public appreciate my efforts. But I doubt it."[1]

This very private merchant, prince to the millions, coined the now-famous marketing slogan Satisfaction Guaranteed or Your Money Back at a point in retailing history when Richard Warren Sears was hard at work peddling a small consignment of pocket watches as a station agent of the Minneapolis and St. Paul Railroad.[2] Young Sears would later appropriate Ward's customer pledge, make it his company imprimatur, and attach it to all promotional and banner advertising.

Before friends, opponents, and politicians tagged him "the watchdog of the lakefront" for his heroic fight to save the lakefront park, Aaron Montgomery Ward had a business to run; a mail order start-up he launched in August 1872 with $1,600 in working capital and the help of his brother-in-law George R. Thorne in a loft space above a livery stable on Kinzie Street midway between Rush and State Streets north of the river. With a firm handshake and a promise to eliminate the middle man, sell directly to the customer at reasonable prices, and always treat people fair, the partners published the world's first general-merchandise catalog and embarked upon this ambitious enterprise against the advice of seasoned veterans of Chicago's flourishing wholesale dry goods trade who predicted a financial downfall.

Their first big break came that same year when the Illinois State Grange appointed Ward purchasing agent, providing him with membership mailing lists and a target audience. Ward capitalized on his good fortune by calling his operation the "Original Grange Supply House" peddling hundreds of agricultural implements.[3] The spring 1874 catalog contained thirty-two pages. In the fall the publication expanded to a hundred pages with sales topping $100,000.[4] In 1889 Ward and Thorne fully incorporated, as Jordan Marsh, Sears, John Wanamaker and Carson, Pirie Scott and Company, all new competitors, entered the catalog business.

The man that *Forbes Magazine* once rated the sixteenth most influential businessman of all time descended from colonial stock. His great-grand-father, Captain Israel Montgomery Ward, served under General George Washington during the War for Independence. The future mail-order king was born February 17, 1843, in rural Chatham, New Jersey, but attended the public schools of Niles, Michigan, during Ward's formative years after his father, Sylvester Ward, moved the family west to buy a local store. The business venture failed and the fourteen-year-old boy went to work manning a cutting machine in a barrel-stave factory for twenty-five cents a day. The family depended on his meager earnings to survive following the calamitous failure of the store. Later he found work as a day laborer in a brickyard. It was hard, demanding work and the memory of it evoked strong sentiment within him for the poor people of Chicago years later.

Ward next accepted an offer of employment from one Captain Boughton, the owner of a barter store in St. Joseph, Michigan, promising five dollars a day plus room and board. Ward, it is said, changed the nature of the business from barter to cash and was so successful that the owner advanced him to store manager at a salary of a hundred dollars a month. Having acquired the requisite experience in merchandising, Ward made his way to Chicago in 1865 to work as a traveling salesman for Case and Sobin, a lamp company. In his wanderings, he tapped the pulse of mid-America, assessing the needs and wants of petty bourgeoisie shopkeepers and the public they served with a mix of detachment and clever passion. He traveled far and wide for Case and Sobin, then later with Field, Palmer, and Leiter from their Madison and Market Street location, and Wills, Gregg, and Brown, a wholesale dry goods company, until they dissolved.[5]

After the Chicago Fire, Ward married Elizabeth Cobb of Kalamazoo, the love of his life, and at the same time launched his catalog business with a promise to his customers that they could pay on easy installment terms, making the purchase of household items and necessities an easier proposition for working class families. He gambled that the American consumer would be willing to purchase goods sight unseen from the pages in a book. The gamble paid off.

On the other hand, he must be held at least partially responsible for the dramatic rise of consumer indebtedness and the glut of credit cards plaguing subsequent generations—an unfortunate consequence of granting easy terms.

In less than ten years, his catalog product line grew from 163 items to 10,000. Americans trusted the quality and reliability of Montgomery Ward and Company products and eagerly anticipated the arrival of the livery wagons delivering catalog merchandise to small towns and villages.

Ward and Thorne opened branch locations in Portland, Oregon; Kansas City, Missouri; Fort Worth, Texas; and New York City. With the value of the business pegged at $40 million per annum and a workforce exceeding six thousand, the partners vacated their cramped headquarters on Kinzie Street to occupy a larger space on Wabash Avenue in 1877. The years passed. George Thorne's five sons assumed prominent leadership roles within the company and countered the growing threat from Sears, Roebuck, whose mantra was "we always undersell," with the promise of superior quality— inferring that you get what you pay for.

In 1886 the partners acquired from the US Warehouse and Merchandising Company valuable property fronting Lake-Front Park near the northwest corner of Michigan Avenue and Madison Street. Ward chose this site "in order to assure that their employees enjoyed sunlight, fresh air and a relatively quiet location in which to work."[6] The eight-story structure erected and opened in 1892 (a year ahead of the World's Fair) became Montgomery Ward's mail-order fulfillment center. Far from being quiet, the catalog house instead became a veritable bee hive buzzing with merchandising activity as frenzied workers jostled with one another to process orders and move them out the door as quickly as possible. A century later, Amazon.com took note.

Work began on an adjoining steel-frame, corner office building destined to rise to the height of 394 feet above the pavement in 1897. The architect crowned the building with an open-air observatory showing off a commanding view of the park. A twenty-two-foot weather vane in the form of Diana perched atop the roof symbolized civilization's progress.[7] For the next few years, the Ward building stood as the tallest in the city.

Preferring the companionship of reserved and refined business and civic aristocrats behind the closed doors of private rooms in the Exmoor Country Club, the Union League, and the Chicago Athletic Association to all else (especially reporters and process servers), Ward had two other great passions in life apart from his commercial affairs: the prized horses he bred at his country home, La Belle Knoll, in Oconomowoc, Wisconsin, and the expanse of public park fronting his Michigan Avenue office from Randolph south to Twelfth Street.

Concerning the latter, one might easily think Ward's lakefront zealotry obsessive. He did however cite historical precedent as his rationale for desiring to keep the swath of parkland free and unencumbered from buildings, and unsightly obstructions. In 1836, just one year before the formal granting of the city of Chicago charter on March 4, 1837, the Board of Canal Commissioners and the United States platted all of the land east of State Street between Madison and Park Row (once an upscale, east-west residential street located during the antebellum period just north of Twelfth Street), exclusive of previously sold lots on Michigan Avenue, to remain forever open.[8] This decision was reaffirmed in court and the original maps declared "legally binding public dedications" in 1839.[9] Five years later the city of Chicago accepted the dedications and agreed to hold the land in trust for the public with the court standing behind the decision.

On account of these easement rights, Ward and Thorne were willing to pay more for their Michigan Avenue land than what another downtown location of the same proportionate size might have cost them in assessed value. They maintained that it was the duty of the city to maintain Lake-Front Park (as it was then called) and to prevent encroachment from any public or private interests.

For many years leading up to the pivotal moment on October 16, 1890, when Ward and Thorne filed suit in the Superior Court of Cook County to enjoin the city of Chicago from erecting any buildings (the construction of wooden scaffolding to load garbage onto railroad cars triggered the legal action), the region directly east of Michigan Avenue and extending to Lake Michigan was desolate, neglected, and unsightly.

The Illinois Central Railroad, having been granted right of way through the submerged land east of the Lake Michigan shoreline filled in the land with passenger and freight yards. The Baltimore and Ohio railroad utilized the Illinois Central tracks for its flourishing passenger business transporting thousands of European immigrants bound for Chicago and a new way of life.

The first challenge to the free and clear doctrine came in July 1864 when the city of Chicago granted permission for the Democratic Party to build a wigwam, a circular wooden amphitheater with a canvass roof at the southern end of Lake-Front Park at Eleventh Street. In this temporary enclosure, the Democrats nominated a peace candidate, the discredited General George B. McClellan as their standard bearer for the national election.

Angry Michigan Avenue property owners filed suit, and the courts granted an injunction—lifted on June 2, 1864, after agreeing to a compromise that would allow the convention to proceed with the stipulation that the wigwam be taken down and removed within six days of the conclusion of the event. The agreement established a dangerous precedent—and offered encouragement to future interlopers that the free and clear mandate might in fact be malleable and open to judicial reinterpretation.

In the aftermath of the Great Chicago Fire, legitimate business owners, gambling dens, saloons, and proprietors of objectionable houses of ill fame erected temporary wooden structures to transact commerce at the north end of the park. The courts granted them wide latitude to reinvigorate the local economy during the period of massive rebuilding, no matter how objectionable the business. Chicago recovered from the fire trauma rendering ninety thousand people homeless. But in the wake of the terrible disaster, the city temporarily cast aside the free and clear doctrine, as fire rubble and debris were dumped into the Lake Michigan shallows and in the expanse of ground adjoining the railroad tracks. The charred embers, twisted steel, and stonework of pre-fire Chicago lie buried beneath the green lawn of Grant Park today.

Although the squalid collection of temporary wooden shacks at the north end of the park eventually came down, Chicago's first permanent convention hall, the majestic Interstate Industrial Exposition Building, opened in 1873 at the present location of the Art Institute to host industrial exhibitions, concerts by Maestro Theodore Thomas of the Chicago Symphony, and a flurry of national nominating conventions that early on established the Windy City as an important staging ground for American politics.

As the fervor over the "free and clear" edict quieted, interested parties capitalized on the deliberate ambiguities of the courts and the Lake-Front Park advocates. The Chicago White Stockings baseball team, an early forerunner of the Cubs, played in the Union Baseball grounds, a wooden grandstand enclosure east of Michigan Avenue at Randolph Street during the 1871 season. The Great Fire destroyed the wooden park, but the owners rebuilt and opened their new park on May 14, 1878. The White Stockings, now a charter member of the newly formed National League featuring the mighty Adrian "Cap" Anson, played home games at the lakefront location through the 1884 season.

At the same time, Battery D of the First Artillery Illinois National Guard built an armory east of Michigan Avenue, reawakening the old controversies over public nuisances in the park. The attorney general of Illinois filed suit in Cook County against the Illinois Central, the city of Chicago, and the United States in a forty-one page complaint. The plaintiffs sought an injunction against any further incursions in the park, including a planned two-story hall for the Trades Assembly and Knights of Labor featuring a saloon, and a gallery. This was simply too much for the Michigan Avenue gentry desiring peace and quiet.

Judge Thomas A. Moran granted the injunction to halt any further construction on May 9, 1883, but for the moment he allowed the temporary structures to remain. The federal government resumed litigation in 1884, this time taking aim at Albert Goodwill Spalding and his Chicago White Stockings baseball team, alleging that the city of Chicago violated its trust as "custodian" of the property by allowing Spalding "to construct a board fence at least ten feet in height, in such manner as to completely shut off said ground from public view or access," further noting that the public was excluded from occupying the location unless they had paid for the cost of an admission ticket.[10]

The matter went before federal circuit court judge Henry Blodgett who ruled against Spalding, ordering that "on or before the thirty-first day of October (1884) next, the said Chicago Baseball Club and the City of Chicago remove or cause to be removed from the said public ground all buildings, fences, and structures of every description and in such a manner as to leave the said public ground open and clear of materials or rubbish of any kind unless in the meantime the court shall otherwise order."[11]

Upon the conclusion of the 1884 season, the White Stockings secured a five-year lease at Congress, Harrison, Throop, and Loomis Streets on the West Side against stiff community opposition from local residents in that community who feared that saloons, gambling houses, and "other establishments of questionable character will follow in the wake of ballplayers."[12]

The successful outcome of the case against Spalding and his directors proved that the forever clear and free 1839 doctrine was legally enforceable in a court of law, thus empowering a man of means and influence to carry the battle forward against future interlopers courting favor with "Big Sandy" Walters, general superintendent of the Lake-Front Park, and a self-interested political spoilsman aligned with 1st Ward Alderman "Bath-house" John Coughlin, if he was of a mind to do so.

Looking back on the verdant parkland of the antebellum period when Chicago's young swains escorted their sweethearts on Sunday strolls, Frederick Francis Cook recalled that "late in the 1860s this guileless Eden was ruthlessly invaded, and thereafter practical interests claimed it more for their own. First the northern part was set apart for a baseball field: then later the Exposition building of 1873 absorbed another slice; and so because of these encroachments—and again because the old boarding houses had nearly all disappeared—the old Lake Front knew its crowds no more."[13]

Sarah E. Daggett, aligned with the red-bearded attorney John H. Hamline; John F. Stafford (owner of a Lake Michigan vessel, John Wilkes Booth's host during his celebrated 1862 Chicago tour, and the superintendent of the Chicago Exposition Building); and other Michigan Avenue property owners joined with hotelier Warren F. Leland, who had waged a continuous war against special interests, the railroads, and prospective developers ever since the Chicago Fire. Together they found their truest champion in Aaron Montgomery Ward, who shared the belief that the parks were for the people.

From a distance, train conductors recalled spotting the ever-vigilant Mr. Leland, a silent sentinel poised at the window in one of the upper floors of his hotel at midnight, indignantly gazing out at their express trains flashing across the park. Curiously, Leland's hotel business directly benefitted from the out-of-town arrivals seeking lodging after stepping off the platform of the Illinois Central depot.

Ward continued his "free and clear" crusade against the Art Institute, scheduled to occupy the former site of the Interstate Industrial Exposition Building in 1891 after the old hall was razed. He deemed the Art Institute an eyesore and demanded that it too be torn down in the name of the free and clear doctrine. However, the Art Institute directors were granted an exception after a majority of the Michigan Avenue property owners, including Ward, consented to a request not to stand in the way of the project. The Art Institute would be the only permanent structure allowed to remain north of Twelfth Street until the formal dedication of Millennium Park on July 16, 2004.

Montgomery Ward and his legal team, George Merrick and Elbridge Hanecy (later a judge and eventually a mayoral candidate) fired their opening salvo on October 16, 1890. Ward, like Warren Leland, enjoyed the pastoral view of the Lake Michigan shoreline from the comfort of his private office. One afternoon, to his dismay, he spotted workers building scaffolding for the purpose of loading garbage into railroad box cars. Citing Judge Moran's earlier decision, Ward demanded and secured removal of the scaffolding.

"They made a dumping ground of the park allowed circuses, mask balls, and anything else there and put up all sorts of unsightly buildings. Without recourse to the courts there would still be merry-go-rounds and whatnots all the way to Park Row," Ward reflected in 1897, seven years into his crusade.[14]

By that time, the city contrived with special interests to erect a temporary post office building at Washington Street, and forged ahead with plans for a second Wigwam between Washington and Madison for the purpose of hosting the 1892 Democratic National Convention despite the annoying and distracting screech of the Illinois Central and Michigan Central trains rumbling past a few hundred feet due east. A police station and engine house went in around the same time to complete the picture. Ward's persistent litigation succeeded in the forcible removal of these buildings.

"The people of Chicago are with Montgomery Ward in the fight he is making," the *Tribune* editorialized on April 16, 1898. "They admire his pluck and wish him success." The Republican-leaning *Chicago Tribune* was especially pleased with Ward after he succeeded in convincing the Chicago Corporation Counsel to prohibit perpetual Democratic presidential nominee William Jennings Bryan from holding an open-air campaign rally in the park under a tent. Bryan was forced to explore other options.

Marshall Field had set aside $1 million in funding to establish a permanent home for the exhibits and collections displayed at the 1893 World's Fair. In honor of the fair, Field and members of his consortium incorporated the Columbian Museum of Chicago on September 16, 1893, encouraging the prominent men of affairs to donate their World's Fair stock to the worthy cause. In this matter, Montgomery Ward provided support with a donation of a thousand shares. The collection would be temporarily housed in the former Palace of Fine Arts in Jackson Park (now the Museum of Science and Industry) until a suitable lakefront location nearest to downtown could be secured. By 1896, pursuant to Chicago City Council ordinances, the title to Lake-Front Park passed into the control of the South Park Commissioners, and in 1899 the legislature renamed the entire space Grant Park.

Mayor Carter Harrison II vigorously supported the Field petition to build the Columbian Museum in Grant Park—well south of the disputed "free and clear" zone and the construction of the John Crerar Library, a notable civic project devoted to furthering the advance of science and technology north near Madison Street. Upon his death in 1889, railroad titan and philanthropist John Crerar bequeathed to the city $2.5 million in his will for that purpose.

Ward was uneasy about the Columbian Museum going in—although he appreciated its stated purpose and understood that it would not impair his splendid lakefront view. For the moment he deferred legal action against Field but fought the Crerar petition tooth and nail, and appealed to the court to sanction John Mitchell, president of the Illinois Trust and Savings Bank (head of the library board) and the South Parks Commission for "outrageous conduct." Judge Theodore Brentano of the superior court upheld the September 1896 injunction and ordered all building materials for the Crerar project removed from the grounds.

"If John Crerar were alive, he wouldn't ask to have his monument erected on public property. He was not that type of man!" thundered Hanecy following the June 26, 1906, ruling. The Crerar Library Board resumed its search for a permanent home.[15]

Meanwhile the South Parks Commission passed an ordinance to build the Columbian Museum—renamed the Field Museum of Natural History on the east side of the Illinois Central tracks on Congress Street, one-half mile south of the Ward building following the passing of Marshall Field I a year earlier. Once again, Ward arose to express his displeasure. Through Attorney Merrick he filed a petition for injunction on February 23, 1907. The South Parks Commission filed a cross-bill to bar Ward from interfering with project construction.

By now the tide of public opinion slowly began to turn against the "Watchdog of the Lakefront." Newspaper editorials criticized Ward as an obstructionist standing in the way of progress. A voter tax referendum to build the museum received overwhelming approval by the public, countermanding his opposition. Circuses and sideshows; armories and train depots; loading docks and a temporary post office; most people agreed that these types of structures were unsightly and objectionable amid the pastoral setting of Lake-Front Park/Grant Park. Practical-thinkers, however, supported the addition of a public museum on the south campus. Accordingly, superior court judge George A. Dupuy found for the defendants, stating that proper park buildings could be built on the east side of the train tracks, but rejected another attempt on the part of the Parks Commission to allow the Crerar Library to go forward.

Stanley Field, a nephew of Marshall Field I and society maven, opened the doors of the $6.7 million museum with its 560 carloads of exhibits carted over from Jackson Park on May 3, 1921, ending a three-decades-old court battle with Ward, his designates, and the lakefront preservationists. In retrospect, did this represent a hard-fought victory for the people or a defeat for "free and clear" (otherwise known as the public dedication doctrine)? The new Field Museum, although situated well south of the disputed

Grant Park zone, weakened the resolve of the preservationists in the years following Ward's death on December 7, 1913, at his Highland Park home. The John G. Shedd Aquarium, whose creation Stanley Field helped inspire, welcomed its first visitors on May 31, 1930, two weeks after the grand opening of Adler Planetarium nearby on Northerly Island, a ninety-one acre, man-made parkway and green space envisioned by Daniel Burnham and opened in 1925.[16]

Chicago's newly formed museum campus south of Eleventh Street taking shape in the 1930s, conformed to the territorial boundaries delineated by Ward in his major courtroom victories. The three museums bookending the south end of Grant Park with the Art Institute, the new $370 million Millennium Park, and the Harris Theater a mile to the north have increased the aesthetic value of the lakefront shoreline. They have fulfilled the mission articulated in the 1909 interview that Ward gave following his victory before the Illinois Supreme Court and Justice James H. Cartwright who decided three landmark cases in Ward's favor—*Bliss v. Ward*, *Ward v. Field Museum*, and *Ward v. South Park Commissioners*: "I fought for the poor people of Chicago, not for the millionaires. In the district bounded by Twenty-Second Street, Chicago Avenue and Halsted Street live more than 250,000 persons—mostly poor. The city has a magnificent Park and boulevard system of some fifty miles, but the poor man's auto is shank's mare, or at the best the street cars. Here is a park frontage on the lake, comparing favorably with the Bay of Naples."[17]

Following the old man's death, control of Montgomery Ward and Company passed into the hands of nephews Charles H. and George A. Thorne and their heirs. Lacking the founder's foresight and vision, the giant mail order and retail operation suffered numerous business and marketing reversals in the lean times to come. By 1918, the company had fallen behind arch-competitor Sears Roebuck. Robert J. Thorne resigned the presidency on August 6, 1920, in favor of Silas Strawn, a company director. James and George Thorne stepped down as directors a year later. Montgomery Ward bankers installed their own man, Theodore F. Merseles of the National Cloak and Suit Company, as their turnaround specialist with mixed results.

Montgomery Ward and Company would engage a number of other "turnaround specialists" in repeated efforts over the coming decades to resuscitate the flagging company before finally throwing in the towel. The financial house of J. P. Morgan, deeply involved with the Ward operation for more than a decade, brought in Sewell Lee Avery (1873–1960), former head of US Gypsum, in 1931, to steer the company toward profitability. A polarizing figure who achieved only short-term success, Avery was involved in stockholder proxy fights and harbored strong anti-union sentiment that resulted in a 1944 battle with President Franklin D. Roosevelt. A controversy involving the Congress of Industrial Organizations led to Avery's forcible removal from his office by military personnel ordered by the US attorney general.[18]

Brusque, defiant, and imperturbable, Avery stumbled in the post-World War II period. While Sears opened new stores in prime suburban locations, Avery played it close to the vest, never fully confident that the economy would fully recover from the cataclysm of the Great Depression. He conserved financial resources but paid a high price for his cautious management style. By the time Ward ventured out into suburbia, secondary locations and picked-over tertiary markets were all that was left to the retailer as revenues continued to sag. Under pressure, Avery stepped down as president on May 9, 1955, at age eighty-one. Other company executives followed him out the door. Briefly, the price of Montgomery Ward stock jumped on the New York Stock Exchange upon the release of this welcomed announcement.

In 1976 Mobil Corporation acquired Montgomery Ward. New marketing strategies were employed. A phalanx of phone-room telemarketers employed by the company's Signature Group in the 1980s pestered beleaguered consumers holding Montgomery Ward credit cards with repeated night-time calls attempting to peddle auto club memberships, insurance products, and home protection plans. Various schemes including specialty store within a store retailing concepts to redefine the shopping experience for customers in the 1980s and 1990s failed, driving the company to the brink. Chief executive officer Bernard Brennan headed the entire operation but profits fell amid a $237 million loss in 1996. Finally, on July 7, 1997, after decades of fractious upheaval, Montgomery Ward and Company filed for Chapter 11 bankruptcy protection.

The company announced it would close its remaining 250 big-box retail outlets on December 28, 2000, resulting in job loss for thirty-seven thousand employees. Today, the Montgomery Ward name exists as an online seller of clothing items and catalog items operated by Colony Brands (formerly Swiss Colony).

It is hard to imagine what thoughts would have churned through the mind of the founder were he alive to witness the slow and painful demise of a business he and his partner had painstakingly started from a Kinzie Street livery stable, or the more recent intrusions upon his beloved green pastures fronting Michigan Avenue. He was an intensely private man who left no written record, journal, memoir, diary, or set of papers expressing his innermost thoughts.

From the moment of his death in 1913 through 1993 and the dedication of artist Milton Horn's bust of Ward and the beautiful Montgomery Ward Gardens along the edge of Grant Park from Randolph to Monroe Streets (moved to the southwest side of Grant Park in 1999 and rededicated in 2005 following the opening of Millennium Park), there had been no public tribute or official recognition given to Ward or his personal crusade as the anointed savior of the lakefront. The inscription reads, in part: "Grant Park is his legacy to the city he loved . . . his gift to the future."

THE HAUNTING OF THE SCHUTTLER HOUSE

f or nearly fifty years a deserted West Side relic of the Gilded Age loomed over the intersection of Adams Street and Aberdeen. The Peter Schuttler residence, now a faded and mildewed remnant of Victorian opulence, once reflected the boundless energy of its owner and his lifetime of industriousness, prudence, and good business sense.

Within two generations, its rotting timbers, lichen-covered porch, and unkempt lawn run riot with weeds carried memories of a former order and abundance—a yard full of roses, hyacinths, and peonies. Water no longer flowed from the beautiful garden fountain—its pipes rusted, its base chipped and eroded.

It was reliably reported by neighbors, onlookers, and police congregating outside the mansion in the year 1913, that the departed former inhabitants haunted this relic of bygone days. Visitors to the magnificent Schuttler homestead—designed in the Louis XVI style by famed architect John M. Van Osdel and built over a three-year period while the Civil War raged—would first pass through a wide veranda and an imported black walnut door.[1] They marveled at the window casings, the artful arrangement of flowers in the parlor, and hand-painted wall coverings conceived by noted Austrian artists personally hired by Peter Schuttler during his visit to the Continent.

Expensive works of art graced the drawing rooms. Upon taking control of the property following his father's death, Peter Schuttler II, a man of cultivated and refined taste, filled the beautiful seventy-eight-foot long adjoining conservatory constructed in the Gothic-Moorish tradition with a collection of imported tropical plants. He hired a German gardener to tend them. "It is difficult to convey an adequate idea of the peculiar beauty and elegance of this portion of the building," wrote an admiring *Chicago Tribune* social critic on December 31, 1869. "It needs to be seen in order to be appreciated. The entire cost is $50,000." Italian stone cutters installed Carrera marble to shape the mantel, fireplace, and grand staircases of the interior living space. The color scheme was a stunning blend of white and gold.

On the southwest corner of the building stood an odd curiosity, a giant tower with a large room that emitted light through imported French window panes on all four sides. From inside this sequestered tower room—a "widow's watch" as such rooms were then known—loomed high over the street. It was in this tower, late at night, when the hauntings were said to have occurred.

Peter Schuttler, original owner, patriarch of the haunted castle, and "the Wagon King of Chicago," grew up with the city, more or less. He was the impoverished descendent of a German aristocrat, born in Wachenheim, a tiny village in the Bad Durkheim district of the Rhineland Palatinate, Germany, three days before Christmas, 1812.

The young man left the region with his worldly belongings contained inside his valise, and immigrated to America in 1834. He settled in Sandusky, Ohio, an industrial town ruefully described by Charles Dickens during his 1842 US tour as "sluggish and uninteresting."[2] Sandusky's meager attractions held little appeal for Schuttler who lasted there nine years as he honed his skill as a wainwright (a tradesman skilled in the manufacture and repair of carts and wagons). He married Dorothy, and there on September 19, 1842, she bore him a son, Peter Schuttler II, who would figure prominently in the unfolding melodrama.

Chicago beckoned, as it had for an entire generation, to ambitious young men chasing manifest destiny and dreams of empire. Schuttler and his family arrived the same year as steel manufacturer Joseph T. Ryerson, incorporator of a factory at Milwaukee Avenue and Clinton that over the next hundred years was destined to become the largest steel service center in the country.

A city of just over four thousand inhabitants in 1840 had grown up around the rotting palisades of old Fort Dearborn, and was the new midwestern vista of industry, commerce, and transportation—and the Hog Butcher to the World. Gurdon Saltonstall Hubbard, fur trader, insurance underwriter, and one of Chicago's "old settlers," packed hogs in the bank building at La-Salle and Lake in a business venture housed in a building airily dismissed as "Hubbard's Folly" by the more established men of commerce. In 1834, the year Hubbard commenced operations, he received five thousand animals shipped in from Vermillion County, St. Clair County, and the Wabash Valley. Following their slaughter, the carcasses were cut and packaged in his house.

In 1845, two years after Schuttler hung out his shingle to announce his presence, Hubbard's operation moved to the North Branch of the River from South Water Street (the city's chief artery of shipment and commercial trade in those days) near where his house was situated. Hubbard gave rise to Chicago's largest and most enduring commercial endeavor, a gigantic, reeking abattoir, making possible the formation of hundreds of related businesses and the city's national reputation as Hog Butcher to the World.

Peter Schuttler, a man of thrift and frugality bordering on obsessiveness except when it came to fitting out his homestead, established his first residence on the North Side near the Gurdon Hubbard holdings stretching along Illinois Street between St. Clair and Pine Street. He opened a small wagon-making factory at Randolph Street and Franklin to service the meatpackers and the carriage trade, but wagon shops were already plentiful in this crossroads of East-West transportation. With so much competition many manufacturers were forced into early bankruptcy, while the best of them managed to turn out only a few hundred wagons a year. By the late 1840s, the city's meatpackers made better use of the Lake Michigan schooners and flat boats to convey the animals upriver rather than relying on slower four-wheel horse-drawn transportation attempting to navigate the muddy sloughs that passed for roads in frontier Chicago.

Schuttler's wagon-building trade plodded along rather unremarkably until 1846 when the Mormon colony in Nauvoo (formerly Commerce), Illinois, dispersed months after its founder, prophet Joseph Smith, was murdered on June 27, 1844, by an armed mob of church dissidents. Facing persistent threats of violence from surrounding communities opposed to the Mormon faith and its practice of polygamy, Brigham Young, senior member and president of the Quorum of the Twelve Apostles, led an exodus of the faithful out of Illinois toward the Great Salt Lake Valley in Utah. The Mormon leader placed an order for Schuttler wagons to transport his followers to the freedom and safety of the West. The lucrative contract with the Mormons enriched the company coffers and established the founder as an up-and-coming midwestern mogul in the overland passenger trade.

Peter Schuttler's business prospects had suddenly turned for the better before the next fortuitous event in his life: the California Gold Rush. Caught up in the gold fever, a generation of adventurers and fortune seekers calling themselves the forty-niners ventured West clinging to a flickering hope of striking it rich. They mortgaged their homes. They sold off their property, and one by one, the pioneers traveling to California via the northern routes, arrived at the factory gate of the Peter Schuttler Company to purchase a sturdy and reliable wagon made from Ryerson steel and solid midwestern timber for the purpose of moving freight and families across the broad expanse of the plains for the sum of seventy-five dollars.

East of the Mississippi River, wagon manufacturing plants dotted the land. The John Deere Company in Moline, Illinois, and the Owensboro

Wagon Company in Kentucky dominated much of the trade, but Peter Schuttler's firm commanded brand loyalty for the quality, durability, and craftsmanship of the product. The Schuttler farm wagon, "Old Reliable," with a special brake invented and installed by his son in later years, opened the West to settlement and would become a staple for the farmers, ranchers, and homesteaders living between the Missouri River and the Pacific Ocean.[3]

Schuttler made a fortune during the Civil War supplying the Union with his army wagons. *Chicago Tribune* publisher Joseph Medill (friend, supporter, and confidant of President Abraham Lincoln) provided the company with a huge competitive edge in the early months of the conflict by promoting the Schuttler wagon in his published editorials.

"Here, for instance, is Schuttler—Peter Schuttler—of sixteen years' experience in wagon building, who has the large steam manufactory on the corner of Randolph and Franklin Streets, not long ago extended by the addition of a four-story brick building," Medill reported on July 20, 1861—just two months into the war. "He has for several years been filling large orders annually for wagons to cross the plains. You may read his name on wagons all the way from the Missouri to the Deseret.[4]

The Mormon emigration calls for several hundred of his wagons every year. These are just the wagons the army wants. Mr. Schuttler has over one-hundred men in [his] employ and can turn out from ninety to one-hundred wagons per week. With a liberal business and capital, it has always been Mr. Schuttler's plan to lay in a large stock of material and keep it long on hand to secure its being thoroughly seasoned and has now of this enough for several thousand wagons. He and his force should be promptly set to work, for their product or some other of its class will be needed, not many months hence, and none better than his can be found in any part of the country."

Flashing his newfound wealth, Schuttler and his bride Dorothy were ordained in the inner circles of the exclusive "prairie aristocracy" of Chicago and with it, came invitations to charity balls, afternoon receptions, fashionable bazaars, card parties, clubland dinners, and cotillions hosted by wealthy elites. Custom dictated that Peter Schuttler fortify his newly found status in society by building a showplace of his own that would reflect his appreciation for culture, refinement, and the ostentatious taste of the coming Gilded Age.

First, there was the matter of securing title to a suitable parcel of land to build this Xanadu. Taking leave of his factory one afternoon, he called upon William Prescott, owner of a land parcel fronting four hundred feet of Adams Street and 256 feet of Aberdeen on the West Side. The location was quiet and out of the way but not so terribly isolated that it was inaccessible to the people who mattered in Chicago. Schuttler was fully aware that society was drifting westward from the lakefront and the residence of William A. Amberg, founder of the stationary firm Cameron, Amberg and Company stood nearby. Mrs. William A. Amberg opened the Madonna Center and the Society of the Christ Child, an institution "which exercises its beneficent influence in the neighborhood of the Near West Side," according to Herma Clark, in one of her serialized reminiscences, "When Chicago Was Young," on December 26, 1943, in the *Tribune*.

Manufacturer Ambrose Plamondon, paterfamilias of a famous clan of Chicago socialites who held an ownership stake in the Cubs baseball team, arrived from Pau, France, in the 1850s to make his mark as a prominent man of affairs. He gave the hand of his daughter Emily in marriage to John Amberg, uniting two influential West Side families that would later form the nucleus of an emerging social network that invited Peter Schuttler and his descendants into their inner circle.

Sizing up this nouveaux riche entrepreneur, German wainwright, Prescott, had his doubts and rebuffed Schuttler. The property was not for sale he declared, in the mistaken belief that Schuttler did not possess the means or wherewithal to meet his steep asking price: $17,000. Prescott stipulated that were it even possible for Schuttler to come up with so vast a sum, he would have to produce it in cash. No checks or bank notes would be accepted. Later that afternoon, Schuttler reappeared carrying a large, heavy sack. Smug and satisfied, he revealed the contents of the package to the astonished Prescott—seventeen thousand one-dollar bills. "Shall I count them out for you?" Schuttler must have quipped.

Dumbfounded, Prescott accepted the money and returned to the city to record the property transfer and file notice of the transaction in the newspapers. Later, with mock contempt, Mr. Schuttler papered an entire room of his new mansion with one-dollar bills until government inspectors informed him that US currency could not serve as a wall decoration and would have to be removed upon pain of prosecution.

Schuttler made elaborate plans for his mansion. His estimated final costs came in at $500,000—$9,159,895.97 in today's money. It is reliably reported that in 1863 he was one of only three Chicagoans to pay taxes on an income of over $100,000.[5]

Although wartime scarcity and deprivation imposed tremendous hardships on the civilian population, Peter Schuttler managed to import expensive brick from Philadelphia at a cost of six cents per piece. He erected a high ornamental iron fence resting on a cement base three feet thick giving the home an austere, if not imposing fortress-like appearance.

In the decades following abandonment of the house by the heirs, neighbors and pedestrians reported that something about the fence surrounding the property gave the place a sinister feeling. Gapers and the morbidly curious for the long-abandoned world stood in awe, as one might revel in the spectacle of the interior chambers of the Versailles Palace in Paris. Charles D. Lunceford, an interior decorator, remembered the gaiety of the home as his crew of workmen stripped the remaining wall fixtures in November 1912. "I remember some of the great social functions," he told a reporter. "It was in the evening a veritable house of a thousand candles. An immense conservatory extended from the back. Beautiful gardens ornamented the grounds. Nobility from European courts visited here, dined under these ceilings and slept in these rooms."[6]

Having died of blood poisoning in December 1864, Peter Schuttler had never been able to fully enjoy the pleasures of his splendorous Victorian castle or see its completion. In the county court of Probate Judge James B. Bradwell (husband of Myra Bradwell, the first licensed female attorney in Illinois), Peter Schuttler II gained control of his father's estate, valued at $200,000 in real estate and $50,000 in cash after the lonely, agoraphobic widow, Dorothy Schuttler, was judged insane.

It would have been unthinkable for Peter to send his mother to an asylum where the ruthless and barbaric treatment of inmates had become a national disgrace. Neither could he give her unmonitored access to the entire household, given her unpredictable behavior. So, twenty-four-year-old Peter confined her to the bedroom atop the tower—the "widow's peak"—where the sequestered and restless woman lived her remaining years attended by nurses. After her death, rumors circulated that Dorothy had committed suicide in the tower—an accusation denied by family members.

"Immediately upon her death, the apparitions, it is said, began to appear in the tower rooms," wrote Mary Dougherty in her retrospective article for the *Chicago Inter-Ocean* in July 1913. "Many old settlers; and not a few of the last generation will readily assure you that often at night they have watched the phantoms flit to and fro past the long French windows and down the marble stairway which can be seen through the side windows disappearing at daybreak." If the ghosts of Peter and Dorothy were lurking about the mansion tower in the months not long after Dorothy's demise, the Schuttler heirs refused comment, and kept it a private matter.

Upon returning from overseas study Peter II married Wilhelmina "Minnie" Anheuser (daughter of Eberhard Anheuser and the sister of Lilly Anheuser, wife of Adolphus Busch of the St. Louis beer brewing empire). The union of the Anheuser-Busch and Schuttler bloodline produced four sons and a daughter—all coming of age during the peak of America's Gilded

Age, a time of excess and ostentation set against the backdrop of rising labor unrest and deepening schisms between the wealthy and the poor.

The Schuttler scion, however, was no idler, living off his father's fortune and good name, but proved to be a cultured and industrious man. He took his four boys into the business, and they enjoyed many fruitful and productive years.

The Great Chicago Fire destroyed Schuttler's Lake Street factory, but as work crews hauled away the rubble, plans were already under way for the construction of a four-story manufacturing plant at Clinton and Monroe Streets that was to be open for business by the spring of 1872. The Adams Street mansion was fortunate to escape the fire's wrath and continued on as the family abode.

In 1877, a former classmate of Peter's during his years in Germany at the Karlsruhe Polytechnic College, Christoph Hotz, settled in Chicago. Hotz and Schuttler soon entered into a partnership, and the two men added a nearby hub-and-spoke factory that stretched for two square blocks between Sebor and Mather Streets along the south branch of the Chicago River. With a total workforce of four hundred men, the plant manufactured twelve thousand wagons a year with assembly-line precision in the postfire period. The Schuttler and Hotz plant became an early forerunner of the Ford Motor Company assembly line, long before Henry Ford conceived the methodical means of mass producing his "horseless carriage."

Hotz built his gilded mansion on the property adjoining the Schuttler home at 301 Adams Street and lived there with his wife Catherine. Within a few years the two influential families intermarried their offspring. Inside the Schuttler home in 1874, Minnie and Peter Schuttler II celebrated the arrival of Peter the III, the young scion they counted on to lead the family and its business enterprise into the new century. In 1870, Catherine Hotz gave birth to a son, Robert S. Hotz.

For the next decade Hotz and Schuttler reaped the rewards of their successful business plan and presided over West Side society. But as the "elegant 1880s" unfolded in Chicago, there were early indicators that the staid and decorous Adams Street sophisticates would soon be forced to make accommodations with urban expansion and relentless industrialization or make the hard decision to abandon their cozy, insular way of life altogether. The new industrial age undercut the pillars of American life and threatened to disrupt the old social order and put an end to the dignified and restrained way of life they so cherished.

Awakened to the threat of clanking, noisy street cars pulled by horses of the West Division Railway Company scheduled to run down the middle of Adams Street, Hotz and Schuttler indignantly protested the incursion and called the property owners together for a meeting at Lower Martine's Hall on Ada Street on October 14, 1881.[7] The private company advancing the new East-West route already served Chicago's most populous areas and had secured the necessary charters and built rail lines over several bridges spanning the south branch of the Chicago River. Under the new proposal, the line petitioned for an exclusive ninety-nine-year franchise along Adams Street.

Residents termed this latest venture "an outrage," that would be certain to bring the *hoi polloi* and "dumb brutes" from the South Side (quoting a *Chicago Tribune* account from October 16, 1881) into their sequestered world of high tea and afternoon socials. Petitions were drafted and sent to the mayor and city council reminding them that earlier street railways had driven down property values in other areas of the West Side, and were there no provisions in the city statutes that clearly defined that Monroe, Adams, and Jackson were to be "free and clear" of objectionable public transportation? The implication of course was that poor working-class families would import the attending social ills of crime, poverty, and homelessness into the neighborhood.

Within two years the line was fully operational over the objections of the neighbors. And gradually the provincial world they once enjoyed faded like a colored postcard bleached by prolonged exposure to the sun. Incidences of crime, as prophesized, escalated. The Hotz and Schuttler homes were twice burglarized and plundered by predawn thieves within a year of each other. The crimes were eerily similar. The burglars forced open windows leading into the parlor and exited with silverware, artwork, and other valuables after overturning furniture and leaving the first-floor rooms in shambles.

The arrival of factories, office buildings, and cheap worker tenements signaled the rise of Chicago's industrial age and altered the landscape of the close-in ante-bellum residential communities. Progress, if in fact the displacement of the old settlers can be called that, extinguished genteel West Side society along Adams Street, slowly at first, then with brute force. One by one society hostesses, their prominent husbands engaged in important civic affairs moved on, and the well-appointed mansions, harboring so many old family secrets, fell into disrepair or succumbed to the wrecking ball. Several years before the old century expired, the Schuttlers disposed of the household furniture and moved away from Adams Street and into a more agreeable North Side residence at 66 Lake Shore Drive, joining recently transplanted society friends and making new acquaintances who happened to lived nearby, including retail merchant prince Harry Gordon Selfridge and his lovely wife Rose Buckingham Selfridge, soon to be London-bound to open their famous Oxford Street department store.

While traveling in Langenschwalbach, Germany, in September 1906, to visit his brother-in-law Adolphus Busch at his summer residence and attend a class reunion, Peter Schuttler II succumbed to a chronic gastrointestinal ailment that had afflicted him for well over a year. A widower since 1901, Schuttler left a sizeable fortune to his five children, three of whom—Walter, Carl and Adolph—took over the family business just as gasoline-powered vehicles for business, commerce, shipping, and pleasure were overtaking the wagon trade, an industry that was entering a steady and irreversible decline.

The old family manse, now shuttered, inspired legends and ghost stories surrounding the death of Peter Schuttler and his sad widow who was beset by mental illness and confined to the sickroom. As reports of apparitions in the tower circulated, curiosity seekers organized ghost-hunting expeditions to Adams Street hoping to glimpse the phantoms through the French windows.

Visitors to Chicago were often encouraged by acquaintances to include Chicago's most famous "haunted house" in their explorations. The caretaker occasionally permitted curious travelers to tour the ballroom, adjacent to the tower room. However, the loudest screams audible to passersby on the street were neither ghostly nor supernatural, but from the startled women whose presence in the house alarmed nests of resident rodents.

The old Schuttler place became more of a scarred relic than a public eyesore. The intriguing, other-worldly tales made it a popular tourist attraction. The presence of uninvited gawkers must have rattled the neighbors coping with the burdens of industrialization, the migration of the moneyed class to better neighborhoods, and the resulting decline in residential property values.

The question lingers: could these paranormal sightings be verified in some way, or were they just urban legends fueled by overactive imaginations? Chicago police inspector John Wheeler, who shot himself through the heart on May 21, 1918, in a fit of melancholy over health issues, swore before his saloon mates that he had observed spectral images while answering a call late one cold winter's night.

"It was on the night of December 31, 1899," he declared. "Everyone was out ringing in the new century. About midnight a riot call came in from the office patrolling the beat on Adams Street. Knowing that it was an unusually exciting night, I thought it best to drive out there myself and direct the movements of my subordinates. When we reached the corner of Morgan and Adams Street, we saw we could drive no further. Being familiar with the history of the Schuttler house, I knew what the attraction was so

I jumped out of my buggy and elbowed my way through the crowd. Sure enough there were strange lights coming and going in the tower windows and for the first time and only time in my life I really believed in ghosts. After some difficulty we dispersed the crowd but for weeks afterwards, ghost stories were in order at the station."[8]

Was it a trick of light or something more sinister? Everyone agreed that the curious old house had a definite odd feeling to it. The Schuttler mansion passed into the hands of a boarding-house keeper who rented rooms to transients by the week and month. The business closed after a few years for reasons lost to history. Unafraid of ghosts, Charles T. Luckew acquired title to the Schuttler and Hotz properties and repurposed the old homestead into a commercial laundry. Luckew paid $125,000, an extravagant sum in those days, to buy the building on May 11, 1906, but fate seemed to conspire against him. The business closed and in its final incarnation before the wrecking ball swung, the promoter of a new venture, the Palace Livery Stable, affixed a sign to the stone archway over the front portals reading: First Class Boarding Stable—Horses Boarded May Be Boarded by the Day, Week or Month.

The finest private residence of the Civil War period west of New York City was no longer habitable. Work horses rested comfortably on beds of hay where Chicago socialites once dined on breast of squab. The neighbors, if they spoke of it at all, called the old Schuttler place "The House of Usher on the West Side."[9] There seemed to be general agreement among superstitious believers in the paranormal that the building had a curse attached to it. A tragic sequence of events over the next fifty years lent an element of plausibility to the whispered rumors.

Chicago Police and medical examiners from the Cook County Coroner's office were at a loss to explain the curious death of fourteen-year-old Richard Schuttler to his father, Peter Schuttler III, at the family home in the Marlborough Apartments at 508 Fullerton Parkway on April 2, 1919. Peter said he heard what he thought to be the sound of an automobile's backfire, and thought nothing more of it. Three hours later he notified Chicago police after finding his blood-soaked son lying on the bathroom floor. It must have been an accident Peter told police. Richard, a student at the Howe School for Boys near Fort Wayne, Indiana, was at home for the Easter holiday. The coroner pronounced the cause of death as "accidental or otherwise."[10]

Carl Schuttler, bachelor clubman and the emotionally distraught grandson of Peter Schuttler I, suffered from what the press described as "nervous troubles."[11] He had just been released from the Sacred Heart Sanitarium in Milwaukee in the spring of 1924, and returned to his private apartment on the sixth floor of the Chicago Athletic Association. His brother Adolph also rented rooms in the fashionable private club serving as a home away from home for many of Chicago's wealthy elites.

At 8:30 P.M. on June 11, his private nurse, Emma Austin, from the Sacred Heart Sanitarium, entered the room and found her patient straddling the sill of the open window. "We had intended to go for a walk," the tearful nurse told police. "As I came into the room I saw him sitting on the window ledge, just as though he were resting there, his back against the jamb and his feet in the room. He was looking down toward the street. As I entered, he half way looked around at me and then plunged suddenly over the ledge. I think he must have fallen out."[12]

Two years passed uneventfully. The Schuttler wagon works, tossed to history's scrapheap by the automobile and the gradual disappearance of horse-drawn teams on city streets ceased production in 1926. Illinois Bell purchased the spacious, 275,000 square-foot plant erected by the brothers in 1903 at Twenty-Second Street and Rockwell Avenue. The company continued to service its existing customers until full liquidation in October 1940 erased the name from corporate ledgers.

The business had passed, but the socially prominent heirs, lived off of their inheritance or found sinecures in other industries. Peter Schuttler IV, the forty-two-year-old son of the last of the family wagon builders, labored as a salesman for a typewriter supply company at 538 South Clark Street. It wasn't much of a job for a young social climber with important connections. His estranged wife, Kathryn Ballard, had divorced him and fled to Michigan with their three children. Down in the dumps, drinking heavily, and living in reduced circumstances, Peter had no other choice but to move back in with his widowed mother, Martha Braun Schuttler, owner of a South Side residential real estate company. Following her husband's passing in May 1941, Martha went to great lengths to wean her son off of the booze—and his liquor-fueled impulse to place random telephone calls to friends and strangers at odd hours.

March 21, 1942. While Martha and her live-in roommate Mrs. Charles Hall attended a lecture, Schuttler, lost in the fog of delirium tremens, threw a fit and attempted to batter down the locked bedroom door. The frightened maid summoned the elevator operator and together they managed to quiet down the tortured soul. They resumed their chores only after calm was restored.

Martha and her friend returned to the Lakeview address in a festive mood that quickly turned to horror as they glimpsed what lay behind the partially closed bathroom door. There they found Peter's lifeless form slumped over the edge of the bathtub. He had killed himself by means of strangulation.

A similar, even more tragic fate awaited the son, Peter Schuttler V, a combat veteran who had survived serious wounds in the campaign to take Iwo Jima in the closing days of World War II. The great-great grandson of the prairie-schooner king of Chicago lived with his young wife, Dorothy, in Skokie, Illinois, the booming postwar Chicago bedroom suburb favored by young white-collar professionals climbing corporate ladders in downtown banks, investment firms, real estate offices, and ad agencies.

Married only three years, Skokie police had already beaten a well-traveled path to the front door of their two-story residence at 9025 Karlov Avenue, responding to reports of domestic violence. It was the kind of home paid for with old family money. Its rustic exterior resembled an abbreviated English Tudor manor house, and bespoke an inherited fortune and understated affluence. Inside, a less than ideal marriage and the husband's penchant for keeping late hours triggered understandable anger and jealousy in the mind of an anxious young wife.

At 2:30 in the morning, July 27, 1952, Peter's automobile lurched to a sudden stop in the driveway facing the street. It was pointed out that it had been exactly ten years and four months since Peter IV used his bathrobe sash as a suicide weapon.

Twenty minutes later (following a furious quarrel), Peter V reached for his .45-caliber automatic tucked inside the drawer of his night table. He placed the muzzle to his temple and pulled the trigger. The Schuttlers' two-year-old daughter was asleep in the adjoining bedroom when neighbors heard the fatal shot fired. Police arrived at the residence shortly before three A.M. and immediately ordered the hysterical wife removed from the premises after a physician provided sedation. "Violent Death Hits Schuttler Family Again," the *Chicago Tribune* somberly reported.[13]

What is one to make of this sequence of tragic deaths? At the center of this Shakespearean ghost story lies a riddle and a family curse (if one is inclined to attach superstitious belief to such improbable happenings). We may never find out. It is a Chicago mystery lost in the fog of time.

STARS AND BARS AND
THE SYMBOL OF A CITY

On the sultry morning of July 12, 1915, Republican alderman James A. Kearns of the Thirty-First Ward rose from his desk in the city council chamber to present an order proposing the formation of a ten-member Municipal Flag Commission, for the purpose of designing an official city flag for the people of Chicago—one that would wave proudly over all civic and public buildings, museums, and sporting venues symbolizing community, the spirit of Chicago, and its enduring motto, I Will.

An earlier attempt to conceive an official iconographic identity for Chicago through flag craft had failed. On the eve of the 1893 World's Fair, Francis Davis Millet, overseeing decorations for the exposition, decided at the eleventh hour that Chicago must come up with official colors—a banner, a symbol, or a flag to complement the patriotic bunting and regalia covering the fairgrounds.

The *Chicago Tribune* embraced the idea and decided to sponsor a public contest. Among the 829 entries, a panel of three judges declared Danish architect Alfred Jensen Roewad's red and white design—signifying the three geographic divisions of Chicago (north, south, and west, divided by the river in the shape of an upside-down Y and framed in a shield)—as the winner. Roewad, an earnest and enthusiastic young immigrant working for the World's Fair Bureau of Construction, earned a hundred dollar honorarium before disappearing into the vapors of history; like so many others, his moment of fame was fleeting.

The celebrated American painter Francis Millet, later the vice-chairman of the US Commission of Fine Arts, fashioned the "Y" into the shape of a pennant. On October 1, 1892, the *Tribune* described the pattern as "forcible, gay, durable, and of great simplicity" and urged its immediate adaptation. That did not happen. The city of Chicago, dismissive and seemingly uninterested, refused to sanction Roewad's winning design, and Millet perished aboard the *Titanic* in April 1912. Chicago would remain flagless for the next twenty-three years.

Among the commission members chosen for this important task of flag design by Mayor Carter Harrison II and Committee Chairman Kearns, were wealthy industrialist Charles Deering, Alderman John A. Richert, a one-time chairman of the powerful city of Chicago Committee on Finance; Mary E. McDowell, founder of the University of Chicago Settlement House and the Women's Trade Union League, Clarence Burley of the Chicago Historical Society, John Fitzpatrick of the Chicago Federation of Labor, Mrs. Louis Torbett, of the Daughters of the American Revolution, and the noted impressionist painter Lawton S. Parker.

Parker invited lecturer, poet, and author Wallace de Groot Rice to develop the rules for an open public competition for the best flag design. Mr. Rice, who later chaired the State of Illinois 1918 Centennial Commission and designed the Illinois flag, was a self-professed expert on flags and heraldry.

All agreed that Mr. Rice, the son of Colonel John A. Rice, the lodging magnate who leased and owned three grand old Chicago hotels—the Tremont House, the Sherman House, and the Grand Pacific—was the right man for this rather daunting commission.[1] In his lifetime, Wallace Rice, with a good eye for historical detail, authored more than ninety books and pamphlets. Over the next eighteen months the committee members left no stone unturned as they entered into an idea-sharing correspondence with important civic factotums in other American municipalities.

They determined that forty other municipalities including Boston, Philadelphia, New York, Cleveland, San Francisco, and Baltimore had already taken the necessary steps and adopted flags reflecting the civic pride of the local citizens.

Lawton Parker directed Wallace Rice, then lecturing students at the Art Institute about the history of flags and heraldry, to draw up a set of twenty rules and guidelines governing the open design competition.

In truth Mr. Rice held out little hope that the public would be able to produce a suitable design to inspire civic pride and stir the senses. But in the true spirit of democracy and inclusion, he invited the public to submit their own ideas. Thousands of entries poured in, ranging from sublime to ridiculous to just plain impractical. Frederic Rex of the city of Chicago municipal library later recalled: "Not more than three of four showed any perception of the prime fact that flags are supposed to fly in the air. Many of them looked okay on paper where every part of the pattern is seen equally well but would not have been easily visible flapping in the breeze at the top of a pole."[2]

Hundreds of flag designs illustrating a blockhouse attached to the palisades of old Fort Dearborn arrived in the mail but none were met with the degree of approbation demanded by Rice or his team. The city of Toledo had just adapted a similar blockhouse image for their flag, as did hundreds of other small towns, state houses, and public parks across the country.

Another curious and imaginative design featured a large black kettle in the center of the flag, emblematic of the "melting pot of the nation" and honoring the tens of thousands of immigrants who had arrived in Chicago. Though well-intentioned, the idea was rejected, as were all of the other submissions, which were deemed unsatisfactory to the trained and critical eye of Wallace Rice.

Chicago, Rice reasoned, should never be satisfied to run with the hounds when it should be leading the pack. In frustration, Mr. Rice declared the public contest a failure, and spent the next six weeks devising more than three hundred different combinations of patterns, shapes, and colors. Working in the living room of his North Side home with color schemes and drawings spread across the entire floor, he brooded over combinations of patterns day and night with the only limitations imposed upon him being the depths of his own imagination.

Approaching the project evenhandedly and without preconception, Rice solicited the opinions of everyone he knew, from family members to the milkman, the grocer, and the delivery boy before producing a rendering that pleased *them*, as Wallace Rice turned out to be his own worst critic.

The final version reflected Chicago through the liberal application of color and symbols. The white band at the top of the flag signified Chicago's North Side. The upper blue band represents Lake Michigan and the north branch of the Chicago River. The broad, white band is the West Side of Chicago, at the time, the largest residential area of the city. The lower blue stripe is the south branch of the Chicago River and the drainage canal, and the lowest white stripe is the South Side of the city. The original design showed only two stars, the first denoting the Chicago Fire and the second, the 1893 World's Fair in Jackson Park.

The colors of the flag added meaning. Blue is the color of water and red is the color of fire and festivity. White symbolizes the admixture of nations, and recognizes the contributions of immigrants to the vitality of the city.

The *Tribune* reported on July 17, 1921, that the "circular emblems depict departmental designs shown on the edge of the flag between the stripes: Health, Police, Fire, Civil Service, Election Commission, Public Service, Board of Education, Public Library, Water, Harbor, Streets, Sewers, Local Improvements, Public Works, Gas & Electricity and Buildings." At some point these symbols were apparently removed and are no longer visible on the flag we know today. On April 4, 1917, just two days before the United

States entered World War I the city council accepted the final report and recommendations of the Kearns Committee and formally adopted the Wallace Rice design to become the official city flag of Chicago.

The flag was warmly received by the public and private interests. The two leading proponents championing its creation earned praise and well-deserved recognition. Alderman Kearns had a long and distinguished career in public life, becoming clerk of the municipal court—which was up to that time the worlds' largest. Interestingly, he established the first public school playground on the South Side.

Wallace Rice embarked on the lecture circuit not long after to explain to Chicago audiences the symbolism of the design. He reminded his listeners that he would be amenable to adding more stars commemorating the next momentous event in our history, be it earthquake, flood, fire, or a great civic celebration.

The long-awaited third star, commemorating the 1933 World's Fair, known as the Century of Progress, was woven into the fabric that same year. Sadly for Mr. Rice and his legion of admirers, he passed away on December 15, 1939, just six days before the city council added the final star to his grand design, honoring Fort Dearborn.

Flag symbolism abounds. Each of the six points on the four stars of the flag represents a central theme, civic virtues, and historical events:

- Fort Dearborn: 1. France, 1673; 2. Great Britain, 1763; 3. Virginia, 1788; 4. Northwest Territory, 1798; 5. Indiana Territory, 1802; and 6. Illinois statehood, 1818.
- The Great Chicago Fire: 1. Transportation; 2. Trade; 3. Finance; 4. Labor and Industry; 5. Populousness; 6. Healthfulness.
- 1893 World's Fair: 1. Religion; 2. Education; 3. Aesthetics; 4. Beneficence; 5. Justice; 6. Civism.
- A Century of Progress: 1. World's Third Largest City; 2. Urbs in Horto; 3. "I Will" Spirit; 4. The Great Central Market; 5. The Wonder City; 6. The Convention City.

The last word about Chicago's enduring civic motto, I Will. Officially *Urbs in Horto*, or City in a Garden, remains the city slogan before the world. It is as old as Chicago, and was adopted with the city charter of 1837. However, as the 1893 World's Fair loomed, the *Chicago Inter-Ocean* newspaper decided that the city should come up with another more easily recognizable phrase in the interest of promoting "civic boosterism" to represent Chicago in advance of the millions of visitors pouring into the city.

Publisher Robert Penn Nixon's *Inter-Ocean* came up with an attention-grabbing motto of its own in those partisan political days—Republican in *Everything*, Independent in Nothing!—and sponsored a contest for a new Chicago slogan, enlisting Bertha Honoré Palmer, queen of Chicago society, and cartoonist Charles Nast to review three hundred entries and choose the winner.

The declared winner, St. Louis artist and sculptor Charles Holloway, adopted his "I Will" catchphrase, affixing the wording to the breastplate of the bust of a goddess figure dressed for battle. The crown on the bust depicts a phoenix rising from the flames, symbolic of Chicago's ascendance from the devastation of the Great Fire, twenty-two years earlier.

Charles Holloway collected a modest honorarium of $200 for his design. Although the World's Fair committees did not officially sanction "I Will" as the motto of the great celebration, Chicagoans admired its simplicity, and the city revived the wording for advertising purposes to promote the 1933 "Century of Progress" World's Fair.

An interesting reinterpretation of Chicago's "I Will" spirit, designed by sculptor Ellsworth Kelly, stands at Fullerton Avenue and Cannon Drive in Lincoln Park. Of course, pundits have had a field day with Chicago's unofficial slogan.

The late Mike Royko, chief culprit of "I Will" sarcasm, asked readers of his newspaper column, "I will . . . but what if I can't?" In his book *Boss: Richard J. Daley of Chicago*, the droll and often querulous Royko suggested changing "I Will" to *Ubi Est Mea* meaning "Where's Mine?"[3]

AMERICA'S FIRST AUTOMOBILE RACE

The Windy City played an important but hidden role at the dawn of the automotive age and the earliest stirring of interest in automobile racing in the United States. Chicago's first motorized competition staged the day after a Thanksgiving Day storm in 1895 is remembered as more of an endurance test than a racing meet, although hundreds of Chicagoans turned out in the frigid weather to witness the start of the spectacle. The contest featured six fearless drivers vying for a gold medal and a generous $5,000 prize offered by Herman H. Kohlsaat, the ambitious young publisher of the *Chicago Times-Herald* who announced the event for November 2, in the July 11 edition of the paper.[1]

After a scheduling delay caused by the unpreparedness of the drivers in readying their machines for the punishing course, the race to Davis Street and Chicago Avenue in Evanston, Illinois, a northern suburb of Chicago, kicked off that blustery morning of November 28 from the Midway Plaisance in Jackson Park near the Palace of Fine Arts that is today the internationally renowned Museum of Science and Industry.

Event organizers originally planned a lengthier, more challenging route to Milwaukee, Wisconsin, and back for the original eighty-three enrolled contestants, but the rough, uneven country roads and an unexpected, howling blizzard that dumped a foot of snow on Chicago streets the night before, forced the *Times-Herald* to scale back the course. "Wrack and ruin were on every hand," the paper grimly reported. "Death hung in the air from a thousand broken wires but luckily passed humanity by. Cable cars were blocked by the wet snow. Every telegraph wire leading out of the city was down or disabled and Chicago sat in the midst of isolation as well as ruin."[2]

Seventy-seven drivers decided to withdraw their vehicles from competition at the last moment, leaving only a handful of contestants including the Morris-Galvin of Philadelphia, and the R. H. Macy and Company machine powered by Jerry O'Connor, who cheerfully boasted, "Our machine has already shown that it can go through mud, sand and snow! It has climbed through the Peekskill Mountains and gone down hills as steep as the roof of a house!"[3]

Frederick C. Haas, the driver of the electric-battery powered De La Vergne built by the De La Vergne Refrigerating Machine Company of New York and a first-place finisher in the earlier Paris-to-Bordeaux race smiled but said nothing. Harold Sturges of Chicago drove his own machine, also an electric; the Duryeas of Springfield, Massachusetts, manned their seven-hundred-pound, four-speed carriage with a top speed of twenty miles per hour; and the H. Mueller and Sons Company team from Decatur, Illinois, positioned their carriage at the starting line in Jackson Park. Each vehicle was manned by a driver and an "umpire" assigned to make notes, attend to necessary repairs, and chart the progress. All had been thoroughly road-tested prior to the start of the race.

Kohlsaat set up three relay stations along the way to chart the progress of the drivers. Oddsmakers favored Elwood Haynes. In an overlapping career, this noted American metallurgist affiliated with the Indiana Natural Gas and Oil Company tinkered with gasoline engines for transportation. He was intent on capturing the top prize. On July 4, 1894, after three years of design-planning, Haynes tested his prized automotive invention—the gasoline-powered *Pioneer* on a country road outside of Kokomo, Indiana. Eight years earlier, German industrialist Karl Benz received a patent for the first motorized vehicle in Germany.[4] With large spoked wheels in the rear and a smaller wheel positioned in the front, the vehicle resembled a children's tricycle—but with a gasoline engine and an electric ignition starter. Benz navigated his seventy-five horsepower, two-seat rig utilizing a tiller to control the direction of the front wheel. The steering wheel did not become a standard feature of an American automobile until after 1898.[5]

Haynes later explained that practical necessity dictated his decision to invent a machine-powered carriage to replace a slow and inefficient horse. He needed to make the rounds of the Hoosier countryside in less time and bragged to reporters that his experimental excursion marked the first trip of a gasoline-powered vehicle driven in America—a dubious assertion in dispute to this day. Haynes and his machine prepared to conquer the world, but Haynes understood that he would first have to demonstrate the efficacy of his vehicle on Chicago's snow-packed streets during the great race.

Automobile, a word unfamiliar to most people in the early 1890s, had not yet entered the American lexicon. The newspaper, unable to provide a suitable name for these motorized carriages, polled its readers, asking them to come up with an identifying moniker. Horseless carriage, the most obvious choice one would think, held no special appeal to readers. Suggestions poured in and eventually the editors agreed upon "motocycle," an interesting if not unusual choice submitted by G. H. Shaver of New York.

Given the terrible weather conditions, the race pitted man and machine against the forces of nature. While en route to the starting line, Elwood Haynes, driving his Pioneer II vehicle, collided with the curb after avoiding a streetcar at Indiana and Thirty-Eighth Street. A damaged axle on the forward wheel kept him out of the race, resulting in Chicago's first recorded traffic accident involving a motorized vehicle. Unamused, a Chicago police officer informed Haynes that he had no legal right to maneuver this four-wheel curiosity on the city streets. The editors at the *Times-Herald* intervened, convincing wary city council lawmakers to pass an enabling ordinance to allow these types of vehicles to share the same space as horse buggies, wagons, and street cars. The Windy City's first traffic regulation passed into law.

The great race kicked off promptly at eight fifteen in the morning. The six fearless drivers who set out on a circuitous fifty-four-mile slog across slick roads that day raced at an impressive average speed of seven miles per hour. "All along the route and at the turning corners from Jackson Park to Evanston and return, hundreds waited patiently until the vehicles came into sight," commented a *Times-Herald* reporter.[6]

The event concluded ten hours and fifteen minutes later after the eventual winner, the prolific inventor, Peoria, Illinois, native Charles E. Duryea, and his brother J. Frank Duryea, crossed the finish line ahead of the second-place finisher, the Karl Benz carriage design manufactured by H. Mueller and Company and driven by H. Mueller's son, Oscar Mueller and Charles Brady King. During the rough ride in biting temperatures Mueller struggled to exit the starting line then suffered exposure in the teeth of a freezing wind and fierce elements. He passed out. King completed the final laps in a losing effort but collected $500 in consolation money.

The other drivers had either gotten lost in the tangle of city streets and arrived late, or overturned their unsteady machines in the early winter snow and slush. The De la Vergne made it only as far as Sixteenth Street before giving up. The Sturgis team gave up at the north end of Lincoln Park and the Morris and Galvin Electronic completed fifteen miles and quit.

Impatient and disgusted by the long wait, the three racing judges stationed in Jackson Park decided to quit after seven hours leaving only two forlorn newspaper reporters to welcome the Duryeas to the finish line to claim their grueling victory. By ten in the evening, the last straggler, the R. H. Macy carriage, made it back safely but with a broken steering gear. The brutal weather conditions tested the resolve of the drivers and mechanics, but against these extreme odds, the Duryea brothers, engineers of prominence, persevered.

Arthur W. White, a Toronto newspaperman serving the Duryea team as a mechanic recounted the perilous ride to reporters.

"At 8:15 A.M. the start was made and we ran without a stop to the corner of Erie and Rush Streets. Here we broke our steering gear by running over a high crossing covered with snow.[7] A wait of fifty-five minutes ensued. From this point we ran to Evanston without a stop arriving there at 12:35 P.M. On the return we were delayed four minutes on Chicago Avenue [near Calvary Cemetery] in Evanston by a sleigh that had tipped over in the street. Continuing, we got onto the wrong road on account of the absence of a sign at the corner of Lawrence Avenue and Clark Street. We ran down Clark to Diversey before discovering our mistake. Then we went up Diversey Street where we resumed the current route. I estimate the extra distance traversed at two miles approximate. While on Diversey near Clark we broke our "sparker" and spent fifty-five minutes repairing it. At 3:30 we resumed the journey. We were delayed fifteen minutes at Drake Avenue and Central Park Boulevard to adjust the machinery and take fuel. Another delay of four minutes occurred at the Fort Wayne [railroad] crossing of Fifty-fifth Street Boulevard. The delay [in] the second relay was ten minutes or so. Three and one-half gallons of gasoline and nineteen gallons of water were consumed. No power outside the vehicle was used. I estimate that enough power was used to run the motor 120 miles over smooth roads. We finished at 7:18 and ran back to Sixteenth Street with our own power. Our corrected time was seven hours and fifty-three minutes."[8]

The team had passed through the West Side neighborhoods of Humboldt Park, Garfield Park, and Douglas Park before heading east on Fifty-Fifth Street to complete the final leg of the race. The Duryea brothers road tested what *they* had claimed to be America's first gasoline-powered automobile inside a garage at 47 Taylor Street in Springfield, Massachusetts, April 19, 1892, by mounting a four-horse-power, single-cylinder engine onto a used horse carriage they had purchased for the modest sum of seventy dollars. The Duryeas called this crude, early prototype of an automobile the "Buggyaut," and they proudly drove it from Springfield to Hartford, Connecticut, for demonstration and publicity.

Their winning Chicago entry—an improved two-cylinder buckboard mounted on a metal frame—was the first to incorporate the use of pneumatic rubber tires. The brake drum was positioned under the seat and controlled by the driver by a wire with a button at the front corner of the seat. The inventors confidently predicted that it could reach a top speed of twenty miles per hour, requiring only five minutes to completely refuel. They estimated their gasoline cost to be less than one-half cent per mile. In completing the race, the machine required only three-and-a-half gallons of drugstore-purchased fuel.

"The response of American inventors to the offer made by the *Times-Herald* has never been equaled in the history of mechanical progress," editorialists beamed. "In June of this year perhaps four inventors were at work on motocycles which possessed any features of practicability. Since that time, 500 applications have been filed at the patent office in Washington on inventions pertaining to this branch of transportation."[9]

The *Yale Review Quarterly* of December 1895 noted: "Thus, amid praise and ridicule, our pioneer motorists made their first feeble assaults upon the barriers of space and time. They were hardy souls. Theirs was the creed of noble simplicity . . . that one man had built, another could keep in motion. Strong in this faith, they suffered, endured and conquered."

Science Magazine noted that "when the prizes were offered on July 11, there were only known three self-driven road vehicles in the United States but there were about seventy-five entries for the contest on November 2."[10] By 1900, the number of autos produced in the United States increased to twenty-five.

A mechanized future was at hand as the nation inched closer to a transportation revolution destined to reshape our way of life in nearly the same fashion as the coming of the internet exactly a hundred years later. Stimulated by their success in the great race from Chicago to Evanston (and back again) the brothers incorporated the Duryea Motor Wagon Company. In 1896, they sold the first thirteen "motor wagons" to the public, marking the first time a "horseless carriage" became commercially available in US markets. For the brothers Duryea, the outcome of Chicago's Great Race and the business enterprise they launched on the heels of their stunning achievement two years later, was not a happy one.

Charles and Frank, embroiled in a bitter argument over which of them deserved the rightful credit for developing the first automobile in the United States (failing to consider Elwood Haynes's assertion that *he*, and not *they* deserved the credit), folded their company and parted ways over issues of ego and irreconcilable differences. Charles, an automotive visionary and something of a genius (if not an audacious self-promoter), held fifty patents during his lifetime. He claimed full credit for the invention of the internal combustion engine, dismissing his younger brother as a shop mechanic and brother's helper who accepted employment from him for three dollars a day.

Embittered auto pioneer Charles Duryea died in Philadelphia on September 28, 1938, from complications of a heart attack. Frank, the cantankerous younger brother, died in Old Saybrook, Connecticut, on February 15, 1967, at age ninety-seven. Neither man expressed interest in reconciliation during their years of separation, not even for the sake of preserving their place in automotive history.

The horseless carriage fired the public imagination beyond anyone's wildest dreams in the 1890s. "It seems only a matter of a short time before motor carriages will be in use by the thousands," the *Tribune* editorialized on September 29, 1899. "The influence of the new vehicles, added to that of the army of bicyclists can scarcely fail to have a tremendous effect in favor of smoother streets and better country roads."[11] That same month, Tattersall's, a raucous, gin-soaked Chicago exhibition hall located on the edge of the Levee vice district at Sixteenth and State Streets (remembered for its six-day bicycle races, circuses, prize fights, brawls, thrills, chills, and legendary pranks by earlier generations of sportsmen and gamblers), sponsored the city's first auto show, featuring sixty "self-propelling," steam-powered, electric, front-engine, shaft-driven internal combustion vehicles.

There would be more legendary Windy City automobile races ahead for Chicago motor enthusiasts including the forty-mile thrill ride of John Burress Burdett and his wife from Thirty-Eighth Street and Archer Avenue on the South Side to the Joliet Courthouse six years later. The couple completed the course in one hour, forty minutes, and ten seconds on October 18, 1901, against fourteen other motorists (but only six others finished the race).[12]

The Burdetts set off at 9:37 A.M., arriving at 11:26. Fighting a brisk and biting wind, the couple crouched low over the footboard of their vehicle. The roads were rough and uneven, inhibiting speed for all the drivers. At the finish line an enthusiastic gathering lining Chicago Street presented Mrs. Burdett with a silver cup and a bouquet of American Beauty roses.

That same year, the Chicago Automobile Club sponsored a day-long competition, inviting daredevil drivers to the old Harlem Race Track at Twelfth Street and Harlem Avenue in west suburban Harlem (now Forest Park, Illinois) to compete for cash prizes and notoriety. In the palmy days of thoroughbred racing before the legislature ordered the major horse tracks to close in 1904 after widespread criminality and the violence of rival gambling syndicates for control of bookmaking operations inspired lawmakers to act, the Harlem track ranked high among the premier racing ovals in the Midwest in the estimation of trainers and owners. Symbolic of the dawn of a new motorized age it is ironic and rather sad that the beloved oat burners that had entertained and delighted the railbirds and race track touts were forced to surrender their prominence to a *horseless* carriage.

However, promoters called off the 1905 event, because, in the words of L. E. Myers on August 22, 1905, "Racing has become too dangerous of a sport; and in spite of precautions, accidents of the most serious consequence will happen. I am much opposed to auto racing."[13]

Meanwhile, in North Suburban Glencoe, the first speed bumps were placed at strategic locations along Sheridan Road and Green Bay Road to deter daredevil motorists from "scorching" (the word most often applied to speed-demon bicyclists of that era who were unmindful of pedestrian safety) through quiet residential communities.

Careless motorists, scorchers, and other speed demons testing the patience of city and state officials hastened state-wide vehicle licensing and regulation following the example set in 1901 when New York became the first state in the Union to register automobiles. In 1907, Sidney Gorham, attorney for the Chicago Motor Club and the author of the state's original licensing bill, acquired the first Illinois license (license no. 1). He held onto the prestigious plate until his death in 1938, at which time it was reissued to George Cardinal Mundelein.

THE HOUSE SIMMONS AND CHICAGO'S FIRST CHRISTMAS TREE

hicago, in its earliest years, was a city in search of Christmas trees. For the hearty souls venturing into frontier Chicago to stake a claim in the marshy land of the "wild onion," there were no indigenous evergreens to be found anywhere along the swampy shallows bordering Lake Michigan, or in the flat prairie land due west of the city.

The placement of the traditional *Tannenbaum*—a decorated fir tree to mark the joyous arrival of the holiday season was a traditional custom in German and French households, but it did not fully resonate among other European ethnic groups settling in the United States before the time of the Civil War.

Britain's Queen Victoria universalized the popularity of the Christmas tree among all classes and Christian people by honoring the cultural heritage of her devoted husband and consort, Prince Albert, born in the Saxon duchy of Saxe-Coburg-Saalfeld (Coburg, Germany), by placing an ornately decorated fir inside of Buckingham Palace. A photographic image of the royal tree, showing off the ornate decorations, lit candles, and items of food appeared in an issue of the *Illustrated London News* in 1848. The British public dearly loved the display and adapted the custom of the tree for their family celebration. Not long after the first splash of publicity in Great Britain, the image of the royal tree appeared in an edition of *Godey's Lady's Book* in America and the ladies clamored to have one of their own placed in the front parlor. The pictorial marked the acceptance of the quaint German tradition of the tree as the newest hallmark of the holiday season.

"In my family the tree was decorated with strings of popcorn and of red haws, or cranberries, chains of colored paper, nuts, fruit, cookies cut in fancy shapes were hung on the branches," wrote naturalist Roberts Mann, superintendent of conservation for the Cook County Forest Preserves, as he looked back on his 1890s boyhood in 1959. Children were told not to eat the morsels of food decorating the tree until the twelfth day of the holiday season. "Illuminated by small candles in tin holders clamped to the tips of branches the tree was a serious fire hazard." Cautious home owners kept a bucket full of sand or water close to the tree just in case. "After 1900 we used strings of tinsel and colored glass balls."[1]

For brothers August and Herman Schuenemann the scarcity of such trees in Chicago opened the door to new opportunity and the birth of an enduring Chicago Christmas tradition.

It was the Age of Sail and the Schuenemann brothers were rugged men of the Great Lakes—hearty souls unafraid of the fearsome winter squalls and other seasonal hazards that sent an estimated two thousand vessels and their cargo to the bottom of Lake Michigan. Ships damaged by storm that did not sink to the depths after foundering ended up in shallow waters where the pounding surf reduced the craft to splinters.

The month of November is the most dangerous month for lake travel because of its unpredictable weather. Before radio, before radar and ship-to-shore communications, boats traversing Lake Michigan and Lake Superior counted on the skipper's trained eye for navigation—dead reckoning. Otherwise the captain and crew were at the mercy of Mother Nature. If a ship foundered and sank, weeks, even months could conceivably pass before the final entry in the log could be recorded, "all hands lost."

The Schuenemann brothers were willing to take on the inherent dangers and risks associated with navigating a craft out onto the Great Lakes for cargo shipment so late in the year. By November, the Lake Michigan mariners, rather than risk the treacherous gales and storms, had prudently dropped anchor to search for seasonal employment in order to get them through the long harsh winter months.

Unwilling to allow their vessel to idle in port for five months, the brothers made the decision to brighten the Yuletide for all Chicagoans by importing freshly cut Christmas trees from the North Woods. The trees were displayed on the dock at the southwest corner of the Clark Street Bridge next to the South Water Street market. The family sold their trees to the general public from that familiar location for many years.

Herman, a jovial man with a ruddy complexion, had a business partner, Captain Oscar Nelson, an old salt of the Great Lakes shipping business who owned and operated two farms in Manistique, the only incorporated city in Schoolcraft County, along the coast of Michigan's Upper Peninsula. The wild, rustic terrain in a natural forest laden with choice, old growth spruce, pine, and fir trees provided them with an abundant harvest. A generation of sailors liked to call these fertile and abundant woods "the green wealth" of the Upper Midwest.

In November 1887, August Schuenemann launched the family's new business venture and brought with him the first load of evergreens aboard a hundred-foot wood schooner, a less than sea-worthy craft. For decades the schooner was the workhorse of Great Lakes navigation, hauling tons of iron ore, grain, lumber, and other commodities in and out of Chicago each year.

Schooner trade was an important catalyst in the rapid development of Chicago as a port city dubbed the "Queen of the Lakes" before the Civil War, although nautical journeys to where the open prairie met the water were fraught with peril.

Prior to the spectacular rise of the nation's intercontinental rail system in the 1850s, the movement of timber to Midwestern sawmills and local markets was dependent on water transportation. The famous three-masted nineteenth-century lumber schooners traversing the Lake Michigan basin were designed with open hulls to maximize storage. The ships displaced two hundred tons and could accommodate three hundred to four hundred tons of cargo.

The cargo loads stretched as high as the sail booms, increasing the chances of capsizing or sinking during deadly Lake Michigan winter squalls. The accumulated ice and snow created a layering effect that weighed the schooner down, until the last critical moments when the craft slipped below the waterline taking down the entire crew. Such hazards severely curtailed Lake Michigan commerce during the late fall and early winter seasons.

The cargo schooners took an awful beating over time. After many years of service, timbers and canvass would rot and necessary repairs were neglected due to the high costs. As they approached the end of their useful life hauling iron ore and other heavy commodities, the captain would attempt to sell the ship to a Christmas tree hauler rather than condemn the old scow to the salvage yard where it would be converted into a barge with its masts cut off.

The Schuenemanns relied on old, decaying schooners like these to conduct their seasonal business. An investment in necessary repairs would cut into their already marginal profit margins. However, in most years their luck held. With a crew of five, August headed north to harvest the most desirable trees. The men loaded the largest of them in a box-like structure on top of the deck with the smaller scrap branches brought below for customers to fashion into wreaths. At other times the trees were positioned upright on the schooner. With the weather cooperating, the captain could expect to reach the Clark Street slip within three weeks' time.

Once the boat had been securely moored, the Schuenemanns affixed a sign to the deck timber reading: The Christmas Tree Ship, My Prices Are the Lowest! The cost of a standard seven-foot tree ranged from seventy-five cents to a dollar. Larger trees, over twenty feet in height, were donated by the family to churches and orphanages.

In the weeks leading up to Christmas, the Schuenemann wives invited Chicago families to come below deck to see their work space, and stay for a light repast. In a small area of the schooner, scraps of evergreen were threaded together by the women and sold as wreaths. They were charming, obliging people, these Schuenemanns, with big hearts, a love for what they were doing, and appreciative of the joyous, wondrous expressions of little children standing on the deck. The fresh scent of pine and spruce hung in the frosty air.

In the winter of 1897, Herman Schuenemann married. He brought his new bride, Barbara, aboard in the middle of the Christmas rush, inspiring a shower of wedding gifts from friends and appreciative customers. The flourishing little business had not made the family members secure and prosperous, but it earned them lifetime friendships and a measure of local fame. In time, other schooner captains sharing the same entrepreneurial spirit launched Christmas tree boats of their own, but none of them were as well or as fondly remembered by Chicagoans of all ages as the Schuenemann family.

The city deeply mourned the tragic death of its gruff old captain, August L. Schuenemann on November 12, 1898, when his schooner, the S. Thal, went down in a ferocious storm off the coast of Glencoe. Just six weeks earlier August had purchased the ship in Milwaukee for the small sum of $650 but he had not bothered to insure the cargo valued at $2,500 or the lives of his men before embarking from Manitowac, Wisconsin, the night before, just as the storm was rising. The bodies of Schuenemann, the first mate, E. Turner Davis, whose wife had lived with the captain in their LaSalle Street home and four other seamen from Sturgeon Bay and Chicago were lost.

Having survived many perilous Great Lakes storms since embarking on his first voyage as a boy, investigators believed that the experienced and knowledgeable forty-six-year-old captain had strapped himself and the crew to the rigging in a last desperate attempt to escape death. August had told his wife many times over the years that by lashing a man to the rigging in this way, it was the surest way to save his men from being washed overboard in the event of a calamity.

A year passed and another Christmas was at hand. Undaunted by the memory of the tragedy a year earlier and with seasonal merriment in full bloom, Herman Schuenemann resumed the Christmas tree excursions and the business grew as Great Lakes fatalities ticked upward. It might have been an omen or portent of things to come, because after acquiring the 125-foot *Rouse Simmons* in 1910, repairs were made to ensure the structural integrity of the craft. Superstitious sailors reported that the *Simmons,* built in 1868, had deteriorated so badly over the summer of 1912 that even the rats had deserted it. The phenomenon of rats abandoning a sinking ship is explainable by science, of course, and not by the belief that rodents have extrasensory powers. Rats most often dwell in the bilge—the deepest part of a ship—where they thrive, undetected by humans. In the event of a sudden leak, columns of rats flee, as their nesting places are disturbed by incoming water. This scurry of frightened rodents occurs long before anyone becomes aware of a problem.

With a crew of sixteen, Captain Scheunemann departed Thompson's Pier in Manistique November 21, 1912, under overcast skies. He had loaded to the gunwales of the schooner with trees. The Manistique lighthouse keeper registered concern about the weather and the approach of a storm, but the captain reasoned that if he were far enough from land when the storm arrived, he would sail before it, without the risk of beating off a lee shore with a worn-out schooner such as the *Rouse Simmons.* Equipped with a fore-and-aft rigging on her three masts that would allow for easier sailing against the prevailing headwinds of the lake, the *Rouse Simmons* had just one lifeboat designed to accommodate five people. Christmas trees covered every square inch of space on the cramped deck.

If all went well, Schuenemann and his men reasonably expected to arrive in Chicago forty-two hours after their departure from Thompson's Pier. Schuenemann also knew that it was late in the year. He could not afford to wait any longer lest the northern end of the lake become frozen, trapping him, the crew, and a cargo of fifteen thousand trees (according to firsthand accounts) in the Upper Peninsula of Michigan until the spring thaws. The captain planned to moor in the Chicago River by Thanksgiving, so there would be ample time to sell off the entire inventory. He would take his chances and hope for a good outcome to his labors.

The heavily loaded *Rouse Simmons* sailed into the choppy waters toward a tragic destiny. Blowing snow obscured the captain's vision as the winds kicked up. The on-board flares and distress signals were useless in the winter squall, but after seven days with no sign of the *Simmons,* a coast guard spotter in Keewaunee reported seeing a three-mast schooner flying its signals. A life-saving crew aboard the motor launch *Tuscarora* quickly sailed from Two Rivers in a desperate attempt to reach the foundering *Simmons* before it was too late. Sadly, the rescue effort was in vain. The ship had disappeared in the foaming wake.

"The tossing waters were as inscrutably silent as to the fate of the schooner as the dull, gray clouds that lowered overhead," commented the *Chicago*

Tribune.[2] As the vessel made its way south, the storm only worsened as ice covered the decks and its Christmas cargo. The violent winds tore apart the sails, and the squall line of snow blinded the *Tuscarora* rescuers. The aging ship was never seen nor heard from again, resigned to the inevitable fate of becoming the "Flying Dutchman" of the Great Lakes.

Back in Chicago, the emotionally stricken Schuenemann family and the families of the sailors, pleaded with the Chicago harbormaster for help but his tone of voice was sarcastic and dismissive. "The boat is just delayed by wind, that's all." He chuckled and told the women he was busy then turned away. With each passing hour the family became more frantic.[3]

Elizabeth Martin solicited the help of Cook County commissioner Daniel Harris, an official mired in a bribery corruption scandal, but Harris neither had the time nor the interest to intervene. Elizabeth made her way to mayor Carter Harrison's office to plea for help accompanied by a member of the Board of Improvements, but a guard outside the door told them to come back the next day. "Think of telling us to come back tomorrow when those men might be perishing in the lake at that moment!" Martin exclaimed. "We never saw the mayor. He never knew we were outside. We went away crying."[4]

On December 4, word reached the Schuenemann family in Chicago that dashed fading hopes for rescue and recovery. Christmas greens and a ship's hatch washed up on the beach at Two Rivers. All was lost. Sixteen crew members and one woman—Captain Oscar Nelson's wife—went down with the *Rouse Simmons.*

Four days later, the *Minerva* and the *Arizona,* two other missing lumber schooners believed to have gone down in the storm, arrived intact, but each was ten days overdue. The captains provided frightening details of the hazardous voyage southward to Chicago. "The *Minerva* had sailed along the western shore, the same course on which was the *Rouse Simmons,* but we saw nothing of it," explained Captain James Ellingsen. "I do not expect to ever see Captain Nelson or any of his men again. He was a fearless man and no other would have stayed on that heavy sea on a bottom like his. But we never will know whether he had the chance to pull to port."[5]

The Lake Seaman's Union appointed a special committee to sell the Christmas trees that had been pulled ashore in fisherman's nets near Pentwater. Recovered trees were shipped by rail down to Chicago where determined family members rented the schooner *Oneda,* similar in appearance to the *Rouse Simmons,* to sell what remained of the seasonal crop. "We will go on with our business," vowed Elsie Schuenemann, the eldest of Herman and Barbara's three children. "The sale this year will no more than pay for the debts caused by the loss of the schooner."[6]

Elsie held out lingering hope for a Christmas miracle, adding: "It seems strange so few trees have been picked up, when there must have been 35,000 trees [by her own estimate] on the ship. I still feel my father must have been saved in some miraculous manner. Otherwise there would have surely been something to tell the story. Perhaps he is on some island with no means of getting away."[7]

Like so many other eerie tales of the lakes and seas, a strange twist of fate and a premonition of disaster saved one crew member from signing on to a rendezvous with death in a watery grave. "Big Bill" Sullivan experienced a feeling of terror and dark dread as the last of the trees were loaded onto the *Rouse Simmons* in Manistique. "I went up with the crew but when it came time to come back with the actual cargo of 15,000 trees, the lake was stormy," he said in a 1934 interview. "I simply had a hunch that's all. It looked bad so I told the captain I would come back on the train. I did. Three days later the *Butcher Boy*, another boat, came in with the news that the *Rouse Simmons* had gone down with all hands on board."[8]

Lake Michigan yielded convincing evidence of the tragic outcome of the *Simmons*, its crew, and Mrs. Nelson. On July 29, 1913, as young Frank Lauscher, the son of a fisherman from Sturgeon Bay, Wisconsin, played on the beach several miles north of town, he found a message tucked inside of a bottle that had washed ashore. The note was hastily scrawled in pencil by Charles Nelson and dated November 23, 1912.

"*These lines were written at 10:30 p.m. Schooner Rouse Simmons ready to go down about twenty miles southeast of Twin River Point between fifteen and twenty miles off-shore. All hands lashed to one line. Goodbye. Captain Charles Nelson.*"[9]

The proof arrived on April 23, 1924. Herman Schuenemann's wallet washed ashore and was recovered by a beachcomber near Two Rivers Point. The original rubber band held the waterlogged billfold together and bundled inside were old newspaper clippings describing other Christmas sailings. The print was still legible.

On the one-year anniversary of the sinking, Elsie presented a written memorial to the *Chicago Tribune* advertising department announcing her mother's intention to honor her husband's memory by keeping alive the traditions of the Christmas Tree Ship.

"Our husband and father spent his life in doing what he could to further the happiness of others. In reverence, honor and love, we do today pay tribute to his memory, and to the brave men who met death with him. We are taking up our father's work just where he left out," Elsie elaborated. "There will be another Christmas Tree ship in Chicago this year. Mother is now up in Northern Michigan superintending the cutting of the Christmas trees."[10]

For many families, the annual Yuletide excursion down to the dock became a cherished custom and rite of passage for the little ones, and Barbara Schuenemann did not wish to disappoint despite her grief.

The following September Herman's gallant widow chartered a schooner and hired a crew of rugged men to navigate the boat through the frigid water of the lake and cut down trees upon their arrival in Manistique. Barbara, believed to be the first woman to head a nautical shipping company, accompanied the men on the voyage. She supervised the felling of the trees while back home daughter Elsie, known to all as "The Christmas Tree Girl," took charge of recruiting a team of Chicago girls to help prepare the bouquets of balsam wreaths before the craft moored in the harbor.

Thereafter, until 1925, Barbara brought her Christmas cargo down from Manistique without failure or mishap except in 1919, when James J. McComb, the Chicago harbormaster, leased her customary dock to another company, forcing her to make arrangements with the railroad to ship the trees into the city. Barbara mistakenly missed the deadline for submitting her permit application. Amid controversy over price gouging by certain unscrupulous competitors, the lot of freshly cut trees was hastily sold to the public from an empty lot up on North Clark Street. "Last year, profiteers charged from $5.00 to $20.00 each and many poor people had to go without them," Barbara said. "This year trees will cell from fifty-cents to $1.50 each."[11]

The Age of Sail along the Great Lakes waterways had run its course by the mid-1920s as the schooner trade all but vanished. The clogged Chicago River, once congested with schooners, freight barges, and excursion steamships, emptied out as years passed. Adjusting to the changing times, Mrs. Schuenemann delivered her trees by rail to a leased warehouse in Chicago beginning in 1925.

Old age and heart disease caught up with Barbara. The Christmas tree lady passed away in her sleep inside the family home at 156 Eugenie Street in Chicago's Old Town neighborhood the night of June 15, 1933. The family laid her to rest beside the empty grave of Herman in Acacia Cemetery, whose modest headstone bears the simple etching of an evergreen tree. Daughters Elsie, Pearl, and Hazel, assisted by "Big Bill" Sullivan, the old salt whose premonition of disaster spared his life, hung up their shingle for the sake of tradition above a tiny store at 1641 N. LaSalle Street the following winter.

The modest little sign read—Captain and Mrs. H. Schuenemann's Daughters—and the business continued, returning increasingly smaller profit margins each season until the final year, 1944. Elsie Schuenemann-Roberts, the spirited woman bound and determined to keep her father's memory and his business alive against long odds, died February 1, 1950. The interstate trucking industry and the railroads assured Chicagoans of a continuous supply of Christmas trees come late November. Plastic trees appeared in department stores for the first time in the 1950s.

Chicago's first family of Christmas trees left behind a quiet legacy that inspired an annual holiday tradition. In 1913, Frank Jordan, a friend and business associate of Herman Schuenemann, donated an ancient forty-five-foot tree that he had cut down deep in the woods during his travels to the Upper Peninsula. In the spirit of good will, Jordan memorialized Herman Schuenemann's life with this gift to the people of Chicago. The first municipal Christmas tree was hoisted atop a thirty-foot pole, with smaller firs attached to the base, at the foot of Grant Park, north of the Art Institute.

At precisely six o'clock, on Christmas Eve, 1913, Mayor Carter Harrison tripped the switch that lit Chicago's official Christmas tree, crowned by the Star of Bethlehem. Lyric opera singers and the Swedish choral societies provided musical accompaniment before an immense throng of 80,000–100,000 people, including 30,000 children who had been awarded free passes by a streetcar company. Not since the great civil aviation meet of 1911 held in Grant Park had so many gathered in one place for a public event.[12]

The lighting of Chicago's municipal Christmas tree remains an annual rite of winter. From late November through the New Year, the brightly decorated tree towers over Millennium Park near Washington Street and Michigan Avenue. All but forgotten in the joyous wonderment of tourists, children, and everyday Chicagoans gazing up at the crown of the tree and the star that rests at its pinnacle, is the saga of the Schuenemann family and the vanished *Rouse Simmons*, a spiritual echo—and a gift—from Christmas past.

Vincent Starrett, a beloved Chicago novelist, book critic, and a cub reporter for the *Chicago Daily News* at the time of the Christmas Tree Ship sinking, applied poetic and elegant verse to the fatal voyage.

> This is the tale of the Christmas ship
> That sailed o'er the sullen lake;
> And of sixteen souls that made the trip
> And of death in the foaming wake.[13]

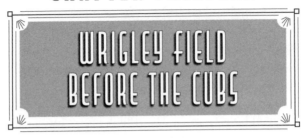

WRIGLEY FIELD
BEFORE THE CUBS

A Richmond, Indiana, blacksmith's son, tiring of the dreariness of small-town living and his clerk's job in the local jewelry emporium, ventured to Chicago in 1893 to visit the World's Columbian Exposition and ride the Ferris wheel, never knowing what it might lead to.

Freed from the shackles of rural Hoosier conformity, the drudgery of shoeing horses in his pop's stable, and selling charm bracelets to the bankers' daughters from the counter of Haner's Jewelry Store, the young man caught a case of "Chicago fever." After sampling the delights of this "Midwestern Athens on the prairie," the lad returned home just long enough to kiss mother goodbye before boarding his Chicago-bound Pullman back to the idyllic dreamland of the "White City," the mesmerizing vision of wondrous inventions, gleaming palaces of commerce, and unexpected novelties that inspired author L. Frank Baum to craft the "Emerald City" of the *Wizard of Oz* in its image.

Charles Henry Weeghman. He was a man of heart and humor, an enterprising and persevering spirit born in the age of "Horatio Alger" positivity. LaSalle Street bankers remembered him as the "luckiest man in Chicago"—until he wasn't. Glib, unfailingly persuasive and charming, Charlie was a nightclub habitué, a movie aficionado, professional baseball promoter, and horse-racing enthusiast who loved beautiful women not so wisely, but perhaps too well.

His speedy rise to prominence began with his first lucky break: an offer for a ten-dollar-a-week job as a coffee boy in restaurateur Charley King's place. King owned and operated a Fifth Avenue (now Wells Street) bistro favored by the overnight reporters writing their copy along "newspaper row." There, Weeghman chatted up the third-shift workers, business and theater luminaries, and the "sports" of State Street's "Whiskey Row," harvesting many important business and social contacts he would use to his advantage.

Charley King promised patrons good home cooking—from kitchen to table in less than ten minutes. Vincent Starrett, legendary Chicago reporter and noted literary maven credited Charley King and his mother Mary King with inventing chicken à la king, a contribution to Western civilization that became the dinner staple of generations of working-class Americans for years to come.

Charles Weeghman, King's youthful, white-jacketed protégé, advanced to floor manager in this way-station for Chicago bon vivants. For eight years Weeghman supervised the "midnight rush" while salting away a portion of his monthly earnings in anticipation of the day when he would sever the bonds of friendship and loyalty with his boss to strike out on his own.

That day arrived in January 1901 when Charley King died. With his $300 savings and $2,500 of borrowed capital from three influential acquaintances, Weeghman opened his own place, a lunchroom counter at Fifth Avenue and Adams Street. The venture proved a hit. With his financial backer William Walker, a wholesale fish merchant and supplier, Weeghman opened six other prototypical downtown diners.

The business was a stunning success, although after just six years Weeghman divested his holdings to his partners for $50,000. He wanted to reach for much more, and had in mind a twenty-four-hour round-the-clock restaurant in the heart of the Central Loop near the theaters at Dearborn and Madison. The 108 chairs filling the interior space of the new "Weeghman's" accommodated five thousand persons daily. Borrowing a page from Charley King's good-food-served-fast playbook, Weeghman's promoted speed and efficient service in a new setup that came to be known as "the one-armed dairy lunch."

Patrons seated themselves in individual chairs resembling an old-fashioned school desk. They ate their meals on a flat wooden surface bolted to the "one-armed" chair. Weeghman's eatery was a forerunner of McDonald's; a fast, affordable dining alternative to white-tablecloth restaurants with food served from a predictable menu that rarely changed.

"Lucky Charlie's" downtown fast-food emporiums clicked with the public. He made a fortune and elevated his social ranking from ambitious coffee boy to tycoon in less than five years. He bought a billiard parlor, played the ponies, and invested in several motion picture theaters. However, a passion for baseball stirred in his blood from his Indiana youth.

In the season of 1911, three things happened. Always the flashy showman, Weeghman mounted an ordinary-sized dinner plate on a pole above the right-field bleachers in the Cubs' West Side Park—385 feet from home plate. He challenged the hometown hitters to aim for the dinner plate, and should one of their home-run balls strike it, he promised the lucky batsman the gift of a restaurant free and clear. One afternoon, the league's top home-run hitter, Frank "Wildfire" Schulte, hit a deep drive that banged off the scoreboard—a mere five feet from the dinner plate. Weeghman sheepishly withdrew the generous offer and removed the plate the next day. But he was far from being done with baseball.

The St. Louis Cardinals were up for sale. Weeghman, his appetite whetted, offered $350,000 for the team and the ballpark. Despite having money in hand, the league rebuffed the Chicago restaurateur. Just who was this upstart young pup the baseball moguls wondered? Their snub only fueled Charlie's burning desire to press on with his ambition to become a baseball magnate. Without another team in the National and American Leagues available for purchase, Weeghman, for the moment, was stymied in his attempt to join the exclusive club of sportsmen.

Charlie next turned his attention to professional billiards, enjoying a limited spectator appeal in Eastern and Midwest cities. A National Amateur Three-Cushion Billiard League, organized in 1910 by retired baseball player Johnny Kling, sponsored professional cue-ball teams playing in eight cities including Chicago. Weeghman, as the avatar of sports oddities, proposed the formation of an "American League" circuit comprised of ten cities with each team playing a home series at the opponent's parlor followed by a second series immediately afterward at the host establishment—back to back. The plan never got past the discussion stage.

In 1913, the same year Kling's National Amateur Three-Cushion Billiard League disbanded, local businessman and perennial baseball promoter John T. Powers established the Federal League from the tatters of the old Columbian League, a failed Class D Midwestern minor league circuit. The Chicago team floundered in competitive play at the DePaul Athletic Field in its maiden season and the league was in disarray. Coal tycoon "Long Jim" Gilmore stepped in to oust Powers and take over league management.[1] He settled a $12,000 debt load and drew up an ambitious plan to lure star players from established teams with the promise of generous payouts.

Gilmore inveigled the fish dealer William Walker and "Lucky Charlie" to buy into a bold scheme to reorganize the Federals as the third major league to be anchored by the Chicago team. "We may have to buy more experienced [players], before the turning point is reached, but the Federal League is composed of game fellows who think they have the right to be in baseball and they will stick," Gilmore boasted.[2]

The Federals had knowingly opened an unwinnable trade war on the American and National Leagues. Amused skeptics dismissed the Feds as "the league of major pretensions."[3] Weeghman and Walker had other ideas though, and with hope and abandonment they eagerly took over the reins of the Chicago club. The partners invested heavily in the acquisition of thirty-three players plucked from major league rosters by coaxing their wealthy chums from the Chicago Athletic Association to sweeten the pot. Joe Tinker, the great Cubs star of the early 1900s, signed on as manager and induced a number of his friends from the rival leagues to join the Federals.

"I was riding the crest in those days," Weeghman reminisced years later. "My string of restaurants were paying big, and to the best of my figuring, I was worth between eight and ten million dollars."[4] On that memorable day, December 27, 1913, Weeghman's fellow investors introduced him to the public as the team president and organizational front man. There were handshakes all around as the proud and beaming owner took a bow and promised the fans an exciting championship team playing in a gleaming new ballpark that all of Chicago could be proud of.

Weeghman and Walker, both shrewd and cunning real estate speculators, turned their attention to a land parcel at Clark and Addison Streets up on the North Side—virgin territory for professional baseball. Several years before, Charles Havenor of Milwaukee, and Joseph Cantillon, a Minneapolis baseball promoter, secured control of the grounds from the Chicago Lutheran Theological Seminary (vacating their building by 1910), with the intention of staking a claim by moving an American Association team to the Addison Street location. They planned a small wooden arena to house a minor league AA team.

However, their ploy fizzled after the Cubs and White Sox successfully blocked them under the terms of baseball's governing National Agreement. Weeghman spied an opportunity and picked up the option. He signed a ninety-nine-year lease in January 1914. The Federals were an "outlaw" league, and therefore beyond the normal rules of baseball governance.

Informed of this alarming development, both the Cubs and White Sox sought an immediate injunction to prevent the Feds from "invading" Chicago and building this new park so close to their home operations. White Sox owner Charles Comiskey relented after Weeghman threatened to take out a lease on the 39th Street Grounds—the former White Sox home field up to July 1910.

Architect Zachary Taylor Davis, designer of Comiskey Park, was hired to draw up plans for the new "Weeghman Park"—future home of the "Chi-Feds." That was to be the team's formal nickname until 1915, when a lucky fan submitted "Chicago Whales" as the winning bid in a newspaper contest to give the Chi-Feds a colorful new moniker.

Five thousand people turned out to witness the historic ground-breaking on March 4, 1914. North Siders were abuzz, and excitement hung in the air.

They defied police and pushed forward to shake Weeghman's hand, solicit his autograph, or simply pat him on the back for the gift of a baseball team. "Lucky Charlie" tipped his hat to the admiring throng. Like all good showmen, he thrived on public attention and actively courted the press.

The Blome and Sinek construction company went to work, promising delivery of the stadium in six weeks. It was a testament to the audacity, nerve, and energy of Weeghman that a concrete and steel ballpark of this size could be built on such an impossibly short deadline. Before the six-week construction schedule expired and the new park delivered, Charlie quietly picked up the final tab of $250,000—and paid for it in cash. As an added touch, he built the first permanent concession stand in an American ballpark. Until this time, strolling vendors sold peanuts, beer, and hotdogs to seated patrons in the grandstand.

Under fair skies before an overflow crowd on April 23, 1914, the Chi-Feds trounced Kansas City 9–1 in their inaugural tilt. Sportswriter Sam Weller observed: "Chicago took the Federal League to the bosom yesterday and claimed it as a mother would claim a lost son."[5] People were turned away at the gate as an estimated 21,000 shoe-horned their way into a stadium designed to comfortably seat 14,000. Songwriter Augusta C. Gebhardt composed *"The Feds Are Here to Stay!"* a peppy little tune she personally dedicated to Charles Weeghman, but there were worrisome signs of the troubles soon to come.

After an early flourish of success, fan enthusiasm waned. Crowds dwindled, forcing Weeghman to reduce ticket prices from the customary fifty cents to a quarter. The writers sarcastically termed it "jitney ball." To lure people into his expensive new stadium, the owner, like all worthy showmen, sponsored an array of promotional events, souvenir giveaways, ten-cent admission days, automobile demonstrations, player testimonial days, and in the 1915 season, a rather shabby attempt to exploit the *Eastland* capsizing in the Chicago River, a horrific tragedy that claimed the lives of 812 people. On July 24, Weeghman announced that the July 29 game against Buffalo would be designated "Eastland Sufferer's Day," promising a nickel-a-head donation to the families of victims. He hired chorus girls to sell flowers at the gate and fully expected to net $10,000. Instead, he collected only $955.14.

The Chi-Feds played well in their first season and finished in second place. Although the owner announced a $20,000 profit at season's end, he had in fact borrowed heavily against his restaurant receipts. Playing under their rather curious new nickname, the Chicago Whales, the North Side team captured the 1915 Federal League pennant on the last day of the season in a dramatic doubleheader showdown with the Pittsburgh Rebels, splitting one of the two games before thirty-four thousand fans.[6] Many thought the Federal League had finally arrived after such an exciting climax, but those in the know predicted the circuit couldn't last. It was a house of cards. The success of the Chicago team failed to obviate the financial strife of the other ball clubs. The league went underwater and bled red ink. In 1915, Gilmore and company spent $300,000 in preinflation dollars on player salaries and signing bonuses. It was simply too much for several team owners facing the specter of bankruptcy. In a desperate gambit, the Feds sought judicial relief in order to survive into the 1916 season and beyond.

Gilmore, Walker, Weeghman, and their combative cohorts labored under the naïve assumption that the federal court would grant them "eleven prayers for relief" through strict adherence to the language of the 1890 Sherman Anti-Trust Law outlawing monopolies. The American League and National League monopoly would surely be broken, they reasoned, the reserve clause contractually binding a player to a team ended, and formal recognition of their right to exist with competitive equality among all teams would be granted. Baseball's future commissioner, the sour-faced federal judge Kenesaw Mountain Landis, adjudicated the matter, but in the end deferred his decision and made no ruling. He feared that if he handed down an outcome favorable to the Federal League it would destroy the shaky underpinnings of organized baseball on which it rested, namely the sanctity of the reserve clause. "Any blows at the thing called baseball could be regarded by this court as a blow to a national institution!" Landis thundered, adding an exclamation point to the entire proceeding.[7]

With that, the war between the baseball moguls ended in a whimper and any hope of peaceful co-existence for the Federal League was shattered. The final settlement between the litigants allowed several league owners including Weeghman to purchase major league teams. With little forethought given to his precarious finances, "Lucky Charlie" submitted a bid for the Cubbies, owned at that time by Charles P. Taft, brother of the former president of the United States. Taft demanded a jaw-dropping sum of $500,000 in cold hard cash. There were other interested buyers, Taft curtly informed Weeghman, from his residence in Cincinnati. The option had to be acted upon quickly.

Minutes before Taft's hard-and-fast deadline expired, Weeghman presented his check to the cashier at the Corn Exchange Bank. It was 2:31 P.M., January 20, 1916. Surrounded by his original stockholders William Walker and Adolph Schuettler of the Chicago Athletic Association and new investors J. Ogden Armour and the wily and pragmatic chewing-gum manufacturer William Wrigley Jr., a beaming Weeghman, became the sixth man to own and operate the ball club. He boasted that he had been a Cub fan all along.[8] Next, he announced his intention to move the Cubs from the West Side Grounds over to Weeghman Park to commence their fabled 102-year residency.

Before the Cubs took the field to inaugurate the 1916 season, Weeghman hoisted the championship flag of his defunct Whales up the pole as a sentimental homage to a lofty dream only partially realized. True, the man behind the bun had built a baseball palace for the ages and had ridden the crest of the wave to instant public acclaim, but in the end he would lose the things in his life most precious to him.

Bessie Webb, Charley King's industrious former head cashier exchanged vows with Weeghman in 1899 but filed for divorce in February 1920 citing his repeated infidelities. She won custody of their seven-year-old daughter following a contentious and often bitter courtroom battle.

Nineteen-twenty was a bad year all around for Weeghman. A day after a Cook County grand jury investigating rumors that eight crooked Chicago White Sox players had conspired to "throw" the 1919 World Series to Cincinnati had issued its subpoenas, Weeghman made a self-incriminating statement saying he had known of the fix all along. While enjoying the company of Chicago gambling boss Jacob "Mont" Tennes at a Saratoga, New York, race track before the World Series kicked off, Tennes advised Weeghman to "play it smart and bet right." "Tennes told me a New York gambler had advised him to bet on the Reds," Charlie revealed, unmindful of how this would make him look. "He said the New Yorker told him the series had been fixed and seven White Sox players had agreed to lay down. He mentioned their names and said the tip was straight but he didn't want it. He liked baseball but wouldn't go in on a crooked deal. I understand in spite of the tip he [Tennes] bet $30,000." Weeghman couldn't remember if he had shared this intelligence with National League president John Heydler before the games began—if he had it might have altered the course of baseball history—but added that he considered "the whole thing preposterous."[9] The embarrassing disclosures only compounded his mounting personal and financial distress.

Years of robbing from Peter to pay Paul (his baseball adventure mostly), had already cost Charlie his team and his livelihood. Citing pressing business concerns, he divested his ill-fated Cub holdings to William Wrigley Jr. on December 7, 1918, just three months after taking the Cubs to the World Series.

After woefully neglecting his restaurant business, which he had entrusted to his older brother, Albert, angry food-industry suppliers demanded immediate payment from the Weeghman Company. Unlucky Charlie admitted he did not have anything left in reserve to settle his overdue accounts, thus forcing the creditors to file an involuntary petition of bankruptcy against the chain in US District Court on August 13, 1920. William Wrigley Jr. rushed in at the eleventh hour to shore up Weeghman's shaky cash reserves by enjoining the creditors to exercise patience before throwing the chain into receivership.

A full reorganization occurred in 1923, by which time Weeghman—his star in eclipse and the "one-armed dairy-lunch" having been supplanted by a new wave of "serve-yourself cafeterias"—severed all remaining connections to the operation.

"Had Weeghman stuck to the dairy lunch business he would still be a wealthy man," Wrigley sighed, although by now the dining novelty had already worn off. "That should have been sufficient warning but the next thing he did was attempt to make a success of motion pictures. Weeghman wasn't a theater man and he didn't understand the theater game."[10]

Before departing Chicago, Weeghman operated two failing Chicago nightclubs, paying little heed to Wrigley's admonishments. He moved east in the early 1930s to manage the Riviera, a locally famous and glitzy "dine and dance" hall atop the Palisades in Fort Lee, New Jersey. As usual Charlie was in his element, table-hopping with the celebrity patrons as they sipped their champagne cocktails in the raucous nightclub setting.

In a strange twist of fate Weeghman returned to Chicago with his second wife, Carol, to die in the same city where he once dazzled. Only fifty-nine years old and refreshed by a recent visit to the mineral baths of Hot Springs, Arkansas, Lucky Charlie suffered a fatal stroke inside his Drake Hotel suite on November 1, 1938.

William Wrigley Jr.'s reputation, fame, and fortune endured; Weeghman's did not. His achievements (and idiosyncrasies) are mostly erased from public memory. (Chicago Cub team publications from the 1940s and 1950s do not even mention his name, although to mark the hundredth anniversary of the opening of the park on April 23, 2014, Cub management invited Weeghman's grand-niece Sue Quigg to throw out the ceremonial first pitch).

Perhaps the unkindest cut to Charlie's fading legacy occurred in 1926 when his former business partner renamed Weeghman Park Wrigley Field after Wrigley purchased the stadium and the grounds for $295,000 in cash two years earlier. "I will prove my point that good baseball is a prime mover of good business," vowed the new owner, whose marketing slogan "tell 'em quick and tell 'em often" pushed billions of sticks of chewing gum and Cubs baseball into the living rooms of Middle America.[11]

THE LAST SUPPER
. . . ALMOST

The elevation of Archbishop Blasé J. Cupich to the College of Cardinals in a consistory on November 19, 2016, at St. Peter's Basilica in Vatican City, brings to mind a near tragic episode in the life of Chicago's much-revered George Cardinal Mundelein (1872–1939). It happened inside the stately dining room of the University Club on the evening of February 10, 1916.

Archbishop George W. Mundelein, a product of New York's Lower East Side, arrived in Chicago from Brooklyn just three days prior to a testimonial banquet hosted in his honor, as he assumed the mantle of leadership of the archdiocese of Chicago. Catholics in Chicago looked forward to a week-long gala with a number of important receptions and welcoming dinners honoring Archbishop Mundelein.

Event planners from the archdiocese considered several downtown venues for the kick-off dinner including the Congress and the Blackstone Hotels before deciding upon the University Club, a warm and comfortable place, as the appropriate venue. The guest list of two hundred plus represented a cross-section of important city elites—the people that mattered. Invitees included seven archbishops, twenty-nine bishops, bank presidents, judges, noted surgeons, former Illinois governors Edward Dunne and Charles S. Deneen, former Chicago mayor Carter Harrison II, future mayor William E. Dever, Arthur Meeker—Prairie Avenue society maven and stockyards magnate, and utilities magnate Samuel Insull.

All gathered to enjoy a hearty feast prepared, in part, by the newly hired assistant chef Jean Crones, a man of intrigue and deadly intention. Traveling under the alias "Jean Cuneone," Crones, a Belgian, had immigrated to the United States from Cologne, Germany, on May 6, 1913. Trained in the culinary arts, he had worked as a night chef in the Arlington Hotel in Binghamton, New York, and other various high-end restaurants in New York City, Buffalo, Staten Island, Philadelphia, Scranton, Pennsylvania, Los Angeles, St. Louis, Cleveland, and Chicago. Remembered as a reserved man with few friends, Crones was interested in amateur photography in his off hours. He studied chemistry, astronomy, and the theoretical concepts of anarchism and the violent overthrow of the government.

The first two decades of the twentieth century were a tumultuous era of American life, marked by continuous strife between labor and capital over the right to unionize, secure a living wage, and the eight-hour work day. There were crippling work stoppages and major strikes in the Chicago stockyards, the coal fields of West Virginia, the Idaho copper mines, and other flashpoints of labor unrest continuing through the early 1920s.

On the eve of World War I, the militant Industrial Workers of the World— the IWW (commonly known as the "Wobblies")–and other radicalized organizations on the far left-wing fringe of the American labor movement, gained momentum. By 1917, membership crested at 150,000.[1]

Crones declared himself a loyal follower, disciple, and comrade of the IWW national secretary William "Big Bill" Haywood (acquitted of the December 1905 murder-by-bombing of former Idaho governor Frank Steunenberg), and the self-professed queen of anarchy Emma Goldman. In those uneasy years, numerous bombings, armed attacks, the murder of President William McKinley and incidents of industrial sabotage inspired social upheaval, widening class division, and societal disruption.

Crones, through his correspondence and association with an anarchist ring calling itself the International Radical Group of Chicago, formed a cell inside a cheap tenement flat located in the once-fashionable Prairie Avenue district at Twenty-Second Street and Prairie Avenue. Although German-born, Crones aligned his ambitions with an inner circle of Italian radicals headquartered in Chicago. With accomplices John Allegrini, a stonecutter, and Dominic Forto, Jean Crones plotted an act of terror targeting the Catholic Church for its perceived injustices against the working men and women of the world.

Later, police discovered that the original plot was far more complex and encompassing than previously imagined. A rash of six fires occurring inside six Chicago churches of different faiths during the previous two years was traced to the anarchist cell that enlisted Crones. If the University Club poisoning attempt proved successful, their plan was to attack religious leaders from other denominations in the same manner. The plot was weeks in the making. It was revealed that during his tenure in Scranton, Crones had enrolled in the chemistry department of the International Correspondence School, run by the Griebel Corporation.

Incredibly, the school furnished its students with instruments and a generous supply of acids and deadly poisons that were sent through the mail by the Technical Supply Company of Scranton for them to work with as they pleased. Jean Crones, a remarkably gifted student according to his instructors, never received a grade lower than 92 in his first thirteen lessons. In lesson fourteen, he mastered inorganic chemistry, detailing the application of various chemicals including arsenic.

Crones continued his correspondence studies after relocating to Chicago early in 1915 and settling into a flat at 2408 Calumet Avenue where he resided for just under a year. Billeted in a run-down apartment at 2201 Prairie Avenue, which he had rented on January 3, 1916, he stocked the shelves with containers filled with various noxious chemicals, test tubes, gas plates, nitroglycerine, guncotton, and a raft of pictures of Emma Goldman, anarchist literature, and flyers.

Police captain Morgan Collins became convinced that Crones intended to carry out a series of bombings targeting several downtown office buildings including the People's Gas Light and Coke Company to augment his nefarious poison plot. Crones's landlady, Mrs. May Zeigenfeus, aka "May Haywood," aka "Blanche Howard," recalled that her tenant was a quiet, exceptionally polite and well-mannered young man who always paid his rent in advance and caused no one any trouble. "I thought highly of him," she said. "He was in his room nearly all the time. He never talked much."[2]

Crones's arrival in Chicago coincided with a labor dispute that had arisen between restaurant owners and waitresses culminating in a walkout. Supplied with a large amount of cash by criminal associates in New York, Crones generously donated money to the cause, and was instrumental in carrying out acts of sabotage by filling salt storage containers in the basements of a number of Chicago cafes with soap, sand, and other harsh abrasives that caused many patrons to become ill.

An informant revealed to police that Crones appeared before an anarchist meeting in May 1915, where the guest speaker assured him that "a chemist could do a great deal in an anarchist movement."[3] He took those words to heart. By day he worked in the kitchen of the Congress Hotel, earning ninety dollars a month. He terminated the arrangement after becoming aware that Archbishop Mundelein's banquet would be held in the University Club and *not* the Congress Hotel.

Crones applied for the job on September 27, 1916, and was hired as the new assistant chef by Edward Lewis, manager of the University Club and the head chef. Former president William Howard Taft, secretary of state William Jennings Bryan, and US senator James Hamilton Lewis were dinner guests of the club during the time Crones was employed there.

By early February the menu for the archbishop's dinner had been prepared and approved. Everyone in the kitchen had access to the menu and the food that was to be served. As the designated "cold meat" preparer, Jean Crones was assigned the task of preparing the chicken and sausage meatballs that would go into the soup. The city dignitaries and religious leaders gathered early and settled comfortably into their seats, awaiting the first course—Chef Crones's soup with his own special ingredient added to the recipe—480 grains of arsenic injected into the tiny meatballs in the chicken broth.

Within minutes, nearly all who had sampled the chef's own consommé, stumbled from their chairs and fell to the floor violently ill. Chaos erupted inside the dining room. "Immediately after the first course I was taken ill," recalled Thomas A. O'Shaugnessey, who was in charge of the artwork and decorations for the dinner. "I was the first to leave the table. I thought it was bad ventilation and went out on the fire escape. I became dizzy, went inside and started downstairs. In one of the lower halls I became deathly sick. An attendant found me and called a physician, who administered an emetic and had me sent to the Ravenswood hospital."[4]

City librarian Henry Edward Legler, banquet host Dr. Francis C. Kelley of the Catholic Church Extension Society, Frank O. Wetmore, president of the First National Bank, one of the men most seriously injured, and Judge John P. McGoorty recovered after days of confinement in their sickbeds. "There were fourteen at our table and twelve became deathly sick," said Judge Denis E. Sullivan. "Explanation that it was ptomaine poisoning never satisfied me. It was too quick in its effects and too universal."[5]

The deaths of several elderly banquet guests that occurred later were traced back to the poisoning. Banker Andrew Joseph Graham, the head of Graham and Sons, who had been a Democratic mayoral candidate six years before, expired on May 1, 1916. In a fortunate turn of fate, the soup had been watered down at the last minute by a kitchen employee concerned that the stock appeared to be spoiled. He threw away four of the five cans of the poisoned stock, but decided to use the one batch that did not look like it had been spoiled. His swift action undoubtedly saved the lives of everyone present.

Dr. John B. Murphy, a physician attending the banquet, administered a mixture of mustard and water and served it as an emetic to the afflicted. The next day, city health commissioner John Dill Robertson declared that the kitchen utensils were unsanitary and infected with verdigris, a greenish-blue poisonous pigment resulting from the action of acetic acid on the copper kettles. However, the theory was challenged and easily disproved. Robertson issued a follow-up report prepared by the city chemist declaring that 3.7 grains of white oxide arsenic had been detected in the analysis of sixteen ounces of the poisoned soup.

Assistant police chief Herman Schuettler, one of the department's most capable and experienced detectives who would rise to the superintendence two years later, was blunt and to the point. "Not one of the men who attended that banquet realizes or knows exactly how close he was to death," Schuettler informed the press. He ordered the department's special "anarchist squad" and scores of plain clothes detectives into the streets to track down the perpetrator of this nearly incomprehensible evil.[6] Schuettler's men discovered that Crones was a frequent speaker at North Side IWW meetings.

Police easily identified Jean Crones under another alias he used: Nestor Dondoglio, the name of an anarchist disciple of Luigi Galleani, East Coast Italian bomb-maker. A search of Crones's (Dondoglio's) apartment on Prairie Avenue turned up chemical supplies that one police detective termed a "laboratory of death."[7] Detectives visited the nearby drug stores and chemist supply houses to determine the origin of the arsenic, and who might have purchased it.

The landlady told police that her polite young tenant with the unusual dark spot over his right eye had returned to the flat around 8:15 on the evening in question in an anxious and worried state. In the company of John Allegrini, he left the building to carry out their evil deed. Allegrini later returned, but Crones had vanished.

The detective squad imposed a citywide dragnet, but efforts to seize the fiend failed. Crones eluded capture and fled Chicago, despite optimistic newspaper headlines announcing his imminent capture and arrest. Police departments from all across the nation were placed on high alert, as fears of a wider conspiracy mounted. A "Red Scare" in America culminated in the prosecution, conviction, and execution of Nicola Sacco and Bartolomeo Vanzetti for the April 1920 murder of a shoe company paymaster in South Braintree, Massachusetts.

For nearly twenty-five years beginning with McKinley's assassination in 1901 by a known anarchist, the nation remained on edge. In Chicago, dozens of men and women with affiliations to subversive groups were arrested and interrogated. Anarchist meetings in the city's neighborhood social halls were raided and closed down, often without warrant. Emma Goldman, acknowledged leader of the national anarchistic societies, publicly condemned Crones and disavowed any connections in stark terms. "That man is not an anarchist. He is a lunatic," she said. "I do not know him and he is unknown to my associates."[8] Meanwhile, Jean Crones penned a series of taunting letters to the press and to Chicago police describing his *modus operandi*. The letters revealed that he had traveled about the country engaged in subversive activities over the course of a few years. He boasted to the authorities of his formidable skills in evading police capture.

In his defiant scribbling, the profligate Crones wrote: "I am proud to be an anarchist. All my work I do alone all the time so police spies do not get the best of me and [do] not get a chance to be promoted."[9] He added a brazen postscript, declaring his intention to continue his university studies in New York, vowing never to be caught. In response the NYPD mobilized the entire force and sealed off every railroad terminal and ferry station. Concerns were raised that Crones might attempt a bombing in Manhattan, but that never happened.

Over time, police arrested various men from around the country because of their striking physical resemblance to Crones. All were eventually released. In May 1919, unconfirmed reports circulated around town that Jean Crones had enlisted in the army during World War I and was assigned to the mess hall at Camp Grant in Illinois before shipping out to France. The soldier who came forward with this startling revelation said that Crones confessed to his crime and added that in the chaos and disorder of wartime, military service provided him with necessary cover and anonymity.

After months of frustration that would evolve into years of missed opportunities, Edward Lewis of the University Club declared, "We have received so many tips to the whereabouts of Crones that proved false we have tired of running them down."[10] Crones remained a fugitive from justice as police scoured the nation's known anarchist haunts in many different locales, following up on dozens of unconfirmed reports of his presence in the naval yard in Portsmouth, Virginia, up through New England. Crones died in 1932 at his Middletown, Connecticut, family home without having ever occupied a jail cell. The avowed anarchist never answered for his many monstrous acts committed in the name of the movement.

Unfazed by the poisoning, Archbishop Mundelein walked away from the ordeal that February evening suffering no ill effects. He explained that he had passed on eating the soup because he was dieting. A second formal reception held in his honor at the auditorium later in the week concluded without incident. Questioned by reporters, Mundelein quipped: "You know, it takes something stronger than soup to get me."[11] Cardinal Mundelein cherished the city of Chicago and its people. In later years he confided to a reporter, "You and I live in the greatest city in the world. The only way they will ever get me to leave Chicago is feet first."[12]

On March 24, 1924, Mundelein became the first cardinal to serve the Catholic Church west of the Alleghenies. Two years later, in June, he hosted the 28th International Eucharistic Congress at Soldier Field—the first ever to be held in the United States. He led the Chicago archdiocese until his passing in 1939 and was honored by the trustees of Mechanics Grove (thirty-five miles northwest of Chicago) in April 1925 when they formally renamed the village Mundelein, Illinois.

It remains the home of the University of St. Mary on the Lake (Mundelein Seminary), the principal seminary and school of theology for aspiring priests serving the Chicago archdiocese and other dioceses in the United States and abroad.

"Lucky" Charlie Weeghman (*right*), flamboyant restaurateur and
the builder of Wrigley Field, poses with James A. Gilmore, president
of the Federal League, the unsuccessful challenger to the American
and National Leagues of professional baseball. COURTESY OF THE
LIBRARY OF CONGRESS, PRINTS AND PHOTOGRAPHS DIVISION.

Archbishop (later Cardinal)
George William Mundelein
(1872–1939) was fortunate to
survive the deadly poisoning
attempt of the anarchist chef
Jean Crones at the University
Club on February 10, 1916.
COURTESY OF THE LIBRARY
OF CONGRESS, PRINTS AND
PHOTOGRAPHS DIVISION.

An enduring Chicagoland roadside curiosity since 1934: the replica Leaning Tower in suburban Niles, Illinois. LIBRARY OF CONGRESS, PRINTS AND PHOTOGRAPHS DIVISION, PHOTOGRAPH BY JOHN MARGOLIES.

Major Lenox R. Lohr (1891–1968) of Chicago business, culture, and philanthropy, managed the Museum of Science and Industry and the "Chicago Railroad Fair: A Century on Wheels" pageant in 1948. COURTESY OF THE LIBRARY OF CONGRESS, PRINTS AND PHOTOGRAPHS DIVISION, PHOTOGRAPH BY HARRIS & EWING.

"Chicago's Sweetheart," torch singer Ruth Etting, achieved international acclaim after launching her singing career at the Marigold Gardens.
WIKIMEDIA COMMONS.

Swaggering tough guy Moe "the Gimp" Snyder married Etting, managed her career, and made her life otherwise miserable.
WIKIMEDIA COMMONS.

Mayor Richard J. Daley, flanked by Rear Admiral Dan Gallery and Father Byrne, led the first downtown St. Patrick's Day Parade on March 17, 1956—nearly fifty-five years since the last one. COURTESY OF THE UNIVERSITY OF ILLINOIS AT CHICAGO. LIBRARY, SPECIAL COLLECTIONS AND UNIVERSITY ARCHIVES DEPARTMENT (RICHARD J. DALEY LIBRARY).

Mayor Richard J. Daley and President John F. Kennedy, shown here in 1962. Daley kindled early interest in a Kennedy presidency by showcasing him at the 1956 St. Patrick's Day festivities in Chicago. ABBIE ROWE, WHITE HOUSE PHOTOGRAPHS; COURTESY OF JOHN F. KENNEDY PRESIDENTIAL LIBRARY AND MUSEUM, BOSTON; WIKIMEDIA COMMONS.

Campaign button for perennial candidate and also-ran Lar Daly, sporting his Uncle Sam costume and deeply held "America First" convictions. COURTESY OF KEN ZURSKI; HTTPS:// UNREMEMBEREDHISTORY .COM/2016/02/01/THE -TIRELESS-CANDIDATE -LAR-DALY-AND-THE-ART -OF-LOSING-ELECTIONS/.

Frenzied young Beatles fans mob Chicago's Midway Airport to catch a glimpse of their idols as they disembark from the aircraft hours before their scheduled concert at the International Amphitheater, September 1964. CHICAGO HISTORY MUSEUM; ICHI-174056; CHICAGO DAILY NEWS, INC.

Anne McGlone Burke with two special-needs children, Pullman Park, Chicago, 1965. PHOTO COURTESY OF ANNE MCGLONE BURKE.

Justice Burke with three para-Olympians at the fiftieth anniversary of Special Olympics in Chicago, 2018. PHOTO COURTESY OF ANNE MCGLONE BURKE.

THE LEANING TOWER WHY?

That metropolitan Chicago shows off a perfectly detailed ninety-four-foot replica of Italy's Leaning Tower of Pisa adjacent to the YMCA straddling the border between suburban Niles and the Windy City is testament to the primal energies of a poised and cerebral man of an earlier generation who was dismissed as a well-meaning eccentric, but who was a business leader with a generous spirit.

Although the locals rarely give it a passing thought as they zoom east and west down busy Touhy Avenue racing past strip malls to the interstate highway, or to the clusters of office buildings, light industry, and motels, visitors to northeast Illinois are usually quite startled by this curiosity of "roadside America" and its equally unusual story.

The oddly placed, incongruous structure is a monument to the early Renaissance and the good people of Pisa. It was conceived in the fertile imagination of Robert Alexander Ilg Sr. (1879–1964), inventor, industrialist, and owner of Ilg Electrical Ventilating Company.

As inventions and inventors go, one might say that Ilg was the direct descendant of Nikola Tesla. Tesla is the "rediscovered" scientist on the minds of twenty-first-century documentary filmmakers, historians, pop-culture enthusiasts, and conspiracy theorists who believe that Tesla was murdered by the government for an alleged discovery of a "super weapon" that could potentially destroy the world. Inside his lab at 89 Liberty Street in New York, Tesla invented a much more practical and verifiable device: the first electrical induction motor.[1]

In 1888, he sold his original design to George Westinghouse, inventor of the rotary steam engine and a principal figure in the "War of Currents," pitting Thomas Edison, proponent of Direct Current (DC) against Westinghouse and Harold Pitney Brown's Alternating Current (AC). In 1889, as Edison's losses mounted and DC gained the upper hand through popular acceptance, acquisition, and financial merger, Westinghouse mounted a prop on the motor shaft to refine and develop the modern electric fan.[2]

In 1905 Robert Ilg invented an electric motor for fans that could work with voltages in both AC and DC currents. Ilg improved the motor cooling design to make motors more easily adaptable for hot air applications. It was an unheralded breakthrough and a catalyst for the launch of a Chicago-based industrial cooling firm and a national product line that ventilated schools, factories, restaurants, gymnasiums, and public buildings decades before the advent of modern air conditioning.

Partnering with Samuel Weis of New Orleans who agreed to provide the start-up money, Ilg incorporated the Electric Ventilating Company in an industrial factory spread across an entire city block at 2850 North Pulaski Road. Ilg set aside part of the building as a testing laboratory for the development of ventilation equipment. The company grew and prospered during the boom times of the 1920s when Ilg and his design team developed a household division that sold the first kitchen exhaust fans and "night cooling fans" (pedestal and desktop fans) to consumers. Commercial window fans gained popularity during this period and were marketed to the public through the Westinghouse distribution network. During World War II, the firm secured lucrative government contracts to build fans and duct systems to eradicate corrosive marine life for the US Navy and merchant marines and electric and gas heaters for the army. The company received the prestigious Navy E Award for its contributions to the war effort.

Hundreds of tradesmen, mechanical engineers, and laborers earned substantial wages in the Pulaski plant making these products during a hectic era that helped define the city of Chicago as the industrial workhorse of the midcontinent.[3] Robert Ilg, idea man, held two patents for an air conditioning and filtering device, and a motor protector for ventilating fans. Laboratory tinkering and inventions aside, Ilg is better remembered for his social legacy and concerns for the well-being of his workforce. He was among the first to offer profit-sharing benefits to employees.

With the intention of maintaining a happy and contented workforce, he landscaped twenty acres of land for employees at 6200 Touhy Avenue in Niles, calling this private wooded recreational area Ilgair Park. The natural country setting for weekend escapes by city folk employed in the factory featured beautiful tree-lined walkways, artistic foot bridges, a manmade lake adjoining a decorative windmill, an observation tower, and a miniature island. Ilg built a home for his family and added two swimming pools, a wading pool, and a picnic grove in this mostly rural setting fifteen miles northwest of downtown Chicago. Ilgair Park opened to the public during the 1920s, with a promotional advertising brochure, "Where Nature Welcomes You Royally."

Before World War II, the close-in suburb of Niles (originally known as Dutchman's Point), was undeveloped farmland, punctuated by small grocery stores, roadhouses, and gambling dives on the western fringe of the village. After the war, rapid suburbanization beckoned aspiring working-class city people into the former Dutchman's Point hinterland, through the lure of single-family home ownership of ranch houses, split levels, and Cape Cods at affordable rates and low taxes. The arrival and resettlement of first- and second-generation Europeans from city neighborhoods quadrupled the population in less than twenty-five years.

When the burgeoning community needed water, a water tower was commissioned by Ilg and built over a period of two years during the depths of the Great Depression (from 1932 to 1934) near the nondescript intersection of Touhy and Mobile Avenues. Not wanting an unsightly steel tower and ugly pump house to mar the tranquility and appearance of Ilgair Park, Ilg solicited bids from structural engineers for a replica of Pisa's famous Leaning Tower, which tilts seventeen feet from the perpendicular with a first-floor diameter of twenty-eight feet. One after another potential contractor walked away from the commission as Ilg was told that the cost would be prohibitive, the probability of collapse enormous, and the risk—frankly, not worth it.

But the inventor-industrialist could not be dissuaded. This leaning tower would serve a utilitarian purpose as a water-storage tower and standpipe for swimming pools, and would be a replica of the twelfth-century relic in distant Pisa, Italy—though, at ninety-four-feet tall—only half its size. Robert Ilg dedicated the tower to the eternal memory of astronomer, physicist, and philosopher Galileo Galilei (1564–1642).[4]

Constructed with great care and attention to detail, the foundation measures twenty-eight feet in diameter, and houses the water pumps used to supply the swimming pools. The California architect promised that the one-piece, L-shaped structure, with the lowest portion buried deep in the ground, would not collapse or fail. It could withstand an earthquake, although earthquakes of a magnitude to knock down the tower are unheard of in the Great Lakes region. Nearby Lake Caldwell, a tiny, placid pond, added to the rustic setting of Ilg's soaring structure.

To enhance his tower, Ilg traveled to Pisa, in northern Italy, in 1935, to purchase five antique, cast-iron bells. Three of the bells were very old, dating back to 1623, 1735, and 1747, with a fourth dating back to 1912. Researchers are convinced that at least one of the bells hung in a church in Cavezzo, Italy, 150 miles northeast of Pisa. Further investigation revealed that the bell of more recent vintage had been cast in a San Francisco foundry.

Mounted in the Tower belfry with the help of Ilg's teen-aged son, Paul, the bells chimed only occasionally in the coming years. However, they were true works of art, greatly admired by out-of-breath visitors who climbed the stairs to the top. Italian artisans had applied a hand-forged seventeenth-century crucifix to one of the bells.

Ilg hired craftsmen to inlay imported Italian tiles on the stairs and a stone relief of Madonna and child above the entrance way that at one time early in the tower's history led to a gift shop. Visitors to the site paid a ten-cent entrance fee to ascend the ninety-four balcony walkway steps of the tower for a far less stunning view of Chicago's sprawling Northwest Side. By 1940, health department regulations stiffened, forcing Ilg to close the swimming pools. The park was also closed. Thereafter, the property went into slow decline. In November 1949, Ilg and his wife, Marie, relocated to their summer home in San Francisco, where they would live out the remainder of their days.

Ilg, who passed away in San Francisco at age eighty-five on Christmas Day 1964, sold his company to Carrier Corporation and donated the grounds, valued at $100,000 in the 1950s, to the Skokie Valley YMCA, which was desperately in need of a permanent facility. The owner attached two important conditions to his gift. A pledge had to be given that the Tower would remain standing and intact until at least 2059. He further stipulated that the new owners should budget at least $500 a year for maintenance and upkeep (failing to take into account spiraling inflation), or ownership would revert to the family heirs.

YMCA workers raised $54,000 for an improvement fund to refurbish the park, but the money fell well short of the $2.7 million cost of construction for a planned nine-story facility with two hundred sleeping rooms, handball and squash courts, a gymnasium, a skating rink, and swimming pools. A new name was given to Ilgair Park—the Leaning Tower Y.

Ground broke on November 11, 1963, and the forty-eight-thousand-square-foot Y opened January 23, 1966. The Leaning Tower, rescued from a rendezvous with oblivion, required costly renovations and upkeep the YMCA could not afford. Robert Ilg passed away on Christmas Day 1964 at the midpoint of construction.

On April 30, 1991, Mayor Nicholas B. Blase, an old-school politician and civic booster who had ruled the roost in Niles continuously since 1961, announced a sister-city agreement with Pisa, Italy (an industrial city of a hundred thousand people on the Arno River), after five years of on-again, off-again negotiation.[5] Cables, letters, urgent appeals from village officials, and US congressman Frank Annunzio had mostly fallen on deaf ears. Apart from the towers—one made of Italian marble, the other, a concrete-reinforced replica, Niles and Pisa had little in common. Niles officials boasted that 40 percent of their community was Italian. After a closer look, however, the estimate had to be revised downward to 25 percent.

The city of Pisa dispatched Monsignor Lido Ferretti to Niles in 1988 to take a closer look at the tower. He sent back photos and drawings, but no decision on the sister status matter could be reached. Then, in 1991, Mayor Giacomino Granchi of Pisa relented and Mayor Blase sent his delegation to Italy to formalize a sister-city agreement. Granchi praised the persistence of Niles and apologized for the baffling five-year delay.

Meanwhile, in that same year, Ilg Industries (reacquired by Ilg Management in 1977), shuttered the doors of the factory after the Northern Trust Company, the firm's main creditor, froze its assets. The venerable old firm with reported annual sales of $10 million and a hundred employees on the payroll faced certain extinction unless a buyer quickly came forward. Late in 1991, the American CoolAir Corporation stepped in to purchase the firm. The Chicago operation then moved to Jacksonville, Florida, and is today, Ilg Industries Division of American CoolAir.

Out of respect for Robert Ilg's memory, and his desire for the tower to remain in perpetuity, Mayor Blase and the village trustees approved a $1.2 million renovation project in 1995, necessary for its upkeep. Year-long improvements were made to the lighting, exterior façade, "piazza" area, four fountains, and a thirty-foot reflecting pool. In an ill-advised agreement made with the YMCA, the village of Niles leased the tower from the owner, prompting growing criticism from village officials as the years passed and problems of deterioration mounted. "For reasons known to God, the Devil and a few politicians, the Village of Niles contracted with the Y.M.C.A. to rent a parcel of land from the 'Y' which included the then-dilapidated Tower," complained trustee Chris Hanusiak to the *Niles Herald-Spectator* newspaper on January 16, 2014. "The Village spent oodles of money to fix it and now it's falling apart. The Y.M.C.A. spends zero dollars but reaps all the benefits."

Expressing understandable skepticism about the tower's long-term value as a local landmark, a minority opinion held out hope that the 1930s-era relic be knocked down along with the YMCA's multistory hotel, paving the way for a full redevelopment of the property as an arts, recreation, and entertainment center.

The trustees spared the Niles Leaning Tower from the wrecking ball by acquiring the property in 2017 for a cost of ten dollars with approval to conduct a feasibility study to see what else might be done to spruce up the appearance of the entire area and make it a destination for visitors, residents, and local artists. The estimated $750,000 cost of renovation will be supported through the creation of a Tax Increment Financing (TIF) district. The ambitious marketing plan, titled "The Leaning Tower and the Touhy Corridor Land Use Plan" gained momentum in 2018.

In July of that year, the village removed the five bronze bells from the belfry. Weighing a combined six hundred pounds, Niles officials shipped them to the B. A. Sunderlin Bell foundry in Virginia for a $53,000 refurbishment and the installation of new clappers, headstocks, and a mechanism for all of them to toll automatically. The restoration project with the addition of four newly cast bells concluded a year later. The historic bells were hoisted into position in early December 2019 and for the first time in decades residents heard their luxuriant sound. No longer may it be asked, "For whom the bell tolls?" It tolls for thee.

Inquiries were soon under way to add Robert Ilg's tower to the National Register of Historic Places. As kooky and offbeat as it may seem to out-of-towners, the Leaning Tower YMCA stands as a monument to one man's fertile imagination, ingenuity, and civic-mindedness that for now, highlights an otherwise drab landscape.

A WORLD'S FAIR OF RAILROADING

for a modest admission price of just thirty cents, Chicagoans of all ages were guaranteed a fun and fact-filled history lesson, with excitement and thrills galore in the warm and languid summer days of 1948 along fifty acres of Park District land in Burnham Park abutting the city's sprawling south lakefront. The railroad fair, a planned exhibition, celebrated the centenary of Chicago's first steam locomotive, the Pioneer, in 1848. The importance of that defining and pivotal event for the future growth and development of Chicago, a city of restless and constant transformation, cannot be underestimated.

It ushered in the era of cross-country travel linking the East with the West and bringing to our lakefront city in the coming decades land speculators, entrepreneurs, promoters, hustlers, immigrant families, and ordinary men and women who dared to dream.

"Chicago . . . is the greatest railroad center in the world!" exclaimed Hollis Field in a 1910 essay. "There are twenty-eight trunk lines of railroad having terminals in Chicago. They come from every point of the compass. No railway passenger passes through Chicago. To continue on his journey in any direction he must debark from his train and seek another. That other train may be under the train sheds fifty feet away; it may be a mile distant at any one of the five union stations in Chicago—Park Row, Dearborn, LaSalle, Union or Grand Central."[1]

A century after the Pioneer chugged into the city, the Chicago Railroad Fair threw open its gates on July 20, 1948, with a ring-a-ding-ding exuberance unmatched since the two world's fairs. Promoters promised enough railroading equipment to satisfy a trainload of little boys, plus many notable feature attractions, including forty-five exhibits and sideshows for young and old alike spread across a mile-long promenade from Twentieth to Thirtieth Streets. The nation's railroads were eager to showcase history and tout their bragging rights at the midpoint of the twentieth century; a time when the passenger airlines were an expensive, if not uncertain, novelty beyond the means of the average commuter and vacationer. The train remained the best and most reliable way to get from one place to another, or so it seemed. The great railroad fair expressed an optimistic belief that passenger rail travel would hold together forever more.

The Santa Fe constructed a southwestern motif represented by six Native American tribes in ceremonial raiment in a setting of cactus and pueblos. The rodeo ring accommodated an anticipated thousand spectators an hour. Construction crews labored around the clock in the early spring months applying finishing touches to a five- thousand-seat grandstand for visitors to observe the fair's main attraction: the hour-and-a-half-long "Wheels A-Rolling" pageant of 220 costumed actors recreating scenes from American history and railroading adventures spanning a 450-foot-wide stage.

A dude ranch allowed visitors to witness cowboys performing rope tricks, and a replica of Sun Valley with an ice-skating rink added to the theme of western expansion. All in all, it was a coast-to-coast historical epoch made possible by the railroads.

"Crazy Horse," a narrow-gauge mining train conveyed visitors to all major attractions, including a replica of the Chicago and Northwestern's original city depot on the north side of the Chicago River at Wells Street (the present site of the Merchandise Mart) built in 1849.[2] Throughout the day, a small movie theater aired classic railroad-themed films including *Union Pacific* and the *Harvey Girls*.

Famous old and original steam, diesel, and electric locomotives and passenger cars of yesteryear and the present day were on prominent display, including the sleek and magnificent Pioneer Zephyr, a gleaming stainless steel Art Deco, diesel-powered passenger train designed by the Budd Company for the Chicago, Burlington, and Quincy in 1934. The Pioneer is now on permanent exhibit at the Chicago History Museum, and the Pioneer Zephyr is showcased at the Museum of Science and Industry. Promoters exhibited the Empire Express No. 999 and replicas of older rolling stock including the Tom Thumb and the John Bull. Mary Brady Jones, the widow of the legendary railroad hero "Casey Jones" (John Luther Jones, 1863–1900), who was immortalized in a popular ballad of the day following his untimely death in the disastrous wreck of the old Cannonball Express, was on hand to answer questions and accept the good wishes of the visitors and promoters.

Despite the future uncertainties of rail versus air travel, a consortium of thirty-eight of the nation's largest commercial and industrial lines vigorously supported this commemoration of the "century of progress"—one hundred years of hauling people and freight across the country with purposeful vision, confidence, and optimism. It was promoted as a "world's fair of railroading." Otherwise, why would they have invested this much time and money in an event one might reasonably describe as a costly marketing and public relations gamble?

The idea for this railroad fair did not spring from the fertile mind of Walt Disney or his creative advisors, but from F. V. Koval, public relations expert and assistant to the president of the Chicago and Northwestern (CNW) line, successor railroad to the old Galena and Chicago Union line, the first railroad constructed out of Chicago following the Pioneer's successful completion of its first run on October 10, 1848. William B. Ogden, Chicago's first mayor, was the driving force behind the organization of the CNW.

The Chicago City Council and Mayor Martin Kennelly enthusiastically endorsed plans for the "Chicago Railroad Fair: A Century on Wheels," with the formal approval of the Chicago Association of Commerce after a closed-door session at the LaSalle Hotel on February 2, 1948. The city's bigwigs unanimously chose Lenox R. Lohr, president of the Museum of Science and Industry to head the planning committee. Lohr, who previously oversaw the Century of Progress program as its general manager, took a leave of absence from his museum duties to superintend this latest lakefront extravaganza.[3]

Thereafter it was a race against time to build and complete the massive fairgrounds (on the site of the 1933 world's fair) by opening day. Forty contractors and their work crews had only four-and-a-half months to fit out the entire campus and provide underground sewage, water, and light with fencing, walkways, and temporary buildings. By the time July rolled around, the project became the city's most ambitious undertaking since the construction of the Century of Progress in 1933, and the timing was right for a summertime extravaganza of this scale and dimension. Chicago had come through the lean days of breadlines and depression and the devastating war that followed.

No new skyscraper had arisen in the central business district since the early 1930s. A housing shortage and a spirit of restlessness made it hard for many returning GIs to adjust to the ordinary routines of postwar living. The skies were blanketed with a grimy haze of industrial pollution that mixed with the stench of stockyards and steelyards. The Cubs and White Sox were well on their way to finishing 1948 dead last in the same season for the only time in city baseball history. The railroad fair swept Chicagoans away from these miseries, if only for a few hours.

Jazz drummer Al Carter—a famous Chicago "first-nighter" remembered as the first man to enter through the gates of the 1933 Century of Progress World's Fair, and the first in line to soar to the observation deck atop the Sears Tower when the building opened to the public on June 22, 1974—held the first ticket to the railroad fair.

It was a big hit from day one. First week's attendance topped 350,000. By early September more than 1.5 million passed through the main gates on Twenty-Third Street. Encouraged by the public response, the committee pushed back the scheduled closing date of September 6 to the end of the month. "Most gratifying feature of the Fair is the fact that more than sixty per cent of the attendance has come from beyond the 100-mile radius of Chicago," beamed Lohr.[4]

Walt Disney, impresario of Hollywood movie magic was one of its most enthusiastic spectators.[5] With animator Ward Kimball, Disney visited the railroad fair after a hasty inspection of Greenfield Village in Dearborn, Michigan. Disney came away with an idea for a theme park of his own—based on a pleasing mix of the science, commerce, and history he had observed in the Midwest—in a self-contained land parcel out in Anaheim, California. In 1955, the Chicago-born showman opened Disneyland with a tip of the cap to the railroad fair of 1948.

There would only be one more railroad fair. Lenox Lohr and his team parlayed their 1948 success by adding the "Cypress Gardens" water show and a newfangled invention called the "Vitarama," a slide-projection system projecting multiple nine-foot high, six-and-a-half-foot-wide images, giving a three-dimensional look inside a large hall constructed for that purpose. The fair of 1949 ended its record run of 2.5 million visitors on October 2. Despite hopeful predictions for a bigger and better fair in 1950, Chicago's railroad show closed out a glorious two-year run, never to return.

A watershed moment in the age of the iron horse, the fair marked the beginning of a slow but sentimental farewell to a magnificent era of leisurely passenger travel poised to expire in a country more and more on the go. The relentless expansion of the commercial airline industry and the construction of the interstate highway system closed out a time and place many still cherish. By 1971 nearly all of Chicago's ornate and glamorous old train stations fell to the wrecking ball, and the legendary trains bearing the names 20th Century Limited, Fast Flying Virginian, Shoreland 400, and Super Chief became faded relics of a bygone era. Who among the throngs of excited children accompanied by their parents could have foreseen at the time that this fair would soon be followed by the apocalyptic demise of the American passenger rail system?

In place of the railroad fair in 1950, the *Chicago Tribune*, with the backing of its publisher, the assertive and antagonistic colonel Robert R. McCormick (with Lenox Lohr steering the helm), threw their resources behind an all-purpose "Chicago Fair." The colonel envisioned this as a yearly event, declaring to his radio listeners on June 18, 1950, the intent to establish the fair as a permanent lakefront exposition, dramatizing achievements in agriculture, commerce, industry, and science with an emphasis on history and the pioneer spirit. However, attendance did not match the numbers achieved by the promoters of the railroad fair, and the outbreak of the Korean War clouded plans for a yearly continuation.

Mainly due to the war, the 1951 event was canceled. Civic backers remained enthusiastic, however, and pushed forward with their plans for 1952, but the means of funding the expensive gala were problematic. Tourism promoters turned to the Illinois legislature to create a "fair fund" to raise $800,000 to meet expenses.

The legislature obliged by imposing a 1 percent state levy on racetrack betting. Mayor Martin Kennelly, encouraged by this rare show of political solidarity between Springfield and Chicago, pushed for a renewal of the fair in 1952, but that never came about. The $800,000 revenue appropriation fell short of the estimated $1 million in additional monies necessary to cover all costs.

Hotel magnates Conrad Hilton and Colonel Henry Crown pledged a sizeable contribution. However, 1952 passed with no Chicago fair. In June 1957, under the leadership of Mayor Daley, a sixteen-day "Chicagoland Fair" welcomed visitors to Navy Pier celebrating the spectacle of progress, industry, expanding job opportunity, and free trade in the middle of America through the stewardship of the Association of Commerce. Puppeteer and children's television personality Fran Allison served as the official fair hostess. A legendary Chicago sportscaster, the genial and upbeat Jack Brickhouse, opened the WGN-TV "Man at the Fair" telecast on the first day with characteristic optimism: "I am speaking from the capitol of a continent!"[6] Few Chicagoans of that feel-good era would dare to disagree with the sentiment.

Two years later, in 1959, the city celebrated the opening of the St. Lawrence Seaway with an International Fair held on Navy Pier, once again sponsored by the Association of Commerce. Today, no one remembers the Chicago Fair, but undoubtedly a different type of fair of more humble origin comes to mind. It is familiar to nearly everyone who has passed through the primary grades and high school.

Perhaps inspired by the 1950 Chicago Fair (but then again maybe not), Schurz High School teacher Robert Schwachtgen came up with a brilliant and motivational idea for a Chicago Public School science fair in 1951. His first competitive event, held in the Museum of Science and Industry, featured just one hundred exhibits with meager prizes offered to the winners. Within five years however, nearly every school-age child tinkered in the garage or basement with dad and mom hoping to perfect his or her own miraculous gadget of the scientific age.

THE WINDY CITY
SONGBIRD

C hicago's sprawling West Side "Valley District," punctuated by a dense cluster of gray-stone walkups, three-flats, saloons, factories, and modest worker cottages, comprised Chicago's "Bloody Twentieth Ward" in the 1920s, the decade of bootlegging mayhem.

It was the bailiwick of Prohibition rumrunners, stickup men, crooked politicians, and champion brawlers in the years leading up to World War II. A young man, if he had any hope at all of escaping the grind of poverty and gang violence had to be nimble, quick on his feet, and possess the ability to think fast and act. The poorly illuminated path to future success for a poor boy growing up in a Valley neighborhood limited the career choices one could make in such a confusing and desultory environment as this. The priesthood and politics were often the best and only hope for an escape. For some, it was the *only* way out.

Early in life, Valley boy Martin Snyder caught an unlucky break. At the age of six, he mangled his left leg in a streetcar mishap that left him with a permanent limp. Thereafter, Valley district wiseacres cruelly tagged him with the unfortunate nickname, "Moe the Gimp." Later in life, the denizens of the Randolph Street theater crowd, whose favor he so desperately coveted, addressed Snyder as "Colonel Gimp." It was neither a term of respect or affection—but derision for a swaggering tough guy with a yen for the footlights who early on chose thuggery and intimidation as his calling card.

Moe Snyder's education never advanced past the fourth grade. He thought it was a waste of time and didn't care much for all that "learnin." He quit school to scrounge a few dollars a week peddling the *Chicago American* on Loop street corners. Snyder advanced to "the circulation department," and was given the job of beating up newsboys and the distributors hawking the rival newspapers during Chicago's violent circulation wars of the pre-World War I era.

It was a hard life, but the glib, fast-talking Snyder made the rounds and established important connections with big-shot West Side politicians circulating through city hall and the county building. One of them, Dennis Egan, served as a bailiff in the municipal court before winning a seat in the Chicago City Council as alderman of the "Bloody Twentieth" Ward. Dennis Egan owned a tough political saloon on Maxwell Street where he employed a number of gang thugs to act as his "street muscle." Egan rewarded his loyal cronies with high-paying patronage jobs in city hall.[1]

This was the world that beckoned Moe Snyder, and Egan recognized the lad's potential and put him to work in the Department of Sanitation. "And den I got a job as an investigator wit' da Prosecuta's office," Snyder recounted to a packed Los Angeles courtroom in 1938.[2]

In city hall and the justice mills of Chicago, he rubbed elbows with assistant state's attorneys, judges, and the criminal mouthpieces that appeared before them. In the thick of things, Moe managed to keep his nose clean and his chestnuts out of the fire. In Chicago parlance, Moe the Gimp was a "well connected man." Chicago in the 1920s, remembered by Genevieve Forbes Herrick as a "Venus de Milo with a crime record; a beautiful face, but she probably lost her arms in a holdup," spelled the world of Moe Snyder and his Damon Runyon-esque chums in those bountiful years.[3]

Like many city hall hangers-on who collected a check for doing as little as possible in that swaggering feel-good era just after World War I, Moe intuitively mingled among the people who mattered. He talked out of the side of his mouth with a cigar firmly clenched between his teeth and a fedora perched at a jaunty angle on the top of his head to disguise a receding hairline. The Gimp was no Rhodes scholar, but he had "street smarts." He bet on the long shot at Lincoln Fields on race day. He had his picture taken in the winner's circle afterward and flashed a certain, undeniable, rough-around-the-edges panache the vaudeville crowd found amusing, just as long as they stayed out of his cross-hairs.

The demimonde congregated along Randolph Street, Chicago's Rialto, where theatrical people buzzed the cabarets and gin joints from Wabash west to LaSalle after the final curtain dropped on the last stage show of the evening. Its living breathing heart was the intersection of Randolph and Clark where the College Inn inside the old Sherman House Hotel was the place to see and be seen directly across the street from city hall.

Years after the footlights had noticeably dimmed on the famous intersection, Snyder confided to journalist John Blades that "the Sherman House was the hangout in the old days for show people. I used to know some bootleggers and I got liquor for people in show business. I had too much sense to be a bootlegger myself."[4] In his capacity as a "song plugger" for recording studios and the publishers of sheet music, Snyder prowled the hotel bars and gained back-stage admittance to the vaudeville houses, show lounges, and ballrooms, where he cozied up to the big stars of the day and their managers. With cigarette lighter in hand, he was quick with a joke and to light up their smoke and would likely say to them, "Now I have dis here little number I'd like to show you dat will work really swell in your act."

"I knew [Al] Jolson, [Jimmy] Durante, Lou Clayton," he bragged. "I worked for a song publisher. [I was] going around to houses like the Majestic and the Bijou at Halsted and Jackson asking the performers to sing our songs. That's how I met Ruth Etting. She was working at the Marigold Gardens."[5]

Ruth Etting. At the peak of her fame, Etting's adoring fans knew her as "Chicago's Sweetheart." She might have belonged to the Windy City, but in the heyday of early radio and vaudeville, her fame was national. Born on a twenty-acre farm near David City, Nebraska, and orphaned at age five, Ruthie went to live with her grandfather, the president of the local bank in town. The child showed great aptitude for drawing. With the blessings and encouragement from her uncle Alex, the mayor of the rural hamlet, Etting left home in 1917 to seek acclaim in Chicago where, for a brief time, she studied at the Academy of Fine Arts.

Etting worked hard to pay for her education. She took a part-time job in the chorus line at the Marigold Gardens, a former German *bierstube* at Grace Street and Broadway formerly known as De Berg's Grove until owner Karl Eitel converted it into a two thousand–seat cabaret featuring floor shows, musical comedy, and dancing.[6] Prohibition became the law of the land in 1920 forcing management to oblige its patrons by providing a leather "sleeve" discreetly tacked underneath each table for the benefit of the thirsty customer wishing to conceal the flask of gin spirits smuggled in off the street.

It wasn't until after eleven P.M.—when the cabaret crowd settled in for the nocturnal merriment performed by dance bands, chorus girls, and baggy-pants comics like Roscoe "Fatty" Arbuckle (motion picture star of the silent era)— that the "steppers and strutters" kicked into high gear. The late-hour scheduling had one advantage though. It freed up time for Etting to put in a five-hour day at a little tailor shop at 72 W. Randolph Street, designing costumes for the performers working up and down the rialto.

Life might have continued on at a dreadfully ordinary pace for this aspiring artist and chorus-line hoofer if not for the roving eye of Martin Snyder who spotted her up on stage one night as he called upon the Eitel brothers with a satchel full of show tones for sale. It was 1921—two years before Karl Eitel closed the cabaret permanently and reopened the Marigold as a boxing hall for club fighters.

Snyder made the approach. He boasted that he was a theatrical agent of local renown and served as singer Al Jolson's personal bodyguard. "I know everyone in this business!" he would have likely said. "Stick with me kid and you'll go places!" Etting earned twenty-five dollars a week at the Marigold and awaited her first big break. Deciding that Moe Snyder might just be her ticket to stardom, she put her trust in his connections. Before the year ended, the Gimp divorced his wife and abandoned his daughter Edith so that he could run off to Crown Point, Indiana, after bullying Ruth into a quickie marriage. They were betrothed by a justice of the peace on July 21, 1921. There was no honeymoon. Snyder booked a hotel room where the newlyweds stayed for one night before returning to Chicago so Ruth could resume her work. Etting paid for the rental.

Back home, Moe Snyder, through the force of his personality, quickly took charge. He scheduled the bookings and haggled over minute details with the producers while Ruth managed the finances. In the early days, before Etting became a star, Snyder huddled in the doorways outside the theaters and cabarets of Chicago pushing a few dollars into the hands of passersby to go inside and clap and cheer Etting's performance, so she would not be embarrassed by empty seats. "I got her a job in the Terrace Gardens [the nightclub inside the Hotel Morrison where Chicago politicians often gathered] and some of the kids dere [sic] used to call her Miss City Hall."[7]

Snyder pulled Etting out of the chorus line and succeeded in making her a celebrity. Her big break in show business came when the College Inn booked her for a series of performances. She was an immediate hit with the collegiate crowd who flocked to the famous nightclub to hear her torch songs. "They packed tightly around the bandstand and swayed gently to the soothing caress of her voice," noted one reporter.[8]

Although he boasted that other major stars clamored for his services as a booking agent and promoter the Gimp insisted that Ruthie would remain his one and only client. What he lacked in manners and charm, he made up for in his willfulness, aggression, and an implied threat of a busted noggin for the hapless manager of the show company if he didn't agree to give his sweetie an even break.

"To him," famed Broadway gossip columnist Ed Sullivan observed, "the world was a battleground rather than an oyster. To him the world was full of real and fancied enemies, and he left his hotel each night ready to do battle with them. He eyed everybody with distrust and limped through the world with a cigar in his mouth, a sour look on his face and the little lady in his heart," Sullivan wrote in his syndicated column, "Looking at Hollywood," published in the *Tribune* on October 19, 1938. Snyder said to Sullivan: "Just why I let her get the divorce, I don't know. I wanted to be nice. Nice? I shoulda' hit her in the topper with a couple of slugs, because she give [sic] me a raw deal. I took her from nothin' and made her a big shot. For seventeen years I've been takin' wrong raps for her and this is the gratitude I get!"

That Snyder was a jealous, possessive, and physically abusive husband has never been in doubt. Etting endured fifteen tumultuous years of marriage to the Gimp. Snyder suffered a fall from grace after his wife scored early and impressive successes as a recording artist and stage and motion picture actress. Moe lived off her earnings, blowing Ruth's dough at crap tables and card games in tawdry Chicago, New York, and Hollywood hotel rooms without apology or regret. "All through our married life he never paid one cent of rent. I paid all the bills," Etting related. "He never worked and he always interfered with mine. And his abuse began right after our marriage. Everyone knew about it and talked about it. But I decided I'd have to go ahead despite his surly manner and rough ways."[9]

The pretty chanteuse reached stardom in the Ziegfield Follies singing "Shine on Harvest Moon" in a slow, lazy style that captivated audiences. Through the 1920s and 1930s, Ruth scored a string of national hits including her signature songs "Love Me or Leave Me," "It Happened in Monterey," "Ten Cents a Dance," "Looking at the World through Rose-Colored Glasses," "Thinking of You," and "No, No Nora." She headlined with Eddie Cantor in *Whoopie* and *Roman Scandals* in 1928 and 1933 respectively and toured throughout Europe.

At the height of her career, Etting appeared on numerous radio programs of local and national origin. She pioneered live performance on the new medium of radio with twice nightly gigs on WLS for more than a year, and later sang in the WGN studios for fourteen consecutive weeks in the fall of 1932 on the locally produced program *Music That Satisfies*. Balaban and Katz invited her to appear on stage in their local movie houses as a featured performer prior to the showing of the motion picture—launching a popular entertainment trend that became standard in the industry from the 1930s up through the 1950s. By now, Ruth had become one of the highest paid stars in the entertainment world.

Meanwhile, Colonel Gimp, an unrepentant misogynist tone-deaf to his wife's sadness and mounting anxieties, broke Etting's spirit and dragged her down emotionally. His bullying and overbearing manner were deeply resented in the business.

Florenz Ziegfeld, who hired Etting for the Follies of 1927 based on Irving Berlin's personal recommendation, had Snyder bodily thrown out of Etting's

New York dressing room during a performance of the Follies one night. He was barred from a number of smaller clubs but kept on making trouble. "Snyder fought with everyone and made my life miserable," Ruth attested. "In defiance to Ziegfeld's strict rule, he persisted in coming back stage at every performance. Ziggy and he had a terrific argument and Ziggy forbade him to even enter the theater. After that he used to hang around at the stage door until I was through each night, grumbling and growling and smoking one cigar after another. Life wasn't any fun. It was terrible drudgery. Work. Go home to a hotel room; get up, rehearse, work and then the same dreary procedure over again."[10]

Scarred by her ordeal the Nebraska farm girl returned to her uncle's home on November 15, 1937, announcing her plan for an uncontested divorce from Snyder on the grounds of mental cruelty and desertion. In the final divorce settlement, Etting gave her ex-husband $50,000 in cash to pay off his gambling debts and half-interest in their Beverly Hills home. She testified that part of her earnings paid for a house given to Snyder's mother back in Chicago.

Then, after final papers were signed and Ruth was at last free of her snarling, manipulative ex, she began a romance with thirty-year-old Myrl Alderman, her piano accompanist, song arranger, and a Hollywood gadfly—a married man thirteen years her junior. Alderman, personally recruited and hired by Snyder in 1932, had a reputation as a ladies' man—a "hound" if the truth be known. After the affair became a matter of public record, Alderman's second wife Alma sued Etting for alienation of affection and contributing to the breakup of their marriage, seeking $150,000 in damages. Alma accused her adulterous spouse of a six-day liaison at a Riverside, California, frog ranch where "they carried on their romance." In scintillating testimony, Marty Seliger, owner of the ranch, accused Alderman of conducting a great number of love affairs. In tears, Alma revealed that husband Myrl had not contributed one red cent toward raising their one-year-old daughter Norma Susanne, as she held up the little tyke to the popping flashbulbs of newspaper photographers for added effect. In her deposition, Etting asserted that it wasn't until July 1938, a year *after* Alma filed her complaint, that Alderman first expressed his love to Ruth. His proposal was accepted in October, with a wedding date scheduled once her divorce from Snyder became final.

It was raw, sensational stuff, but the court ruled in Etting's favor and Alma's complaint was dismissed on December 21, 1939. Back East, Moe the Gimp, hearing rumors that Etting and Alderman had been keeping company at football games and prize fights, was livid with jealousy and rage. A prize fight no less! He phoned Ruth from New York with a deadly threat, saying he would fly back and kill her.

The hot-tempered, controlling Snyder decided to kill Alderman instead. He located his intended victim inside the NBC studio on Melrose Avenue in the west end of Los Angeles during the early evening of October 15, 1938. At the point of a gun that he later claimed to have won in a New York City card game, Snyder forced Alderman to accompany him to Etting's alabaster-white home facing the San Bernardino Mountains at 3090 Lake Hollywood Drive "to settle an old score." Inside the home Snyder found his twenty-one-year-old daughter, Edith, whom Ruth had hired as her personal secretary. Eyeing the gun, Edith screamed at the father she detested. "Shoot me if you will daddy! Go ahead!" Snyder told his daughter to shut up and scram.[11]

In the music room, he ordered them to be quiet. But when Alderman arose from the chair and attempted to speak, the Gimp fired a shot into his stomach. He later blamed his actions on drunkenness and asserted that he had only fired in self-defense.

In the confusion, Etting raced upstairs to retrieve a revolver from the bedroom nightstand. Panicked and wild-eyed, she trained the weapon on Snyder, but the Gimp knocked it loose before Ruth could squeeze off a shot. Edith Snyder retrieved the loaded gun and pointed it at her father.

"I've got my revenge. Now you can call the cops!" Moe snarled, seconds before fleeing the residence. Edith chased him out of the front door and fired several errant shots into the night, thankfully missing her mark. Snyder banged on the door of screen star Wayne Morris, announcing that there had been a shooting and for Morris to summon the police. In the police lockup hours after the dramatic shooting, Snyder lost his swagger, telling the cops that he had gambled away a fortune because of the torment the divorce case had caused him. "The ashes of love our love are very cold now," he murmured. "The little lady has hung one on me. But it doesn't matter because all of the old flames are dead—the torch has gone out. I only hope Mr. Alderman gets well and they find some happiness together."[12]

Alderman survived his wounds. Nearing the end of Snyder's trial for attempted murder in December 1938, Myrl exited St. Vincent's Hospital and flew to Las Vegas with Etting where they were betrothed in a wedding chapel ceremony. It had been brought to light that the couple secretly married in Tijuana, Mexico, five months earlier. Now it was official and out in the open. Informed of this development from inside his jail cell, the disbelieving Snyder grumbled to a reporter, "That would be a bum joke to play on a guy."[13]

It was no joke, and despite a vigorous defense put up by Jerry Giesler (attorney of choice for stars caught in the legal crosshairs of 1930s Hollywood), Snyder was found guilty of attempted murder. He won a new trial on a technicality July 24, 1940, but by now, Myrl Alderman and Ruthie had moved on with their lives and declined to appear as prosecution witnesses in the second trial. With no other recourse, Moe was freed by the Los Angeles district attorney. Chastened and despairing, Snyder limped back to his old Chicago haunts to pick up the pieces. He had lost the love of his life to another man. Daughter Edith died of natural causes in a Chicago hospital on August 4, 1939, leaving behind a few worthless trinkets to Ruth Etting, with no mention of her estranged father in her one-page will.

The Gimp came away from his recent travails a broken man. From time to time he was spotted selling newspapers at Frankie Pope's newsstand at Clark and Randolph. This once dapper figure of Chicago nightlife and the local race tracks lived as a down-and-outer at the old City Hall Square Hotel, and worked for a time in the city water pipe extension bureau. John Blades located him in 1975 working as a mail sorter in city hall. Snyder was seventy-seven years old, suffering from chest pain, and verbalized his intent to "take a dive" out of the window of his hotel room. In a regimented world, the "devil-may-care" attitude of Snyder completely evaporated. He expressed contrition for his misspent life and his treatment of Etting and generously praised Mayor Richard J. Daley for giving him a job when others would not. "You've heard of Christ?" he asked. "You've heard of Moses? Daley belongs with them. The Three Musketeers."[14] Snyder lived out the remainder of his days in Chicago and died at the ripe old age of eighty-seven on November 9, 1981.

Myrl Alderman, accused of a romantic tryst with actress Dorothy Lamour inside a Hollywood bar by the first Mrs. Alderman and a rebuttal witness during her alienation of affection lawsuit against Etting, sustained war wounds in the service of his country. He died in 1966 after twenty-eight years of marital contentment with Etting who made a brief comeback in March 1947 after signing on for a three-week singing engagement at the Copacabana in New York. "I thought it might be fun to see if I'm forgotten," she informed columnist Louella Parsons.[15] Ruth was fifty-one and had no lingering desire to renew her singing career once her contract ended. She retired to her husband's home in Colorado Springs and faded into obscurity until MGM commenced production on *Love Me or Leave Me*, the cinematic retelling of the famous love triangle starring James Cagney as Snyder, Doris Day as Ruth Etting, and Cameron Mitchell as Myrl Alderman (his first name changed to "Johnny" in the script).

The motion picture earned six Academy Award nominations including one for James Cagney as best actor (his last) and came away with a win in the category of Best Motion Picture Story. Unamused by Daniel Fuchs's screenplay and Charles Vidor's direction, Snyder lost his temper. "They had a scene that showed me shooting that guy in the back. You can bet your underwear I didn't do that. He pulled a gun on me first. To give you an idea of how God damned silly they are, it's my left leg that's on the bum, and Cagney is walking round all through that movie dragging his right leg!"[16] If we accept Snyder's word at face value, how was it possible for Alderman to have brandished a gun at the Gimp when in fact Snyder aimed the gun at *him*?

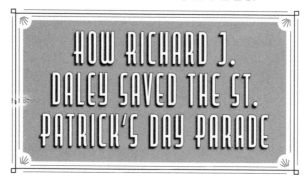

HOW RICHARD J. DALEY SAVED THE ST. PATRICK'S DAY PARADE

I n this most Irish of cities where the wearin' of the green, the drinkin' of the Guinness, and St. Paddy's Day merriment carries on from dawn's early light . . . to dawn's early light . . . it is a curiosity of our wonderfully Gaelic heritage that downtown Chicago skipped the parade and its attending revelries from 1901 until 1956. From the horse-and-buggy era to Buddy Holly, State Street merchants shared the blame for nixing the glorious celebration of the Irish diaspora and Ireland's patron saint, who, according to ancient legend, drove the snakes from the *auld sod*.

The St. Patrick's Day parade, as identifiable with city tradition as Mrs. O'Leary's cow, the Chicago Bears, and the Water Tower enjoyed a long and celebratory run beginning in 1843. A jubilant procession of 775 marchers and the colorfully festooned paramilitary Montgomery Guards strutted down rough, unpaved Clark Street to St. Mary's Catholic Church where parish priests conducted a mass shortly before the day's important business commenced—the day-long singing, drinking, and storytelling inside the Saloon Building at Clark and Randolph—Chicago's first city hall.

In 1836 Captain J. B. F. Russell's three-story-tall wood-frame Saloon Building at the southeast corner of Lake Street and Clark celebrated a grand opening. Curiously, the hall did not have so much as a bar for a thirsty citizen to wet his whistle. In the frontier days, the word "saloon" served as a derivative of the French word *salon*, signifying a meeting place or hall. Unquenchable beer-soaked Chicagoans it is said gave added meaning to the word.[1]

As immigration crested in the 1850s and 1860s and membership in the Irish fraternal societies and religious orders increased its ranks, parade day grew more lavish. Irishmen, with shamrocks in their coat lapels and democracy in their hearts paraded the streets to the tune of "Garry Owen" and "Wearing of the Green."

Chicago's proud Irish citizenry "chanted 'America!' to the tune "*God Save Ireland*,'" observed one reporter in 1896. "The sky, the street corners, the

women's bonnets—everything reflected Irish green with American trim-
mings and there wasn't a child of the *auld sod* who could tell which was
Ireland, and which was the United States. St. Patrick was only a symbol,
an excuse for national celebration."[2] The parade was just the warm-up to a
city-wide celebration featuring dance parties in the town markets that continued until three or four in the morning. Couples pranced merrily to the
lively tunes laid down by fiddlers, flutists, and pipers from all sides of town.

Officially, St. Patrick converted the Irish homeland from paganism to
Christianity in the fifth century, and the day of celebration actually marked
his death—not his birth. To current and former generations of Chicagoans
on the outside of the Church, the legend of the patron saint is lost or imma-
terial amid the parade pageantry. The important thing is the display of Irish
pride before the eyes of the world. Chicago mayors often declared a public
holiday and urged employers to give workers the day off out of respect for
the wishes of city hall. In 1897, the fraternal societies unexpectedly called the
whole thing off because they had "exhausted their treasuries in benevolent
work" during a rough winter, a time when so many who were rendered
homeless and starving were on the public dole.

The big parade resumed in 1898 and continued on for three more years.
However, with much regret the time-honored custom ended following a
stupendous 1901 gala the lads remembered for years to come. Major Bob
Monahan, parade grand marshal, astride his prancing horse led the procession out of Haymarket Square at Randolph and Des Plaines Street on the
Near West Side. An estimated forty thousand marchers circled around the
Loop, headed east down Jackson Boulevard to Michigan, west to Wells Street
and the reviewing stand outside the County Building where Mayor Carter
Harrison, the political potentates, and Archbishop Patrick A. Feehan, the
venerable prelate, tipped their hats.[3] The throngs of spectators saved their
loudest applause for the heroes of the Irish-American Ambulance Service,
recently returned from the Boer War in South Africa.

Amid the patriotism and good cheer, there were larger concerns that had
to be taken into account. The blustery March weather imperiled the health of
the old-timers. The archdiocese fretted over the number of reported deaths
stemming from pneumonia and related diseases of the lung and dissuaded
the Irish fellowship societies from renewing the permits for another year.
The *Tribune*, on March 16, 1911, commenting on the disappearance of tradition, offered another reason. "The old-timers, the men who marched behind
the band are fast passing away. The American born or 'country born,' as
he is called by those from across the Atlantic, would prefer to ride in an

automobile than step out to the strains of an inspiring air. That is one reason why the St. Patrick's Day Parade was abandoned in Chicago."

Without a parade to call their own the Irish societies hosted holiday feasts, choral performances, and theatrical productions, in the big downtown hotels and out in the neighborhoods with traditional religious observance at old St. Patrick's Church at Randolph and Des Plaines Avenue. During the 1936 services, an estimated 450,000 Irish-Catholics attempted to crowd into the ancient church. The annual Celtic Ball at White City, the famous South Side amusement mark of yesteryear hosted 15,000 Sons of Erin belonging to the United Celtic-American Societies at a gala ball held each year.

Minus the raucous street celebration of former years, matters were never quite the same. The Irish Fellowship Club, founded in 1901, sponsored the largest and most notable gathering in town, the annual St. Patrick's Day dinner. Louis Sullivan's majestic Auditorium Theater and Hotel provided a staid and decorous backdrop for the thousand tony, cash-paying patrons of high social ranking who attended each year. In 1907, Vice President Charles Fairbanks arrived by train bringing with him tidings of good cheer from President Theodore Roosevelt.

Chicago's proud South Side Irish revived the lost parade tradition in 1951 by inaugurating their own pageant of green, white, and gold (the colors of the Irish flag) along Seventy-Ninth Street in the Gresham community to Loomis Avenue near Hanley's House of Happiness. At that time, the neighborhood was 75 percent Irish.

The South Side parade, a grand and opulent 1950s public display, competed with a heavily promoted West Side parade along Madison Street. The West Siders began their annual celebration in 1952 when the St. Mel's High School Band and a contingent of marchers set off from Madison and Hamlin en route to the Keymen's Club Ballroom a half-block distant, where the Crossroads of Irish American Entertainment in America met up. The event grew in popularity among first- and second-generation residents who had emigrated from the west of Ireland and settled nearby. Merchants and important civic leaders representing the neighborhood Irish parishes showed their respect and reverence for the teachings of St. Patrick and the homeland struggle to break free from centuries of oppression from Great Britain.

If not for the determination of the Daley clan of Bridgeport to set matters right, memories of the famous downtown affairs of yesteryear might have faded into the vapors of history. Richard J. Daley, the first Chicago mayor born in the twentieth century, began his long and artful twenty-one-year reign in April 1955 by defeating Republican challenger Alderman Robert

Merriam by a hefty 708,222-vote margin. That magical number became Mayor Daley's license plate number through his six terms of office. A deeply devout family man interwoven in his Bridgeport community and bungalow living, Daley dined at home each night with his wife, Eleanor Guilfoyle, whom he wed in St. Bridget's parish in 1936, and their seven children. His daily routines rarely, if ever, varied.

Daley revered his Irish-Catholic faith and heritage. His sense of place in the ethnic melting pot of Chicago was firmly established at an early age—ordinary living in familiar surroundings amid his working-class roots. "I'm a kid from the stockyards," he often boasted. As a young man finding his way in the urban milieu, he had toiled in the packinghouses along Halsted Street—doing grim, physically draining menial labor, until establishing political connections through his early participation in and seventeen years of leadership (1927–1945) with the Hamburg Athletic Association. Hamburg, founded in 1904, was a social and political gathering place for Bridgeport's rough-and-ready young bloods—many of whom went on to obtain prominence in city politics and civic affairs.

City hall discussions between political factotums and the St. Patrick's Day Parade Association to revive the downtown gala stalled after five years, amid complaint and opposition from the State Street merchants who feared jam-packed sidewalks and a significant loss of revenue with so many bagpipers, floats, and politicos, their arms linked in fraternalism, passing in review. It took this new mayor to end the logjam and reinvigorate the parade.

Daley was most persuasive, according to the recollections of Daniel P. Lydon, executive director of the Plumbing Council who eagerly accepted appointment as parade coordinator—a position he held for many years. Without delay "Hizzoner" the mayor moved forward and organized a planning committee of prominent Chicagoans. Daley of course served as honorary chairman and would lead the March 17, 1956, march with shillelagh firmly in hand. The grumbling heads of the State Street department stores were not the toughest hurdle to overcome, but the West Side and South Side Irish parade organizers who stood in opposition to merging with the downtown group. The West Siders finally agreed to cast their lot with the mayor, but the Seventy-Ninth Street South Siders held firm. When the dust settled there would be two parades on two separate days. South Side pride demanded it.

The night before the big parade, Mother Nature dumped four unwanted inches of snow on Chicago. In a frenzy, Dan Lydon called Daley early the next morning, wondering if it would be wise to postpone. Unbeknownst to Lydon, Daley had already activated the snow removal fleet from the Department of Streets and Sanitation. They were already on the job. The march kicked off promptly at 10:00 A.M. And what a sight for Irish eyes it was! Rear Admiral Daniel V. Gallery, hero of the high seas and the man responsible for the capture of the U-505 submarine placed on permanent display at the Museum of Science and Industry in 1954, served as grand marshal.

An estimated 250,000 people gathered under brilliant sunshine as the parade kicked off at Wacker Drive and State Street and proceeded south past the Chicago Theater where the musical *Carousel* played. A police motor squad of 105 vehicles escorted the smiling Mayor Daley, followed by a carful of Daley family members; "all of the little mayors" were there, quipped Elgar Brown of the *Chicago American*, not knowing just how prophetic his words would be.[4] Irish consul general Sean Ronan (the guest of honor at the 1960 parade), of the Irish Legion of Honor—a delegation of Chicago's most important officials and bigwigs trailed the procession. All along the way, Irish pride was fully displayed as thousands of spectators sang traditional folk songs of the homeland in unison. They greeted twenty-five military and civic marching bands and a cascade of lavish floats. WGN-TV broadcast the parade live into thousands of Chicago homes.

The parade stopped at St. Patrick's Catholic Church, founded on Easter Sunday, April 12, 1846, with two octagonal spires representing the Eastern and Western branches of Catholicism, celebrated its hundredth anniversary in 1956.[5] The ancient Romanesque structure that had been a sanctuary for nineteenth-century Irish immigrants, survived the Chicago Fire. His Eminence Samuel Cardinal Stritch celebrated Solemn Pontifical Mass before an overflow crowd. A traditional corned beef and cabbage dinner followed. The pastor, Father Thomas P. Byrne, remarked that it had been a long time since old St. Pat's had been filled to overflow. The community had been uprooted years earlier, and warehouse buildings encircled much of the church grounds in the years before urban gentrification took root, allowing the parish to revive.

Later that evening, the Irish Fellowship Club hosted its annual banquet at the Sherman House at Clark Street and Randolph (now the site of the James R. Thompson State of Illinois Building). Luminaries from public life, including former governor and presidential aspirant Adlai E. Stevenson II; Senator Everett McKinley Dirksen; Mayor Daley, (recently elected as the club's fifty-sixth president); former mayor Martin Kennelly whom the Democratic regulars had dumped in favor of Daley a year earlier; Samuel Cardinal Stritch; and no one would ever forget, the keynote speaker of the evening, Senator John F. Kennedy of Massachusetts.

Mayor Daley's political intuition told him that the handsome young politician would delight and dazzle Irish Chicago. In Kennedy, the mayor recognized a rising star in the national political arena and with it came the chance to install an Irish Catholic in the White House for the first time in the nation's history. What better time than the present to introduce the charming and urbane JFK of the national Democratic Party to Chicago?

JFK, his wisdom, charm, and wit on full display, reminded his listeners that "all of us of Irish descent are bound together by the ties that come from a common experience which may only exist in memories and in legend, but which is real enough to those who possess it. And thus if we live in Cork or Boston, Chicago or Sydney, we are all members of a great family which is linked together by the strongest of chains—a common past."[6]

On that wintry St. Paddy's Day, Mayor Daley could take rightful credit for uniting Chicago's Gaelic past with the present while helping to sow the seeds of destiny for the next president of the United States.

The greening of the Chicago River, another tilt to Irish ingenuity, came six years later, during the visit of Robert Briscoe, Lord Mayor of Dublin to Chicago. The plan was hatched in 1962, the year Chicago first enforced water-pollution controls in the river. A plumber testing the city's wastewater system injected a green dye into the water in order to trace the discharge point. City engineers pronounced the experiment a success. And that gave way to a moment of inspired genius.

Stephen M. Bailey, parade chairman, business manager of the Chicago Journeyman Plumber's Local 130, Dan Lydon, and Chicago port director John Manley, hit upon the novel scheme of turning the river into a lovely shade of green for St. Patrick's Day. They cautiously predicted the compound purchased from a plumbing supply house would last from four to five hours. Mayor Daley heartily endorsed the plan, suggesting that they should take it even one step further. In an excited tone of voice that seemed to echo the optimism of Daniel Burnham's long-ago phraseology that one should "make no little plans" the mayor allegedly proclaimed, "Let's dye Lake Michigan!" The plumbers cast a wary look at one another and advised Daley that turning the lake green would be a feat of engineering that not even the brightest minds and sharpest thinkers in the Streets and Sanitation Department could ever hope to pull off. The Chicago River would have to do.

After fits and starts, and plodding through the muck and morass of the Chicago sewers, a hundred-pound mixture of fluorescent dye previously used by the military in rescue operations, was dropped into the river, completing the Windy City's picture-perfect Gaelic green nod to St. Patrick.

Summoning the press to his office, Bailey, in characteristic Irish blarney, informed reporters of his plan. "The Chicago River will dye the Illinois, which will dye the Mississippi, which will dye the Gulf of Mexico which will send green dye up the gulf stream across the North Atlantic into the Irish Sea, a sea of green surrounding the land will appear as a greeting to all Irishmen of the Emerald Isle from the men of Erin in Chicagoland U.S.A.!"[7]

He was only kidding of course. The Chicago River retained its green hue for a full week.

It worked so well that on the eve of St. Patrick's Day in March 1965, Bailey extended a generous offer to dye the alabaster white Wrigley Building shamrock green, but Philip K. Wrigley, in a huff, said absolutely not. "I don't think P. K. likes the Irish," Bailey sighed.[8]

The tradition carried over to succeeding generations. Mike Butler, who served under seven different Chicago mayors in various "Streets and San" assignments, closely guarded the secret recipe of the nontoxic powder. He carefully stored it away in the family garage until it was needed. The powder, called "Irish leprechaun dust" by Tom Rowan, a former special projects coordinator in city hall and a close friend of the Butler family, is actually orange until it is churned in water after a hand-sifting through an old-fashioned kitchen flour sifter.[9]

Parade planners, the city of Chicago, and its robust Irish-American community from Mount Greenwood north to the Wisconsin border never forgot Mayor Daley's historic role in resurrecting Irish family traditions. In the modern day, the parade no longer traverses State Street, but instead winds its way down Columbus Drive and Grant Park. The second Mayor Daley rescheduled it for the first Saturday before St. Patrick's Day, because so many Chicago teens were caught skipping school on March 17 in order to sneak downtown and do what teens like to do best—act out.

On the occasion of its fiftieth anniversary, on March 12, 2005, the hale fellows, well met of the Irish societies officially dedicated the St. Patrick's Day parade to the memory of the late mayor. It was an appropriate and ironic tribute. In that same year, Daley's beloved White Sox finally broke through and delivered to Chicago its first World Series championship since 1917. From somewhere on high, Irish eyes must have been smiling down on *that* passing parade.

HE RAN FOR HIS LIFE

The full measure of a person's life is not necessarily what awaits at the finish line, but rather the lengths he or she will go to to promote, sacrifice, and defend a sacred belief. "Sometimes people believe in little or nothing, and so they give their lives to little or nothing," said Joan of Arc, heroine of France during the Hundred Years War.[1]

Swimming in the rough crosscurrents of American politics, Lawrence Joseph Sarsfield Daly, a furniture jobber overseeing a marginal business from the backyard garage of his modest brick home and a Halsted Street business address, provides a modern Joan of Arc parable. Scrupulously honest in expressing his opinions, it is true that Daly believed in something . . . but in the final tally, he gave his life to nothing.

In West Pullman, a South Side enclave of sturdy eight-hundred-square-foot single-family ranch houses owned by ex-GIs returning home to good-paying jobs in the nearby steel mills, Lawrence Daly sold bar stools, raised five children, and ran for president on a self-styled "America First" platform.[2]

Clad in a homespun red, white, and blue Uncle Sam costume that he wore on the hustings, Daly was an uncomplicated man, a mid-twentieth-century hybrid of Don Quixote and Donald Trump. Rejected by educated elites, this tall and lean political upstart forged ahead, never abandoning the hope of achieving happier outcomes while recognizing the futility of his cause and accepting the inevitability of spectacular failure with stoicism and good humor.

Born in Gary, Indiana, to working-class Irish American immigrants in 1912, there was nothing remarkable about Daly's background, apart from the hardships of family life thrust upon him after his mother passed away when he was only five. Their father temporarily placed Lawrence and his brother John in the local orphanage. His dad—employed as a policeman and firefighter in this sooty industrial town of fifty-five thousand, attempted to make suitable living arrangements for his boys.[3] In Gary, people toiled in the steel mills and inhaled the sulfurous fumes wafting westward from Lake Michigan over the residential neighborhoods all day and all night.

Up through the 1950s, the temporary exile of a child to the confines of an orphanage amid family travail, divorce, the death of a parent, or the result of an unwanted pregnancy was a fairly common practice, albeit a searing emotional ordeal for the victimized youngsters. At the age of seven, with his dad's affairs in order, Lawrence relocated to Chicago's South Side. An outgoing, friendly lad flashing a frenzied whiz-bang entrepreneurial spirit, Daly went to work for a street vendor, peddling fruit and vegetables to housewives, earning two dollars a week at the end of World War I. By the fourth grade the ambitious boy secured his own route. "I wasn't the only kid working," Daly told long-time Chicago journalist Hal Higdon years later. "A lot of kids peddled. But I was the only one who ever rented a horse and wagon."[4]

He earned eighteen dollars a day—an impressive sum in those days for a young man with minimal schooling and few useful connections to help further him along. What Lawrence Daly lacked in social importance, he made up for with unrestrained chutzpah. The boy purchased five thousand bunches of carrots for a half-penny a bunch. Whether Daly managed to unload the carrots and turn a profit before spoilage set in cannot be ascertained.

The 1928 candidacy of New York governor Alfred Emanuel Smith, the Irish-Italian Democrat and first Roman Catholic to seek the presidency, became Daly's political baptism and the spindle on which the thread of his lifetime compulsion for attaining public office spun. At age seventeen, the red-headed young hustler tacked up campaign posters for Smith in his Irish-Catholic South Side neighborhood in the belief that Prohibition violated a person's right to enjoy the abundant fruits of life, liberty, and a foaming glass of lager. Governor Smith was a "wet" in his beliefs, and that suited Lawrence Daly just fine. "A man should have the chance to drink a glass of beer," the sixteen-year-old Daly believed—by now, wise to the ways of the world.

Becoming active in Sixth Ward politics, Daly boosted the Democratic aldermanic campaign of John F. Healy in the city election of 1931. The *Chicago Tribune* dryly noted, "[Healy] shows promise of developing into a useful alderman." Then, with Daly's help, Healy bolted the Democratic Party and won election as a Republican. He held on to his seat in the city council for the next eight years until his ouster at the hands of Republican foe Patrick Sheridan Smith.[5]

At the end of the 1931 campaign, Alderman Healy, already feeling invincible in his city council sinecure, turned his back on his most ardent precinct worker, and failed to support Daly's bid for the highly coveted post of Sixth Ward committeeman, a job of enormous political "clout" (that famous bit of Chicago slang applied to all who *have* influence as opposed to those who *desire* it).

Daly was only twenty years old and too young and callow to even think he could move up the rungs of the ladder so quickly. But he never flinched in his zeal to attain elective office. He set out to unseat the old Sixth Ward Democratic warhorse James M. Whalen, sanitary district trustee, and powerful political acolyte of Mayor Anton Cermak, until an assassin's fatal bullet cut Cermak down in Miami's Bayfront Park on February 15, 1933.

Before he could challenge Whalen, it was first necessary for Daly to collect the seven hundred required signatures to fill his nominating petitions. "I went out and got all the signatures of the neighbors from my old fruit and vegetable route," Daly related. "I needed seven-hundred names and I filed 1,200." The Chicago Board of Elections notified him that one of the Whalen people "objected," claiming "they were not in order."[6]

"I got all the signatures myself," the young candidate sulked. Nevertheless, the election board threw out the petitions over Daly's strenuous objections. In other words, you're not a candidate until the city tells you that you are. Whalen would go on to win his re-election bid, but Daly, his incensed opponent refused to let the matter die quietly. Daly paid a University of Chicago attorney ten dollars to file a declaratory judgment with the Cook County Superior Court in a bid to block Whalen and save his candidacy. Judge William J. Lindsay of the superior court listened to the arguments from both sides and promised to "take this case under advisement and announce [my] decision on April 11th."[7]

This presented a huge problem. The city had scheduled the primary election for April 10. With a shrug of the shoulders Daly went back to the streets and collected seven hundred more signatures—for a write-in campaign. On April 11, the day *after* the election, Daly appeared before Judge Lindsay, an unsuccessful candidate for Cook County state's attorney in 1928. Lindsay owed his judicial appointment to Whalen. "Petition granted!" the judge thundered, but the ruling was of little consequence and it came one day too late for Daly.[8]

Shifting his focus away from politics for the time being, Daly launched a new business venture—"Daly Brothers Furniture Movers." It was a generous thing to do, to include his brother in this scheme considering that John Daly worked in the steel mills and had little or no dealings with the new business.

The lure of politics drew Daly back into the hunt during the early winter months of 1938 when he filed to run in the Democratic primary as a candidate for Cook County superintendent of schools pitting him against the incumbent, Noble J. Puffer, and another unknown, Milton Monson. Daly listed his affiliation as "unattached"—meaning that he was neither sanctioned nor supported by the invincible Patrick Nash–Ed Kelly "Machine"— the ruling bosses of Chicago from 1933 to 1946—who drew up the slate of candidates for every election, promising jobs and other considerations in exchange for votes in a heavy-handed fashion.

"Once in a while the people get on their hind legs and demonstrate that they do not like dictatorship in any form—and the Nash–Kelly Machine is a dictatorship!" snorted Judge Edmund K. Jarecki, long-time Chicago reformer and good-government spokesman who fought a futile battle against both Democratic and Republican machine politicians in his quest to deliver honest and open elections.[9]

In this election for the $17,000-a-year post of county superintendent of schools, the cash-strapped Daly had little of his own money to squander on a losing campaign, but in the belief that Christianity should be taught in the public schools, he forged ahead. High school dropout Daly handed out his literature on street corners, and managed to convince many first- and second-generation Irish to vote the name—and what better name than Daly in this, the most Irish of American cities? Fun but all in vain. Puffer sent his "unattached" opponents down to defeat, but Daly's surprising showing would stand as his best ever.[10]

Charles Regan, an acquaintance from the Healy aldermanic campaign enticed Daly into his career calling—the barstool business. Regan invented a seat cover easily slipped over the barstool. Regan needed an unabashed promoter, a glib pitchman to promote the lasting benefit of a product of dubious value. Who would buy this and for what purpose? Daly had an ingenious idea.

Looking back on it years later, he waxed poetic with Scott Simon of National Public Radio. "You know I run a barstool company. Business is okay but the glory days were back when I was young in the thirties. Bookies needed stools. You know why? They couldn't sit on desks and post the numbers on blackboards. So they sat and stood on stools. The cops knew where all the betting parlors were, 'cause they'd bust them. When they'd bust them, I'd tell the cops. 'Give me an address and you'll get fifty cents for each stool we sell' [Daly promised police]. The cops would raid them every few weeks."[11]

Daly admitted that he wasn't much of a businessman. The money put food on the table for his wife, Alice, and the five kids, but the fear of syndicate goons turning up at the door of his Vermont Street bungalow one night posed a serious risk to his life and limb. After the stuttering Regan died, Daly took over the operation and expanded the client base to include schools and churches. This true-blue moralist and polemicist for the stars and stripes painted his automobile to match the colors of the flag. He took to heart the words of his heroic inspirer General Douglas MacArthur. "Only those are fit to live who are not afraid to die!"[12] Daly dutifully filed MacArthur's name for president in the Illinois primaries beginning in 1936, but the general withdrew it from consideration in the proscribed ten-day window. If MacArthur's example had taught Daly anything, it was, perhaps, that lost causes are the only ones worth fighting for.

Daly kept the home fires burning for the general. In March 1952, after being fired by President Harry Truman for meddling in affairs of state and his conducting of the Korean War, MacArthur drew strong support from the political right wing for a run at the presidency. "That year I filed MacArthur's name again," Daly said. "It was the closest he ever came to leaving it on the Illinois ballot. But after an exchange of telegrams he finally withdrew. He thought it unwise at the time."[13]

Undeterred and unrelenting in this endless parade of confrontations, Daly identified a slate of electors in MacArthur's home state of Wisconsin who were agreeable to supporting the general's candidacy, but MacArthur had no interest. Minus the general's approval of his latest stratagem, Daly placed advertisements in nineteen Wisconsin newspapers in search of a man of the same name—Douglas MacArthur—but his time-consuming attempt yielded no results.

Daly scoured the Chicago phone book and came up with forty-two-year-old General McArthur—"General" was truly his first name—a tank inspector for Wilson and Company in the Chicago Stockyards. Daly asked if he might borrow the man's name for placement on the ballot. General McArthur, an African American and the father of eight, chuckled, saying he had no problem with that because he too admired the famous war hero. He stood four-square behind Daly's platform and vowed that as the next president he would "defend American freedom and Christian civilization from the satanic scourge of godless communism."

Humorless *Chicago Sun-Times* editorial writers, seemingly unaware that these shenanigans were commonplace in city elections dating back to the Civil War, blasted Daly for subverting the electoral process. "Two days later the Attorney General says our man cannot be certified," lamented Daly. "Not enough electors. We could have gone to the Wisconsin Supreme Court but we did not have the money."[14] All in all, 1952 was not a good year for Daly—a strong supporter of Wisconsin senator Joseph McCarthy during his ill-advised campaign to expose communist sympathizers in the government—who by now had shortened his first name from Lawrence to "Lar."

It is commonly believed that the name change was made as a sop to Swedish American voters living in his district. However, Chicago's Swedish settlement concentrated far north of West Pullman, in the Andersonville-Edgewater communities. The correct Swedish name, if that was Daly's true intent and purpose, is "Lars," not "Lar,"—an old Irish nickname for Lawrence used by his father and grand-uncle back in the old country.

With it, Daly introduced a new middle name "America First." It was the height of the Joseph McCarthy era and communist paranoia engulfed the nation as the Wisconsin senator's smears and accusations of red infiltration at the highest levels of the armed forces and in the government ruined reputations and shattered lives. "I lacked money. I lacked organization," Daly explained. "Your only hope of making any possible dent in the vote is to seize on a certain policy—America's interests first in politics and to attract attention to yourself. So I chose the sartorial emblem of our country, the Uncle Sam suit, complete with goatee, beard and everything."[15]

Daly hired a Lithuanian seamstress to hand sew his Uncle Sam getup. In a low moment early in 1958, a thief pilfered the precious commodity. To Daly, it was an incalculable loss akin to Superman losing his cape and Popeye running out of spinach. The costume was a source of pride and strength that emboldened him before the voting public. Donning the costume, Daly transformed from mild-mannered businessman into a ferocious campaigner unmindful and uncaring of whom he might offend by his words.

Lar recovered the costume after placing an advertisement in the *Chicago Tribune* promising a reward for its safe return. A caller telephoned to say that he would return the suit upon receipt of the reward—fifty dollars. Daly directed him to a park bench a few hundred feet south of Buckingham Fountain in Grant Park and told the man to come by after midnight and he would find the money taped underneath a park bench. Daly patched up the frayed suit and resumed the frantic pace of life. "I carry a pistol," he warned, just in case someone else contemplated kidnapping the patriotic garb a second time. "I've got a reputation for not putting up with any foolishness!"[16]

Lar went through two or three of the signature costumes every year promoting a nonexistent coalition and a mixed-up right-wing agenda that called upon police to execute known drug peddlers if they refused to leave town within seven days of receiving the order to clear out. Concerning witnesses invoking the Fifth Amendment during interrogation sessions, Daly offered up a simple solution for dealing with these obstructionists. Send them to prison! On the other hand, he favored legalized gambling.

In his printed literature and promotional advertising, Daly introduced a cartoon character he dubbed "Dr. Cyclops," a disheveled, wild-eyed kook in coke-bottle glasses conjuring in the candidate's mind a horde of unpatriotic, atheistic, left-wing university intellectuals who were intent upon destroying American values and hide-bound tradition. During a campaign for state superintendent of public instruction he billed himself as the "champion of Christian education and good old-fashioned American school standards." Dr. Cyclops on the other hand stood for "the crack-pot elements who favor the God-less, silly and harmful system of progressive education."[17]

Claiming the moral high ground, Daly bellowed: "Teach the Christian religion to all Illinois public schools with clergymen of the three communions of Christianity; Catholic, Protestant, and Eastern Orthodox as teachers. I hope to drive home first the issue of America first. You're faced with one choice. The issue now is national survival. Your choice is America first or death!"[18]

It was customary for Daly to circulate petitions for elective office and wait until the last possible moment to arrive in Springfield and hand deliver his signatures. That way, harried election officials coping with tight deadlines would be less inclined to check the validity of his signatures as they might have, days earlier.

In the heat of a 1954 campaign he blew out a tire halfway to the state capitol. His spare had not been properly inflated. It was no simple matter to get back on the road and arrive at the secretary of state's office before the five o'clock deadline, but after the emergency truck arrived on the scene, he persevered and drove the rest of the way at breakneck speed. Denied access to the locked office, Lar Daly wrapped a handkerchief around his fist and smashed through the glass of the window, alarming security personnel who had rushed to the scene. Demanding to see Dan Butler (chief clerk of the index department under Secretary of State Charles F. Carpentier), Daly breathlessly informed the guard that according to the hands on his watch he had beaten the deadline. Moments later Butler advised the frazzled America First campaigner that it was 5:01—too late to file.

This wouldn't be the first or last time Daly faced a tough challenge to his signature petitions. During the 1948 national election he presented thirteen petitions for a range of candidates including former racket buster Thomas Dewey, Senator Robert A. Taft, the éminence grise of stolid postwar Republican conservatism and another personal favorite, the headline-hunting Harold E. Stassen, former governor of Minnesota, arguably America's most famous perpetual candidate in the postwar years. Stassen espoused the same freedom-loving, mom-and-apple-pie patriotism as Daly, but achieved better results.[19] The petition bid on behalf of Stassen and the others failed of course.

Daly, the father of three sons and two daughters and the avatar of political jabber, took potshots at politicians on both sides of the aisle. Driven and nearly blinded by his quest, Daly ran for a stupefying number of offices on both party tickets making it impossible to label him a committed Republican or occasional Democrat, although more often than not he parachuted into the GOP camp to the chagrin of the party bosses. He drove through Chicago streets in a specially equipped sound truck to broadcast his odd mix of libertarian and archconservative messaging to the befuddled people on the sidewalk. During the McCarthy era, Daly begged President Harry Truman to grant him the privilege of becoming the only civilian permitted to accompany the flight crew of the air force bomber that was expected to drop an atomic bomb on Moscow. Truman was unresponsive, and the invitation, of course, never came.

Who was America's greatest president? Certainly not Harry Truman in the opinion of the offended and unapologetic Daly who had been denied the use of Truman's Los Angeles hotel suite during the 1960 Democratic Convention after the ex-president decided at the last moment to bypass the entire event. "George Washington was the best!" Daly fired back. "He had the greatest problems of all. He and the whole gang were threatened to all be hanged from a yard iron."[20]

A frequent target of hecklers during public appearances, Daly drew loud guffaws one night after methodically running through his political agenda, point by point. "Point one . . . Point two . . ."[21] A wiseacre in the crowd urged him to remove his Uncle Sam hat and reveal point three. At the 1956 Republican National Convention in San Francisco, Daly marched through the Fairmont and Mark Hopkins Hotels where the delegates had congregated, displaying a banner reading "I Never Did Like Ike!" with reference to President Dwight D. Eisenhower who had earlier called Lar's failed demand for equal airtime ridiculous.

Lar Daly's big moment in the national spotlight finally arrived in 1959–1960. He secured enough votes that year to run in both the Democratic and Republican city primaries in March, and scored a media victory after forcing WBBM-TV (the CBS Chicago affiliate) to grant him a half hour of equal time under the provisions of section 315(a) of the Communications Act of 1934, after his namesake Mayor Richard J. *Daley* delivered his annual report to the city over the air. The FCC ruling is famously known as "The Lar Daly Decision."[22]

H. Leslie Atlass, Chicago radio pioneer who cofounded WBBM Radio in 1923 as a two-hundred-watt station before rising through the ranks to become CBS vice president of the central division called the law poorly written. "Our attorneys have decided that a citizen must be given equal time if he shows he is qualified to hold an office and is making an effort to be elected. This means he could be no more than a write-in candidate if he can prove his efforts."[23]

After Mayor Daley appeared as a guest on the Norman Ross *V.I.P.* program that aired over WBKB-TV on January 4, Sterling "Red" Quinlan, the legendary Chicago television executive explained, "We cannot censor the program. Lar Daly might push Norman Ross aside and turn it into a monolog. He told us he intends to ask for funds on the air. How can we stop it?"[24]

With the law—at least temporarily—on his side, Lar filed for the 1960 New Hampshire presidential primary as a Democratic candidate for president five minutes before the 5 P.M. deadline. Daly's name appeared on the ballot with Maryland hillbilly singer Elton Britt, Chicago ballpoint pen manufacturer Paul C. Fisher, and John F. Kennedy of Massachusetts.

After Kennedy's fifty-two-minute-long prime-time appearance on the *Jack Paar Show* on NBC, June 16, Lar Daly again appealed to the FCC for help and they upheld their earlier stipulation that Daly was "a legally qualified candidate" entitled to equal time. "This ruling by the FCC makes me ashamed for the first time, to be a part of the entertainment industry," groused Paar. "This ruling by the FCC abuses the decent principle of equal time. It makes an absurdity of equal time."[25]

Lar Daly showed up at the studio in full Uncle Sam regalia. The audience booed and heckled Daly mercilessly for his criticism of the genial, grandfatherly incumbent president, whom he called a "poor excuse" and for making a direct appeal to the public for campaign contributions, forcing an apology from Paar at the conclusion of the show. Only then did the audience applaud.

Daly said he knew that wearing the Uncle Sam suit would hurt him, but since it was his trademark, he'd wear it on his first national TV appearance. Nearly six hundred people sent in letters and cards and donations in response to his appeal for money that totaled $151.17. Daly also received a phony check and three death threats.

Author Hal Higdon said, "Lar Daly is a likeable person, but one of his major flaws in his character is that when he gets in front of a microphone, he begins to shout and threaten in an attempt to intimidate the audience. With Lar Daly as his own best friend, he doesn't need enemies!"[26]

Following his verbal judo with Paar, Daly filed a lawsuit against Illinois governor William G. Stratton demanding $5 million in punitive damages for violating his civil rights after the secretary of state removed him from the 1960 senatorial primary ballot. Daly's petition, with the names of 5,125 signatories, was mostly fraudulent and the case was thrown out. A cut-rate liquor store, an automobile dealership, a vacant lot, and a florist shop were listed as private residences.

Daly never abandoned hope, even after his political future had come and gone. If there was an election to lose (or a lawsuit to be filed), he was Johnny-on-the-spot with petitions in hand. Only once did the indefatigable campaigner claim a legitimate victory. In 1973, he rose, like Banquo's ghost, to haunt the Republicans with a stunning primary win in a special election for the Seventh Congressional District. How could this have happened? He ran unopposed in a Democratic district.

As the years passed, scraping together the money necessary to finance his costly misadventures became insurmountable. Down on his heels and beset with financial problems from all sides, Daly stopped wearing his signature costume altogether, and, according to several accounts, either pawned or sold it to raise cash.

In his final bid for elective office in March 1978, Daly challenged Republican incumbent and party moderate US Senator Charles Percy in the primary. Percy, the taciturn former chairman of Bell and Howell Corporation, whose daughter Valerie had been brutally murdered in a still unsolved September 1966 home invasion, faced only token opposition in the primary and general elections. Surprisingly, Daly polled 74,779 votes, one of his highest recorded totals.

Suffering numerous physical ailments that robbed him of the use of his hands, Lar Daly passed away April 17, 1978, at Little Company of Mary Hospital in Evergreen Park. Those who gathered for the funeral service at Holy Founders Catholic Church in Calumet Park affirmed the words of the Reverend Mark Dennehy, who praised the refreshing political naiveté of the deceased. "This was a good and sometimes misunderstood man . . . the embodiment of Don Quixote . . . who sought the forum, not the victory, to press his ideals."[27]

Calling him a player in a "walk-on character part," a *Tribune* editorial published April 19, 1978, conceded that "to his eternal credit, [Daly] was not a hater. He stood for what he believed, and if other people could not understand how simple everything really was, that was their problem, not his."

CHAPTER TWENTY

ALL IN A HARD DAY'S NIGHT

We remember 1964 as the year of the "great divide," the unambiguous endpoint of the "nifty fifties" and the dawn of the "swinging sixties." It was the year of the Warren Report and the Gulf of Tonkin resolution, authorizing the president to deploy troops into South Vietnam without congressional approval. It was an epic year that lives on in memory in so many ways.

In Berkeley, under the informal leadership of a coalition of University of California student activists, the Free Speech Movement set in motion an unprecedented decade-long struggle to end an unpopular war that divided the nation. The struggle to abolish institutional segregation and the abuses of Jim Crow in the South took on greater urgency amid the protest of a new and increasingly vocal generation born after World War II. The times, as it has often been said, were indeed "a-changin'."

The message echoed across the land. It foretold a great social revolution among young people asking hard questions, invalidating old ideas, and re-inventing our popular culture in such a way that rattled established values, attitudes, and the 1950s conventionality of an older generation—the parents of the baby boom.

It all happened so fast. Four mop-topped lads from Liverpool invaded America and they changed the world we thought we knew in profound and remarkable ways.

Three key Beatle dates signaled the arrival of the 1960s insurgency. On December 10, 1963, Walter Cronkite—not Ed Sullivan—introduced the Beatles to a nationwide audience during an evening broadcast of the CBS Evening News. The segment drew attention to the showmanship of the band, and the fanatical devotion of British teens that appeared to the reserved Mr. Cronkite to border on mass hysteria.

On January 31, 1964, when, after only a few weeks on the Billboard Hot 100 and the WLS Silver Dollar Survey in Chicago, "I Want to Hold Your

Hand" zoomed to the top of the rock and roll charts.[1] WLS nighttime platter spinner Dick "the Wild I-Talian" Biondi is believed to have been the first American rock and roll deejay to give the Beatles radio airplay in early 1963 when he introduced "Please, Please Me" to his Chicago listening audience.

Nine days after hitting number one on the Chicago charts, the Beatles performed on the *Ed Sullivan Show* and "Beatlemania" overtook the nation. Ed Sullivan, the stone-faced former Broadway gossip columnist dismissed the Beatles as a "novelty act," but group manager Brian Epstein inveigled the doubting Sunday night toastmaster to commit to airing three taped appearances on consecutive weeks in the winter of 1964. Suddenly and inexplicably, the "Fab Four," clad in their pipe-stem trousers, pointy shoes, and Carnaby Street "mod" haircuts, were headliners from coast to coast and around the world.

The other key date: September 5, 1964. The Beatles, after bypassing Chicago in their whirlwind trip to New York City in February, played the International Amphitheater in the midst of a dizzying, non-stop national tour that kicked off on August 19 at the Cow Palace in San Francisco. It was the Beatles' first full-blown tour and the schedule called for thirty-two shows in twenty-three cities. If the concert pace was grueling and the boys homesick, the financial reward was sweet. At the Indiana State Fair, the quartet carted away $85,231 for two sets. When the Beatles left Milwaukee and headed for Chicago, they received a staggering check in the sum of $1,000 per minute for a thirty-minute performance. Inquiring minds at the Internal Revenue Service demanded to know if they were a foreign corporation and therefore exempt from paying US taxes—pegged at $42,000. In today's dollars the 1964 tour earned the group the hefty equivalent of $7.5 million.

It was Labor Day weekend in Chicago, marking the end of summer and the beginning of a new school year. *A Hard Day's Night* continued its long run at the Woods Theater downtown, and thousands of youthful Beatle worshippers—teen-aged girls mostly—had spent much of their summer vacation cajoling, contriving, and pleading with their parents to purchase scarce concert tickets priced at $5.75 each. Scalpers demanded a then-unheard-of sum of forty dollars per ticket. Chicagoland dads considered the hefty ticket price outrageous, while still wanting to please their precocious daughters. The scalper price was under-the-table and nonnegotiable. Some were lucky and got to go, most were denied.

Not since Elvis Presley breached the gates of the Windy City on March 28, 1957, had there been such a rock and roll frenzy as this.[2] Opinions were sharply divided. Jealous of the obsessive attention showered on John, Paul, George, and Ringo by their girlfriends, adolescent boys naturally found much to scorn. They vented their displeasure in a series of letters to the Beatle editor of the *Chicago American*, the afternoon paper whose star columnist, the middle-aged, middle-of-the-road square, Jack Mabley, had been assigned the frightening task of introducing the lads to thirteen thousand screaming youngsters inside the amphitheater.[3]

"[Charles] Darwin would turn green at the sight of those mutated floor mops, otherwise known as the Beatles," griped Daniel Sobieski in his letter of protest. "Don't get me wrong, they aren't good for nothing. NASA could always send them up to the moon to make sure it's safe for the astronauts, or you could put whiskey kegs around their necks and send them to the Alps!"[4]

School administrators and nervous teachers reacted with a mix of caution, negativity, and yes, even acceptance. At Joliet East High School, principal James Risk permitted WLS to pipe in Clark Weber's morning show over the public address in order to "make the students think a little more positively about school," but only before the start of class.[5]

In Mrs. Bailey's fifth-grade classroom at Onahan School on Chicago's far Northwest Side, the girls scribbled "I love the Beatles" five hundred times on sheets of loose-leaf notebook paper when the teacher wasn't watching and sent it off to the contest promoter promising a "Beatle Prize" to the school submitting the most entries. That summer the Chicago White Sox were locked in a thrilling, three-way pennant chase with the Yankees and Orioles. In the stench of the nearby stockyards, mortal combat raged against the "Yankee evil empire" as the American League lead changed hands daily. Sadly and tragically for number one Sox fan Mayor Richard J. Daley and thousands of other loyal Pale Hose rooters, it ended unhappily for the South Siders on the last weekend of a stoic but unforgettable baseball season.

Meanwhile, at Pierce Elementary School in the Far North Side Andersonville community, Denise and Ellen Janda hung on every word written about the Fab Four that appeared in their fan magazines. They kept a scrapbook of news clips, worshipped at the altar of George Harrison, but would have to wait another year until the Liverpool long-hairs returned to Chicago to play Comiskey Park before they could swoon before them in person. "For my thirteenth birthday [in 1964], my parents promised me a bike," Denise recalled. "But I wanted their first two LP albums instead, *Meet the Beatles*, and *Introducing the Beatles* for $2.99 a piece at the Sears record department. My parents got off cheaply."[6]

Chicago braced for the invasion of the Beatles by imposing Kremlin-like security at the key checkpoints: O'Hare, Midway Airport and the International Amphitheater. Fearing a riot of a hundred thousand screeching teenagers and mass pandemonium, Colonel Jack Reilly, Mayor Richard J.

Daley's long-suffering director of special events canceled preliminary plans for a civic center reception. He took elaborate precautions to "protect" the city by appointing a mobilized task force.

After reading published accounts of mobs of fans descending on the airports and hotels of other American cities, Reilly decided that it would be prudent to covertly move them through Chicago following their Milwaukee concert and a wild melee the night before. It was shaping up to be a real cloak and dagger caper.

At which airport would their chartered four-engine Electra aircraft touch down? Colonel Reilly kept them all guessing. Early reports suggested that it would be O'Hare at four thirty in the afternoon. The unsubstantiated rumor drew a vanguard of five hundred teens to the terminal. The last-minute change to Midway Airport, however, left the befuddled O'Hare fans in an uproar, and angered Ringo Starr, who, according to one account, telephoned the presidents of the Chicago fan clubs to alert them to Reilly's "bait and switch" tactic. The police detail at O'Hare breathed a collective sigh of relief. "Thank God they are going to Midway," said Lieutenant Harry A. Smith.[7]

At approximately 4:40 the Electra taxied down the runway at Midway to the Butler Aviation terminal. There to greet them were five thousand fans and sixty police officers. Some hoisted banners reading "Ringo for President!" Nineteen-sixty-four was after all, an election year. Others wore Beatle sweatshirts and Beatle buttons. All were in a highly festive, emotional state.

They screamed and jumped up and down, hoping to catch a glimpse of their heroes. About a dozen emboldened teenaged girls scaled the four-foot-high cyclone fence and made a desperate, mad dash for the waiting limousine there to whisk the lads off to the Stockyards Inn and a scheduled press conference with bemused members of the media. A battery of wheezing, uniformed police officers carrying billy clubs chased them down seconds before they overtook the limo. The Beatles waved to their fans and disappeared inside. The girls just kept screaming.

The storied Stockyards Inn, a Halsted Street landmark since 1934 had welcomed President Dwight Eisenhower, movie stars, and scores of foreign dignitaries in its better days. Strictly white tablecloth. Martinis, shaken, not stirred. The arrival of the Beatles, well that was quite a departure from the dignity and decorum of the place.[8]

Stately and regal, and adorned by three hundred oil paintings in wood-paneled dining rooms, the Stockyards Inn seemed an unusual venue for a media blitz such as this one. Pity the poor dining patrons looking forward to a late lunch or early dinner of prime rib slathered in horseradish sauce that had to be turned away.

The wait staff and busboys braced for a mad-cap press conference attended by reporters, ingenious fakers impersonating reporters, and members of Beatles fan clubs who had bribed security guards with gifts to gain entry. A farcical interview, if it was in fact an interview, followed.

Munching on a prime rib sandwich, Paul McCartney said he looked forward to seeing some famous Chicago gangsters festooned in fedora hats and top coats but criticized city officials for the tight security measures put in place to separate the quartet from their fans. "It seems to me that we are being protected to a ridiculous extent!" A reporter then asked: "What would you do if a crowd broke loose?" George Harrison replied: "We'd probably get killed!"[9]

John Lennon complained of a sore throat. A reporter asked Harrison what he thought of American girls. "They're the same only they speak foreign—I mean, with a different accent." Another scribe asked the Beatles where they wanted to go after Chicago. "Home," Lennon replied.[10]

Outside the Amphitheater, a long line had already formed. Twenty-four hours before concert time, eight enterprising teenaged girls hid out inside the women's washroom until the arrival of the cleaning crew. Security officials were at a loss to explain how they managed to sneak past the major checkpoints, but obviously the girls came prepared to camp out all night with their bags of sandwiches, snacks, and a change of clothes. They were told to go home.

The International Amphitheater, the customary venue for livestock shows, 4-H Club competitions, prize fights, and national political conventions since the hall opened in 1935 following the great Stockyards Fire, resembled a military encampment. Expressing their concern for kids in the event of injuries or a riot, a phalanx of 230 police officers, 160 Andy Frain ushers, 40 private detectives, 150 Chicago firemen, and doctors and nurses manned the first aid station. Nothing quite as terrible as a riot occurred over the next three hectic hours, although as a precaution, six fans were dispatched to the Evangelical Hospital for emotional and physical exhaustion.

The doors swung open at 6 P.M. and 13,260 Beatle worshippers swarmed past the ushers. The mood was electric, the throng of fans restive. At eight thirty Jack Mabley stepped up to the stage to introduce the four opening acts. At that moment, a cascade of nonstop, unrelenting screaming commenced.

Mabley, the ardent defender of mom, apple pie, and Republicans favored the tunes of his big-band youth—Tommy Dorsey, crooner Russ Columbo, and Glen Gray and his Casa Loma Orchestra. Recalling that September night, he said, "I walked out there not knowing if I'd be struck dumb or would manage to stumble through my assignment."[11] Poor Jack. He could not hear one word of his welcome remarks or his introduction of the warm-up acts: the Bill Black Combo with his distinctive Memphis sound, the Exciters, the early 1960s soul of Clarence "Frogman" Henry and songstress Jackie De Shannon.

It is doubtful that anyone else heard them that night either, amid the earth-shattering noise of the amphitheater. At 9:45, Jackie De Shannon hustled off the stage to make way for the Beatles—who were forty-five seconds late.

Mabley, frazzled and in a near panic wondered what he should do next if they failed to show up. Where were they? He repeated his introduction. "Here's the Beatles . . ." and finally the band bolted on stage from an enclosed stairway. "They came in one of the sloppiest entrances I have ever seen," groused Mabley. "It didn't matter. They walked on stage, looked around, found their instruments and then went to work."[12]

For the next thirty-four minutes the group performed a range of their hit songs, beginning with "You Can't Do That," and closing with "Long Tall Sally." In between, sheer bedlam rained down. Flashbulbs popped and fans showered the stage with teddy bears and jelly beans as a show of affection. Ringo loved jelly beans, but he didn't appreciate being pelted by them. He used his cymbals like a fly swatter to deflect them. Meanwhile, perspiring Andy Frain ushers struggled to restrain the girls in the balcony from tumbling over the railing.

All too quickly, it was over. The quartet that ushered in the *true* 1960s, were nudged toward a waiting limousine minutes before the girls inside the Amphitheater scampered over to the parking lots to hunt them down. The Beatles rushed back to Midway for their next gig in Detroit, twenty-four-hours later. No Chicago gangsters in fedoras to meet and greet along the way. No time for food or a bit of chatter with the awestruck presidents of the local Beatle fan clubs. For the exhausted "Fab Four" there was not a moment of spare time to pause and reflect on the dark side of overnight fame. Their 1964 fans may not have known that relaxation for these cheerful, irreverent lads was not possible without a little help from pills and alcohol—uppers and downers. The city of Chicago? It was just another hard day's night on the journey to rock and roll nirvana.

The Beatles are a phenomenon in the music-making culture, separating the old order from the new in clothing style, evolving political activism, socialization, and the art form itself. Inspired by the Beatles example, a generation of mid-to-late-1960s Chicago-area "garage band" imitators, including the Buckinghams, the New Colony Six, the Cryan' Shames, the American Breed, Shadows of Night, the Flock, the Ides of March, and CTA (a jazz-rock fusion band later renamed Chicago), signed contracts with national recording labels. All went on to achieve varying degrees of celebrity, fame, and national prominence. In a larger sense, the Beatles became the prime mover of musical evolution in the same fashion as the New Orleans jazz men and Mississippi Delta blues and gospel singers who moved north in the 1910s and 1920s and redefined popular taste, thus inventing a uniquely stylized, signature "Chicago Sound."

Jack Mabley, acerbic and skeptical, had the last word. "The Beatles are a parody. . . . Twenty-five years from now the Beatles will just be something that happened a long time ago."[13]

CHAPTER TWENTY-ONE

HUMANITY IN THE HEARTLAND

Before she helped change the world, Anne McGlone Burke, a bartender's daughter, grew up in modest circumstances in a three-bedroom flat at Forty-Seventh and Ingleside in the South Side Kenwood community. Although she did not suffer the extremes of poverty and want in this working-class neighborhood that was undergoing a profound demographic shift from white to black in the post–World War II years, Anne's life was richly defined by her family, the parish of St. Ambrose, and a deepening passion for team sports, baton, piano playing, and tap dance.

At the age of ten, she moved with her parents, George and Helen Mc-Glone, to Sixty-Third and Washtenaw, straddling the Gage Park and Marquette Park boundary line in the heart of the city's Southwest Side "bungalow belt" where thousands of second- and third-generation Irish Americans settled after World War I.[1] "I suppose you can say that I was an average student earning average grades," Burke reflected. "I was never an 'A' student nor did I excel in academic studies."[2]

During her years of parochial education at St. Rita Grammar School and Maria High School, Anne Burke suffered from a distinct, language-based learning disability of neurological origin known in the day as "word blindness." For many years there was no clear understanding of the syndrome we know today as dyslexia, an affliction that affects 20 percent of all school-age children in the United States.[3]

Minus a viable early identification methodology by teachers and administrators, otherwise bright and informed school-age children suffered and fell behind the learning curve in reading comprehension. Well-meaning teachers assumed that their dyslexic pupil showed laziness or simply required more time for their reading skills to fully mature and develop. "Your child will pick it up in time," a teacher might advise concerned parents. Without remediation or a clearer understanding of what was really going on within the child, the dyslexic student often became a problem student— disruptive, depressed, despairing, and lacking motivation to continue. For some, dyslexia is a matter of word-letter reversal—"was" becomes "saw." Others may see letters positioned upside down or just one word contained in a sentence differently.

"Reading comprehension was always a challenge for me because dyslexia takes away a person's ability to read rapidly and effectively," Burke relates. "I read my sentences backward, from right to left. You can imagine what that must have been like." Thankfully, Anne's parents did not pressure her to achieve As at all costs. "I was a 'C' student. My mom and dad were very understanding and accepting. They encouraged me to pursue what I loved best—art, baton twirling, tap dancing and sports—without placing unreasonable demands upon me."[4]

Anne McGlone Burke had a wonderful mentor in Sister Henrietta at Maria High School (an all-girls' high school near Marquette Park on the South Side named for Maria Kaupas (the future Mother Maria of Lithuania and founder of the Order of the Sisters of St. Casimir) who encouraged her early interest in these subjects. "Why don't you become a gym teacher? Do what you love," Sister Henrietta advised Burke.[5]

Anne took her words to heart and volunteered to become a recreation leader at the Chicago Park District while still in high school. "Sister Henrietta helped me to believe in myself. . . . She changed my life." In 1962, with the help of a $500 scholarship awarded to her by the Chicago Park District, she attended classes at George Williams College with the hope of attaining a college degree.[6]

However, George Williams College moved to Downers Grove in Chicago's far western suburbs. It was an impossible commute for Anne, so, for the moment, she was forced to put her college plans on hold in order to apply for a position as a physical education teacher in the Chicago Park District. She worked at several parks from 1963 to 1965 before applying for a new position as a Special Recreation teacher. In January 1965, the district assigned her to West Pullman Park.

In her work with young people, Anne took note of the tragic plight of special needs children suffering from intellectual disabilities—youngsters cruelly and callously shunted aside, or locked away in institutions, many of them degrading sinkholes of despair. In a revealing 1946 essay published in *Life Magazine*, Albert Q. Maisel declared America's mental institutions "a shame and a disgrace."[7] What chance did a child confined to such an environment have? "You did not see them playing in the parks with the other children," he remembered.[8]

They were hidden. They were forgotten. They were the ignored and excluded children of the shadows. And if they were noticed at all by the other kids playing in the park, mockery and ridicule inevitably followed. Anne wondered if something more could be done to bring them out to the public parks and involve them in games and recreational activities to build their self-esteem through inclusion. "I asked myself, why can't we give them the same opportunity to run and jump, bounce a basketball and catch a baseball? Wouldn't it make their lives just a little more enjoyable and meaningful?"[9]

During the same month, the Joseph P. Kennedy Jr. Foundation awarded the Chicago Park District a ten thousand dollar grant to allow the board to invite these children into ten public parks to be given the same opportunity to experience the ordinary joys of childhood all young people deserve. It was called the Special Recreation Program, and Anne looked forward to teaching these children how to run, to throw a ball, to ice skate and to swim. "However, neither I nor any of the other Special Recreation Program teachers had acquired the necessary formal training to work with this segment of the population, simply because this kind of training did not exist previously," Burke said.[10]

That is, until Dr. William "Bill" Freeberg, formerly associated with the Kennedy Foundation, invited Anne and nine of her colleagues down to Southern Illinois University at Carbondale to attend specialized training sessions at the Touch of Nature Environmental Center, derived from the Shakespearean quote, "One touch of nature makes the whole world kin!"[11]

Dr. Freeberg had returned to SIU in 1949 to establish curriculum specialization in outdoor education after becoming the first person in the country to complete a doctorate of recreation.[12] Working with SIU president Dr. Delyte Morris and the board of trustees, Freeberg acquired for the university, 150 acres of land from the US Fish and Wildlife Service along the western shore of Little Grassy Lake to build the center. It is one of the first recreational camps in the nation established for disabled communities.[13]

McFetridge, a seventy-three-year-old veteran Chicago labor leader and previous head of the Building Services Employees International Union, became the new parks chief in August of that year, bringing with him former Notre Dame all-American gridiron star Dan Shannon as his vice president.[14] In an emotional speech given to a packed room of civic leaders at the Palmer House following his installation, McFetridge, a member of the Chicago Building Commission and president of the Marina City Building Corporation (owner of the iconic "corn-cob"-designed residential towers adjoining the Chicago River), promised to "provide a childhood for every child in Chicago."[15] "I never had a childhood myself," he confided to his Palmer House listeners, recounting boyhood hardships of going to work at an early age to help support his family.[16] To fulfill his promise to the children of Chicago, Bill McFetridge solicited fresh ideas and new thinking. Anne invited McFetridge and Shannon to visit West Pullman Park and gauge the work she was doing.

"I do not believe that up until that moment, either of them had any prior dealings with an intellectually disabled person," Burke believes. "They wanted to find out how many children like this resided in Chicago. I told them I did not know. There were no reliable data points to draw upon. It was anyone's guess."[17]

The challenge before them, and one that Burke could not have anticipated, was to overcome the extreme reluctance of parents to bring their children out of the shadows and into the parks to have fun, to socially interact with one another, and to learn.

Many parents were embarrassed and hesitant about taking such a step. They feared their children would be stigmatized and suffer public ridicule and teasing. In order to convince them that a new day was dawning in Chicago and in America, Burke, with the help of park supervisor Randy Herman, placed ads in the community newspaper and called parents on the phone urging them to consider enrolling their children in the Park District program.

Anne made personal visits to their homes in an effort to convince parents that the program was inclusive and beneficial to the well-being and personal growth of their children. She assured them that bullying and ridicule from the other kids in the park would not be tolerated.

It took a great deal of time and effort to overcome such deep-seated parental misconceptions and anxiety, but slowly her informational campaign began to yield positive results. The other kids in the park so greatly feared by the parents, proved to be welcoming, supportive, and encouraging. They volunteered to help the park counselors with coaching and instruction, and as the weeks passed the fear of bullying abated. Everyone got along in the spirit of inclusion, teamwork, and social acceptance.

Then, in the summer of 1967 park district president William L. McFetridge invited Burke to leave West Pullman Park and join his team in the administration building adjoining Soldier Field along the Chicago lakefront.

Meanwhile, Burke, McFetridge, and Shannon brainstormed various concepts and ideas aimed at encouraging wider participation in the city parks and a meaningful way to engage disabled children. "So I presented them with a plan for a one-day city-wide event—a track meet for intellectually challenged children—and they were very supportive. 'You can make it work, Anne,' they assured me."[18]

The task ahead would be daunting, but McFetridge and Shannon recognized the enormous possibilities. Identifying a funding source to make it all happen in a compact period of time, well, that was an entirely different matter. Anne's thoughts drifted back to Dr. Freeberg and his pioneering work with the Kennedy Foundation.

At Freeberg's urging, Anne attended conferences of the National Parks and Recreation Association and the National Association of Health, Education and Welfare. It served as an invaluable learning experience and even more importantly a potential funding source.

"Bill urged me to personally reach out and contact Mrs. Eunice Kennedy Shriver to seek financial assistance and the support of the Foundation for our event."[19] Eunice Kennedy Shriver, married to R. Sargent Shriver, former president of the Chicago Board of Education (1955–1960), the first director of the Peace Corps, and the United States Ambassador to France, held a deeply personal commitment to furthering the cause of inclusion for the intellectually disabled through therapeutic sports participation.[20] Eunice's sister Rosemary had been born with mild retardation. Mrs. Shriver publicly acknowledged this private family matter for the first time in the September 1962 edition of the *Saturday Evening Post*.

The sisters were deeply devoted to one another during the time they spent together, and as they grew up, the highly competitive Kennedy siblings actively engaged in athletics at the family compound in Hyannis, Massachusetts.

However, Rosemary's condition only worsened following a frontal lobotomy. For much of her remaining life, she was confined to a Wisconsin rest home.[21] Her sister's hardships inspired Eunice's call to action. In 1957, Shriver took over leadership of the family foundation. In the coming years she gave generously to research programs, national conferences, and programs acting on behalf of the mentally impaired. The foundation donated $1 million to establish the Joseph P. Kennedy Jr. Laboratories for Research on Mental Retardation at Massachusetts General Hospital. It became the first research center in the world focused on mental retardation.

Leveraging family connections with brothers John and Robert to create a presidential panel on intellectual disability, they drew attention to substandard conditions in the nation's mental hospitals. Senator Ted Kennedy helped write the Americans with Disabilities Act (ADA); Eunice's activism pushed the envelope forward.

Each year, beginning in June 1962, Mrs. Shriver conducted a free-of-charge summer camp for children with disabilities at Timberlawn, the three-hundred-acre Kennedy estate near Rockville Pike in Montgomery County, Maryland. Consulting experts, including Dr. James N. Oliver of England, whose 1958 study demonstrated that physical activities for children with intellectual disabilities had a positive effect that carried over into the classroom, worked with camp attendees and endorsed programming objectives at "Shriver Camp."[22]

Like Anne Burke back in Chicago, Eunice swam in the pool with the youngsters, played ball, personally supervised recreational activities, and made this much more than just another exercise in *noblesse oblige* by a prominent American family.

Accompanied by Steven Kelly, handling public relations for the park district, Anne flew to Washington, DC, hoping for the best but unsure of what to expect or the likely outcome. After all, these *were* the Kennedys, American royalty. It was only the second time in her young life that Anne had ever flown in an airplane.

"And so I met with Mrs. Shriver in December 1967. I was just twenty-three years of age and very nervous and excited as you can imagine," she remembered. "In my meeting with Mrs. Shriver, I gained the sense that I was a part of something very meaningful, perhaps even historical. It was a life-changing moment."[23]

Eunice Kennedy Shriver had already contemplated the start-up of a series of sporting events patterned after the Olympics for the disabled, but it was just a drawing- board idea kicking around with no official actions taken up to that point, until Anne Burke's arrival. In Washington, Anne found a sympathetic and understanding ally open to all possibilities. Importantly she had tremendous contacts to tap in to around the country. The two women agreed that the track and field meet Anne and her colleagues envisioned for Soldier Field in July 1968, should become much more than a one-day event. "This is bigger than Chicago," asserted Eunice. "With Chicago behind this program it can succeed as a national event."[24] Shriver envisioned a series of athletic competitions—to be scheduled biannually and to continue over a period of years. After witnessing the success of the Soldier Field games she set her ambitious plan into motion.

Because of its proximity to the rest of the nation in the American heartland and the Kennedy family's deep ties to the city both personally and professionally (family patriarch Joseph P. Kennedy owned the Merchandise Mart and had opened the Joseph P. Kennedy Home for Exceptional Children in Palos Park, Illinois, a south suburb of Chicago.

For eight years, Eunice and Sargent Shriver resided in a duplex at 2430 Lakeview Avenue during his tenure as president of the Chicago Board of

Education, and Chicago became the logical choice to host what was originally billed as the "National Olympics for the Mentally Retarded."[25] Anne Burke was most persuasive. The Kennedy Foundation agreed to underwrite the venture with a check for $25,000.

Soon, donations and service offers poured in from the city's four major professional sports teams, the White Sox, Cubs, Bears, and Blackhawks. The Illinois Sesquicentennial Commission agreed to supply commemorative medallions to every participant. The Chicago Fire Department hired a dozen clowns to entertain the children while the park district set up a petting zoo. Continental Air Transport Company arranged for thirty buses to pick up participants at O'Hare Field and deliver them to the Olympic Village, set up inside the LaSalle Hotel. Future Mayor Richard M. Daley, the son of "Hizzoner" Richard J. Daley, and young political up-and-comers Thomas Hynes, James Houlihan, Neil Hartigan, and Anne's husband, Edward Burke, volunteered for chauffeur duty between the LaSalle Hotel and Soldier Field.[26]

Anne Burke marshaled park-district resources and chose the sequence of athletic events to be included in the program. Although the Department of Health, Education and Welfare (HEW) in Washington declined to endorse the event, the plan came together nicely and became official on March 29, 1968, when Burke, Mrs. Shriver, and Bill McFetridge convened inside Mayor Daley's office in Chicago's city hall to announce the birth of Special Olympics. McFetridge called it "a great step forward in taking care of retarded children." Eunice said that "they have the same urge for physical activity and the same need to experience fun and success through play."[27]

Anne Burke added: "The Soldier Field set-up may be superior to any Olympic arena ever seen. We'll have our own Olympic flame above the south scoreboard where they had the Pan-American games flame in 1959. In the same arena with the track events, we'll have the swimming pool, a basketball court, and a Teflon rink for ice hockey. We have the Great Lakes Naval Training Band and 2,000 helium-filled balloons will be set loose in place of doves during the opening ceremony." Chicago hosted the third Pan American Games and the first to be held in the northern hemisphere on August 28-September 7, 1959.[28]

Not everyone in Chicago viewed this event with the same degree of enthusiasm and equanimity. Chicagoan Avery Brundage, the crusty fifth president of the International Olympic Community and the owner of the LaSalle Hotel, angrily dismissed the very idea of Special Olympics as demeaning to the reputation of the games.[29] Chicago Tribune Charities accused committee members of exploiting the participants by putting them on public display—which of course was the last thing in the world Burke and her colleagues would have sanctioned if they believed it to be even *partially* true.

Nearly a thousand athletes from twenty-six states and Canada converged upon Soldier Field, July 20, 1968, to compete in two hundred events including the fifty-yard dash, broad jump, high jump, swimming races, field hockey, and baseball throwing.

The musical accompaniment of a marching band filled the spacious lakefront stadium as "James," the seventeen-year-old young man carried the Olympic torch and lit the forty-five-foot flame that honored John F. Kennedy for championing research, education, and support for the disabled. The parade of athletes marched proudly past the reviewing stand where they were extended a warm welcome by Governor Sam Shapiro, Mayor Daley, Bill McFetridge, and Eunice Kennedy Shriver who had just flown in from Paris to represent the foundation. Holding aloft their school banners the young people entered the stadium to the musical accompaniment of the Great Lakes Naval Band.

Anne McGlone, wed to Edward M. Burke—who was recently installed as Democratic committeeman of the Fourteenth Ward and logged fifty-plus years of unbroken service to the community as alderman—marked the history-making moment with her new husband. It was a glorious sun-lit morning, filled with hope, inspiration, and the promise of brighter tomorrows.

The only thing missing amid the flutter of flags and banners, sunshine and optimism . . . were the people. Despite the promise of free admission, Greater Chicagoland stayed away. "Other than athletes, chaperones, families, the volunteers and organizers, security, members of staff, and the dignitaries, the stands were empty, absolutely empty."[30] After so much careful planning, it had to be a disappointing revelation for Anne Burke.

The newness of the games, public apathy, and unfamiliarity with the lofty goals of the fledgling movement had undoubtedly kept spectators away, although Chicago media turned out to report on the daylong competition and cite the personal involvement of professional sports greats Rafer Johnson, Paul Hornung, Bob Mathias, Stan Mikita, Ralph Metcalfe, Gary Erwin, Johnny Lattner, Ziggy Czarobski, Howard "Hopalong" Cassidy, Joe Giardello, and Olympic gold medalists Dianne Holum and Canadian skating star Barbara Ann Scott in making this happen.

As honorary chairman, Mrs. Shriver opened the games by proclaiming: "Let me win, but if I cannot win let me be brave in the attempt." Eunice Shriver's universal message of hope, of triumph, and inclusion resonates today in the faces of the special athletes around the world.[31]

After awarding a thousand medals to winners and participants, a chorus of "Auld Lang Syne" followed. The Special Olympics torch was extinguished at 6:05 P.M., but the end of the day signaled a beginning. "Our purpose here today is to secure a pledge that all retarded children will be given this chance in the future," Mrs. Shriver proclaimed.[32]

Turning to Mrs. Shriver, a beaming Mayor Daley remarked, "Eunice, the world will never be the same after this." By 1969, communities from all across the nation organized regional events. It had been decided to schedule Special Olympics every two years and local programs annually. Daley's optimism echoed across the land and his words soon became a self-fulfilling prophecy. In 1971, the US Olympic Committee granted approval to incorporate the name "Olympics" into the mission, vision, and official designation of the Special Olympics.[33]

Anne Burke, who overcame childhood dyslexia to become an attorney and later a judge on the Illinois Appellate Court, is today an Illinois Supreme Court justice. In June 2018, as the Special Olympics approached its Golden Anniversary and a series of commemorative events were scheduled along the Chicago lakefront near Soldier Field, Burke received a special invitation from Pope Francis to visit the Vatican for a special ceremony honoring the courage of Special Olympians, with Papal thanks given to the many volunteers, organizers, and coaches deeply involved in the movement since its inception.

Looking back on those formative years, as she helped to renew and re-shape the democracy of sport through inclusion and active participation of those previously stranded on the sidelines, Anne remembers occasional eruptions of infighting and jealousy among Special Olympics officials as to who deserved the most credit for the birth of the movement in the months and years after the 1968 inaugural games.

She concedes that the whole is far greater than the sum of its parts—a concept of Gestalt psychology—that applies to the historic rise of the movement. It is not possible for one individual to own the life-affirming Special Olympics. Each person—uniquely motivated by his or her interests and a sincere desire to work for humanity and to change the world—played starring roles.

Since 1968, the growth of the games has been nothing short of remarkable. In 1977 the first Special Olympics World Winter Games were held in Steamboat Springs, Colorado. Eleven years later the International Olympic Committee officially recognized Special Olympics, and in 2003 the first Special Olympics World Summer Games were held abroad in the host city of Dublin, Ireland.

By 1998, Special Olympics became the largest, amateur sports organization for people with disabilities in the world. Today, more than 5.7 million athletes, coaches, volunteers, and partners, are involved in the program representing 192 nations. Its legacy shall forever stand as an "inclusion revolution."

In a stirring speech, R. Sargent Shriver, honorary chairman of Special Olympics some years back, remarked: "We are the only worldwide, comprehensive sports organization which rises above nationalism. We do not, thanks be to God, rank countries by the number of medals won by their athletes. We do not fly national flags or play national anthems. We do not send away a majority of our participants with no rewards at all, no medals, no citations, for their efforts. Special Olympics builds people up. We don't knock anyone down. Special Olympics rewards human beings, not nations.[34]

"They remain a beacon of hope in a troubled world and a common thread to unify and bring people of diverse backgrounds, abilities and disabilities ... together under the flag of peace and understanding." "Everyone has the power to change the world effectively and emphatically," Anne Burke said. Quoting Marian Wright Edelman, the founder of the Children's Defense Fund, Burke adds: "If we don't stand up for children, then we don't stand for much."[35]

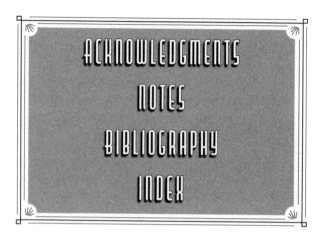

ACKNOWLEDGMENTS

NOTES

BIBLIOGRAPHY

INDEX

ACKNOWLEDGMENTS

I extend thanks to Sylvia Frank Rodrigue, for her critical insights and suggestions through multiple drafts, my skillful editors Wayne Larsen and Lisa Marty, and Linda Buhman, Jennifer Egan, and Judy Verdich for help in obtaining illustrations—the Southern Illinois University Press team that shepherded this book through to publication.

Additional thanks to Ken Zurski, author of *Unremembered*, Karl Kageff, formerly of SIU Press, Pamela Olander, a constant source of encouragement; fellow authors Dick Bales and Thomas Frisbie, and the many dear friends and past colleagues from the Society of Midland Authors and the Chicago writing world. A final note of thanks to Justice Anne M. Burke of the Illinois Supreme Court whose commitment to the mission of Special Olympics has shaped a brighter world for children and adults with intellectual differences.

NOTES

INTRODUCTION: TWENTY-ONE
TALES OF OLD CHICAGO

1. As cited in Richard C. Lindberg, *Quotable Chicago* (Chicago: Wild Onion Books, 1996).

CHAPTER 1. THE BROTHERS BOOTH

1. *Baltimore Sun*, April 17, 1865.

2. *Chicago Tribune*, November 6, 1857; also, November 26, 1857.

3. *Chicago Tribune*, November 6, 1857.

4. "The Funeral Services Held Yesterday at St. Paul's Church," *Chicago Tribune*, November 19, 1881.

5. John Wilkes Booth was born at Tudor Hall, his parent's farm in Bel Air, Maryland, on May 10, 1838. He and his brother Edwin were the illegitimate sons of Junius Booth and his mistress Mary Ann Holmes of England. John was the ninth of ten Booth children, and made his stage debut at age seventeen on August 14, 1855, at Baltimore's Charles Street Theater portraying the Earl of Richmond in *Richard III*.

6. Prentiss Ingraham, "Wilkes Booth's Last Burial," reprinted in the *Chicago Tribune*, February 26, 1899.

7. *Chicago Evening Journal*, April 17, 1865.

8. *Chicago Tribune*, January 21, 1862.

9. Frederick J. Glahe, called "the father of the free lunch" operated the McVicker's saloon until his death on February 18, 1911. Barkeeps in those days provided thirsty patrons with free sandwiches and other fare for the price of a beer. In desperate times, for many homeless or otherwise impoverished persons, the saloon lunch marked the difference between starvation and life-giving sustenance.

10. *Chicago Tribune*, December 19, 1862.

11. Letter from Booth to Keach quoted in John Rhodehamel and Louise Taper, eds., *Right or Wrong, God Judge Me* (Urbana: University of Illinois Press,

1997). Also: *To Make a Fortune: John Wilkes Booth Following the Money Trail.* Clinton, MD: Surratt Society, 2018.

12. Quoted in the *Chicago Evening Journal*, April 15, 1865, and the *Rock Island Evening Argus*, April 21, 1865, and printed verbatim in *The Trial of the Alleged Assassins and Conspirators at Washington City, D.C., May and June 1865: For the Murder of President Abraham Lincoln; Full of Illustrative Engravings* (Philadelphia: T. B. Peterson and Brothers, 1865; digitized by the Indiana State Library and available at Internet Archive, http://www.archive.org/details /trialofallegedas00john). Also, Dion Haco, *The Assassinator of President Lincoln* (New York: T. R. Dawley, Publisher for the Million, 1865), 39.

13. Terry Alford, *Fortune's Fool: The Life of John Wilkes Booth* (New York: Oxford University Press, 2015), 250.

14. "The Booth Dynasty," *Los Angeles Times*, March 28, 1897.

15. Ibid.

16. Robert H. Fowler, "The Tragedy at Ford's Theater," quoted in http:// washingtonoddities.blogspot.com/2018/06/campbell-hospital-near-washington -dc-by.html.

17. The shooting of Booth haunted Thomas "Boston" Corbett, a man of zealous religious conviction bordering on fanaticism and dementia for the remainder of his life. On the night of July 16, 1858, after feeling "lustful" toward two New York prostitutes he observed on the street, Corbett returned to his residence to castrate himself. A doctor's attention saved him from bleeding to death. After the Civil War had ended, Corbett became a full-time minister at the Siloam Methodist Episcopal Mission in Camden, New Jersey, where the townspeople regarded him as something of a minor celebrity. Wherever he went, strangers approached him for his accounting of the Booth shooting and an autograph. Public speaking opportunities followed, but inevitably Corbett disappointed his audience by launching into a sermon demanding repentance and salvation. While working as the assistant sergeant-at-arms in the Kansas House of Representatives on February 15, 1887, he drew a pistol on the Speaker of the House, clearing the chambers. Although no one was wounded in the fray, the court ordered Corbett institutionalized in the Topeka Insane Asylum. The mentally unhinged ex-soldier ("Lincoln's Avenger"), who had been incarcerated in the notorious Andersonville prisoner of war camp during the Civil War, escaped from the institution on May 26, 1888, and disappeared. He is believed to have died in the forest of Hinckley, Minnesota, in 1894, although no one can verify this with any certainty. See the June 1929 issue of *Scribner's Magazine*.

18. The first Booth Theater, built between 1867 and 1869, was demolished in 1883.

19. Veteran actress and theatrical manager Laura Keene (d. November 6, 1873), brought her company to Chicago for the return engagement of Tom Taylor's eccentric farce *Our American Cousin* at Aiken's Theater on May 22, 1873. The comedy fell out of favor with the American public following the assassination of Abraham Lincoln, but eventually the production enjoyed a revival. On February 12–13, 1935, the Chicago Historical Society sponsored two performances given by the Goodman Memorial Players in the museum assembly hall to commemorate the anniversary of Lincoln's birth.

20. "Edwin Booth, Gentleman; A Man among Thousands," *Baltimore Sun*, December 30, 1906.

21. The partnership owned two other Chicago theaters, the Randolph and the Bijou. In July 1922, Jones signed a contract with Paramount Studios agreeing to show only Paramount-produced movies at the McVicker's.

CHAPTER 2. THE FAMILY O'LEARY

1. "The Fire: West Division," *Chicago Times*, October 18, 1871.

2. *Chicago Journal*, October 21, 1871.

3. Henry Raymond Hamilton, *The Epic of Chicago* (Chicago: Willett, Clark and Company, 1910).

4. Quoted in Karen Sawislak, *Smoldering City: Chicagoans and the Great Fire 1871–1874* (Chicago: University of Chicago Press, 1995), 44.

5. "The Organ of the Petrolbuse," *Chicago Evening Journal*, October 23, 1871.

6. "Mrs. O'Leary's Cow Story Refuted by Old Reporter," *Chicago Tribune*, January 21, 1915.

7. "Kin of O'Leary Absolves Cow in Fire of 1871," *Chicago Tribune*, October 8, 1933. The story was originally reported in the *Tribune* of September 26, 1903, "Centennial Eve Reveals Truth of Great Fire: Mrs. Mary Callahan Tells How Gathering of Merrymakers Innocently Caused Terrible Disaster."

8. "Last Survivor of O'Leary Fire Family Is Dead," *Chicago Tribune*, December 26, 1936. Before she died, Mrs. Ledwell affirmed that Denis "Peg-Leg" Sullivan pounded on the back door of their parents' home on DeKoven Street to alert them to the fire in the barn.

9. Clerk of the City Council City of Chicago, *Chicago City Council Journal Proceedings*, November 7, 1871.

10. "Linked to Chicago's Two Worst Fires: The Family O'Leary (A Tale of Mostly Jim the Gambler)," *Chicago Tribune*, March 31, 1935.

11. "Centennial Eve Reveals Truth of the Great Fire," *Chicago Tribune*, September 26, 1903.

12. Interview with Sollitt published in the *Chicago Tribune*, June 24, 1894, "Tales of Early Days."

13. "Centennial Eve Reveals Truth of the Great Fire," *Chicago Tribune*, September 26, 1903.

14. "Chicago Fire Refugees Relive Time of Terror: Relish Stories of Former Hardships," *Chicago Tribune*, October 10, 1928.

15. Ibid.

16. "True Story of Chicago Fire Told at Last," *Chicago Tribune*, October 20, 1927.

17. "Chicago Tragedies," *Chicago Tribune*, August 24, 1885.

18. "Puggy Is Here," *Chicago Tribune*, September 28, 1885.

19. "Rushes to Ireland on Bet: Wager Due to Fizz Talk," *Chicago Tribune*, December 17, 1908.

20. "Rushes to Ireland on Bet: Wager Due to Fizz Talk," *Chicago Tribune*, December 17, 1908; "In the Wake of the News: Big Jim O'Leary," *Chicago Tribune*, February 1, 1925.

21. "Jim O'Leary's Eye to Easy Bets Gets Crossed," *Chicago Tribune*, December 23, 1918. Detailed accounts of the Freda Welchman murder can be found in the *Tribune*, December 22, 1918.

22. "In the Wake of the News: Big Jim O'Leary," *Chicago Tribune*, February 1, 1925.

23. "Back of the Yards Says Goodbye to Jim O'Leary," *Chicago Tribune*, January 27, 1925.

24. "O'Leary Who Would Bet on Anything, Dies," *Chicago Tribune*, January 23, 1925.

25. "Jim O'Leary Jr. Is Eloper," *Chicago Tribune*, January 29, 1910.

26. "Linked to Chicago's Two Worst Fires: The Family O'Leary (A Tale of Mostly Jim the Gambler)," *Chicago Tribune*, March 31, 1935.

CHAPTER 3. FOUR BUTCHERS
TRYING TO GO TO HEAVEN

1. Archibald Clybourn (1802–1872) opened Chicago's first slaughterhouse in 1827. During the 1832 Blackhawk War, frightened citizens living outside the palisades of the fort took refuge inside. Clybourn and John Noble fed the entire population.

2. Samuel Allerton (1828–1914), a descendent of Mayflower pilgrim Isaac Allerton, bought his first cattle shipment at the Merrick Yards on Cottage Grove Avenue in 1856. The twenty-five story Allerton Hotel (now the Warwick-Allerton) is a Chicago landmark, opened in 1924. Radio personality Don McNeill hosted his popular "Breakfast Club" program in the Cloud Room during the 1960s.

3. "Greatest Cattle Market the World Has Ever Known! Frontier Supply Post Unhurt by Rivalry," *Chicago Tribune*, October 10, 1904.

4. See: Kansas State Historical Society, "Kansapedia," www.kshs.org/kansapedia /joseph-mccoy/17219, for a good account of Joseph McCoy (1837–1815) and his times.

5. Quoted in Donald Zochert, "Heinrich Schliemann's Chicago Journal," *Chicago History Magazine*, Spring-Summer 1973.

6. "A Card to the Public," *Chicago Tribune*, October 14, 1886.

7. "They Find Awful Filth," *Chicago Tribune*, January 18, 1890. The town of Lake, inclusive of Hyde Park and continuing west to the stockyards, was once a suburb of Chicago until its annexation in 1889. By the 1930s, the Southwest Side community gained a new community name: Back of the Yards.

8. "Bubbly Creek's Doom Finally Decided," *Chicago Tribune*, October 17, 1919.

9. Quoted in "Bubbly Creek's Fortunes Might Finally Be on the Rise," *Chicago Sun-Times*, December 28, 2018.

10. "Foes of Bubbly Creek Vent Ire of Alderman Martin," *Chicago Tribune*, June 30, 1915.

11. Quoted in Richard Lindberg, "The Rise and Fall of Chicago's Greatest Industry," *Chicagoly* Magazine, December 19, 2017.

12. Ibid.

13. "Pulpit Praise of Armour," *Chicago Tribune*, January 14, 1901. After relocating to Chicago from Milwaukee where he worked in the commission business, Phillip Armour established the firm of Armour and Company in 1868. Upon his death, Armour bequeathed to his widow Malvina Belle Ogden Armour the sum of $15 million for philanthropic enterprises.

14. Richard Lindberg, *Quotable Chicago* (Chicago: Wild Onion Books, 1996), 45.

15. At the time of Morris's passing, his estate executors estimated his net worth to be $25 million. His Chicago operation comprised forty buildings with a floor space of sixty acres. At its peak, Morris and Company opened a hundred branches across the United States. The firm merged with Armour in 1923.

16. Libby McNeil and G. H. Hammond were two other prominent packing-house firms.

17. See Paul Charles Bourget, *Outremer: Impressions of America* (London: T. Fisher Unwin Paternoster Square, 1895), 165.

18. Quoted in Arthur Meeker, *Chicago with Love* (New York: Alfred Knopf, 1955), 99. Arthur and Grace Murray Meeker, important social and civic leaders for more than a half-century, resided at 1815 Prairie Avenue, down the street from the Philip Armours.

19. "Linked to Chicago's Two Worst Fires—The Family O'Leary: A Tale Mostly of Jim, the Gambler," *Chicago Tribune*, March 31, 1935. Backed by James O'Leary, Captain William P. Clancy resigned his post as police inspector in

charge of the stockyards on January 27, 1912, in order to run for a congressional seat in the Third District.

20. Howard, Jonas, "The Greatest Cattle Market the World Has Known," *Chicago Tribune*, October 10, 1904.

21. Upton Sinclair, an outspoken advocate for the downtrodden, received a $500 advance from *The Appeal to Reason* to serialize a magazine story about working conditions in the meatpacking houses. For six months he worked undercover in the plant, recording his impressions and crafting a powerfully written and sensitive tale serialized from February 25 through November 4, 1905. Sinclair published his novel in book form as *The Jungle* with Doubleday in 1906. The novel rallied the public and Congress to enact key legislation and government regulation including the passage of the Meat Inspection Act and Pure Food and Drug Act. Writing in *Cosmopolitan* in October of the same year, he observed: "I aimed at the public's heart and by accident I hit it in the stomach."

22. "John B. Sherman's Plans," *Chicago Tribune*, November 12, 1899.

23. James G. Watt, secretary of the interior declared the iconic limestone gate a national historic landmark on May 29, 1981, nine years after its inclusion in the National Register of Historic Places. The firefighters who perished while battling the deadly infernos of 1910 and 1934 are depicted in a monument to the fallen directly behind the gate.

24. The John B. Sherman home in the exclusive Prairie Avenue district was just the second commission for Burnham and Root in their distinguished careers.

CHAPTER 4. ELISHA GRAY
AND THE TELEPHONE

1. Irish scientist John Tyndall (1820–1893), conducted scholarly research into light, sound, and radiant heat, and was one of the nineteenth century's most acclaimed and brilliant scientific minds.

2. "The Telephone: The Trial of Mr. Gray's Wonderful Invention," *Chicago Tribune*, January 5, 1875.

3. Ibid.

4. Ibid.

5. New Yorker Enos M. Barton (1842–1916), widely known in engineering circles, arrived in Chicago in 1869. He entered into a business partnership with Elisha Gray the same year, and was named secretary of Western Electric in 1872, the firm he helped cofound. He advanced to the vice presidency in 1887, later becoming president, then chairman of the board.

6. General Stager became president of Western Electric Manufacturing following the 1872 business reorganization. By 1880 the firm had grown into the largest electrical manufacturer in the nation. In its formative years, Western Electric battled companies operating under the patent obtained by Alexander

Graham Bell for primacy in the fiercely competitive telephone industry. In 1881 the Bell companies absorbed Western Electric into its expansive monopoly and kept the plant open as an equipment supply and telephone production factory, dropping "Manufacturing" from the company name. General Stager continued as president until 1885.

7. Boyd Crummins Patterson, "The Story of Elisha Gray," Boyd Crummins Papers, edited and prepared for publication by assistant professor Frank Merrill for the Historical Collection of Washington and Jefferson College Library, Washington, Pennsylvania, 1969, 31–32.

8. Alexander Graham Bell demonstrated the practical advantage of his pole magnet telephone at the 1876 Philadelphia Centennial celebration.

9. Zenas Fisk Wilber previously served in the Civil War with Major Marcellus Bailey.

10. *Baltimore Sun*, May 22, 1886.

11. Ibid.

12. "Professor Bell's Denial," *Baltimore Sun*, May 24, 1886.

13. See United States v. American Bell Telephone Co., 128 US 315 (1888), argued October 9–10, 1888. The full name of the case is Amos Emerson Dolbear et al. v. American Bell Telephone Company; Molecular Telephone Company v. American Bell Telephone Company; American Bell Telephone Company v. Molecular Telephone Company; Clay Commercial Telephone Company v. American Bell Telephone Company; People's Telephone Company v. American Bell Telephone Company; Overland Telephone Company v. American Bell Telephone Company (128 US 320).

14. "Elisha Gray: The Inventor of the Telephone Discourses of Its Greatness," *Chicago Tribune*, September 1, 1882.

15. In 1909 George Hughes, a native of North Dakota, converted an oil cookstove inside his shop on South Dearborn Street into the first electric range. The Hughes Company evolved into Hotpoint. In post–World War II America, Hotpoint turned out six hundred thousand ranges a year in just one of its Chicago plants. Eugene McDonald of Zenith began his career as an automobile mechanic earning six dollars a week. A former naval intelligence officer during World War I, McDonald and two friends tinkered with a ham radio station, giving it the call letters 9ZN. The "ZN" prefix inspired the corporate name, Zenith.

16. *Chicago Tribune*, September 1, 1882.

CHAPTER 5. THE FIRST POLICEWOMAN

1. "Little Victims of Vice," *Chicago Tribune*, September 9, 1888.

2. The Illinois School of Agriculture and Manual Training School (a nonsectarian home and school) reported that it had taken 1,780 boys from the streets and found homes for 1,526 of them between 1887 and 1896.

3. "Brains Stunted by Child Labor," *Chicago Tribune,* August 15, 1906.

4. *Chicago Tribune,* February 14, 1888.

5. The *Chicago Times* contradicts the *Herald* and the *Tribune* in their description of the Gaughan family's economic situation. Various accounts describe the family as "middle class." The *Times* infers that Owen and his wife raised their children in abject poverty. It is probable that the latter description is closest to the truth.

6. Laid out in 1866, Forrest evolved into an important Illinois railhead linking Chicago to Kansas City for the Toledo Peoria and Western Railroad and the Wabash Railroad, constructed in 1880. By the 1920s, the importance of the railroad diminished.

7. "A Murderer Caught," *Chicago Times,* February 29, 1888. Also: "Zeph Davis Captured," *Chicago Tribune,* February 29, 1888.

8. "Zephyr Davis' Crime," *Chicago Tribune,* March 31, 1888.

9. Louis Lingg embraced Chicago's flourishing underground anarchist movement and joined the International Carpenter's and Joiner's Union. He lent his support to a campaign shortening the workday to eight hours, one that targeted rising labor unrest at the McCormick Reaper Works on the city's southwest side. A planned rally denouncing the heavy-handed tactics of the Chicago Police at Haymarket Square (Randolph and Des Plaines Streets) the evening of May 4, 1886, resulted in the deaths of seven uniformed officers after a bomb, hurled from the vestibule of a nearby factory building, exploded in a police column sent in to disperse the meeting. Two other bombs were to be exploded at two North Side police stations as a diversionary tactic that same day, but the alleged bomb thrower lost his nerve. History records this watershed event in American labor history as the "Haymarket Riot." On November 10, 1887, the day before the convicted Haymarket men were to hang, Lingg, the youngest of them, committed suicide by exploding a dynamite cap in his mouth. He blew off half of his face but lived just long enough to pen the words *"Hoch die anarchie!"* (Hurray for anarchy!)

10. Ibid.

11. Kirk Hawes (1839–1904), for twelve years a judge, won election to the superior court in 1880 becoming its chief justice on November 23, 1891.

12. *Chicago Times,* May 13, 1888.

13. *Chicago Times,* May 12, 1888.

14. "Zeph Was Ready to Die," *Chicago Tribune,* May 13, 1888.

15. Ibid.

16. "A Big Unfeeling Crowd Sees Him Die," *Chicago Times,* May 13, 1888.

17. Rick Barrett, "Resurrecting the Lost Legacy of the Nation's First Policewoman," unpublished research report. Edward M. Burke files.

18. "Women Will Watch," *Chicago Times,* July 26, 1889.

19. Ibid.

20. Journalist, social reformer, and early leader of the civil rights movement Ida B. Wells-Barnett (1862–1931) was one of the founding members of the National Association for the Advancement of Colored People (NAACP). Wells drew attention to the evil specter of racial lynching in the South through her investigative reporting. She published her findings in a pamphlet entitled *Southern Horrors: Lynch Law in All Its Phases*. Wells-Barnett emerged as the leading spokesperson of the nineteenth-century civil rights movement. Lucy Louisa Flower (1837–1921) organized the Illinois Training School for Nurses. During her thirty years of active engagement in educational and civic club life, she advocated for manual training classes in city high schools, and the introduction of kindergarten courses to primary school.

21. "Protecting Female Employees," *Chicago Tribune*, December 16, 1891.

22. "The Only Woman Police Sergeant in the World," *Chicago Tribune*, August 7, 1904.

23. Ibid.

24. "The Only Woman Detective on the Chicago Police Force," *Chicago Tribune*, October 28, 1906.

25. Ibid.

CHAPTER 6. WHERE TIME BEGAN

1. The Dearborn Astronomical Observatory, a five-story structure, opened in April 1866 on a ten-acre tract of land near the Chicago lakefront for the benefit of students at Chicago University (not to be confused with the University of Chicago), to gain an appreciation of practical astronomy and the cosmos. Jonathan Young Scammon, president of the Chicago Astronomical Society, and Thomas Hoyne secured a six-ton, twenty-three-foot-long "equatorial" telescope considered the largest refracting instrument in the world at the time. Scammon spent $30,000 of his own money to build the observatory tower (composed of two independent buildings), which he named in honor of his wife, whose last name was Dearborn. The observatory, one of only five of its kind in the United States at the time, suffered repeated financial setbacks and a chronic shortage of endowment monies through the first decades of its history after Jonathan Scammon could no longer bear the financial burden of its upkeep. In November 1887, several years after the original Chicago University went broke, Northwestern University purchased the telescope from the Chicago Astronomical Society and relocated it to Sheridan Road in Evanston where it was housed in a newly constructed tower.

2. Allen G. Debus, ed., *World Who's Who in Science: A Biographical Dictionary of Notable Scientists from Antiquity to the Present*, 1st ed. (Chicago: A. N. Marquis, 1968), 5. Cleveland Abbe (1838–1916), nicknamed "Old Probability"

for the accuracy of his weather reports long before weather reporting became an exact science, was appointed to head the US Weather Bureau on January 3, 1871. To deliver accurate and reliable weather forecasts, Abbe pushed the railroad companies to adapt standard time zones.

3. Sandford Fleming laid his proposal, to establish a new prime meridian for the world 180 degrees from Greenwich to form the basis of standard time, before the Imperial Academy of Sciences of St. Petersburg in 1880. The academy unreservedly endorsed Fleming's proposal. On January 9, 1881, the Canadian Institute provided similar approval.

4. Chicago's official local time was ten minutes slower prior to the formal adoption of Central time on November 9, 1883.

5. "Standard Time," *Chicago Tribune*, November 20, 1883.

6. Chicago's mercantile and lodging moguls were less certain about the hotel's future and its prospects for success in 1871. Its distance from the city's business center and the shabby surroundings in this squalid brothel and crime district south of Madison Street and west of Clark, known as "The Patch," foretold financial failure. The six-story hotel and the remnants of the old slum district were destroyed in the Great Chicago Fire. The replacement Grand Pacific, built at a staggering cost of $1.5 million by three major railroads, was designed by William W. Boyington and opened in June 1873. The addition of the new board of trade building across the street and a score of office buildings nearby shifted the business district to LaSalle Street and increased business. For many years, the hotel enjoyed a first-class patronage. In February 1890, John Drake, who acquired the property in 1874, sold the hotel but not the land to Levi Z. Leiter, former business partner of Marshall Field I, for the sum of $403,000.

CHAPTER 7. THE SCARLET LETTER VERDICT

1. An air of mystery and doubt surrounds Leslie Carter's alleged suicide attempt. Contemporary sources allege that it was accidental, but the evidence is not 100 percent conclusive. However, given his state of mind, a suicide attempt seems highly probable.

2. *Chicago Tribune*, September 26, 1908.

3. Her date of birth is a matter of historical dispute. In various accounts the year given is 1862.

4. "Planning a Yacht Expedition," *Chicago Tribune*, April 26, 1889.

5. "Mrs. Carter to Carter," *Chicago Tribune*, November 27, 1887.

6. Ibid.

7. "Leslie Carter's Answer," *Chicago Tribune*, May 12, 1888.

8. "Mr. Carter Steps Down," *Chicago Tribune*, April 27, 1889.

9. Ibid.

10. Emmett Dedmon, "An Ardent Temperament Rather Than a Weak Will," *Fabulous Chicago: A Great City's History and People* (New York: Random House, Inc., 1953), 211. Also: "Mrs. Carter's Denial," *Chicago Tribune*, March 1, 1888.

11. "The Imperturbable Maid," *Chicago Times*, April 24, 1889.

12. "Letters Read in Court," *Chicago Tribune*, April 26, 1889.

13. "Platonic Kyrle Bellew," *Chicago Tribune*, May 8, 1889.

14. Ibid.

15. "Carter versus Carter," *Chicago Tribune*, November 19, 1887.

16. Ibid.

17. "Maid Follows Mistress on the Stand," *Chicago Tribune*, April 23, 1889.

18. "Leslie Carter's Answer," *Chicago Tribune*, May 12, 1888.

19. "Leslie Carter's Answer," *Chicago Tribune*, May 12, 1888.

20. Emmett Dedmon, "An Ardent Temperament Rather Than a Weak Will," *Fabulous Chicago* (New York: Random House, 1953), 213.

21. "The Famous Trial Begun," *Chicago Tribune*, April 18, 1889.

22. "Pleading for Carter: Luther Laflin Mills Makes a Great Speech for His Client," *Chicago Tribune*, May 15, 1889.

23. Nathaniel K. Fairbank provided the financial means necessary to build the Chicago Club, arguably one of the city's most prestigious and elegant private dining venues, which opened in 1876.

24. Edward Gilmore (d. 1908) the proprietor of New York's famed Academy of Music, acquired the lease to P. T. Barnum's Hippodrome (later Madison Square Garden), and renamed it Gilmore's Gardens, where many of the leading musical acts and orchestra leaders of the late Gilded Age performed, including Maestro Theodore Thomas, conductor of the Chicago Symphony Orchestra.

25. "As Mrs. Carter Tells It," *Chicago Tribune*, June 19, 1896. The David Belasco papers are on file in the Billy Rose Theater Division of the New York Public Library for the Performing Arts. Playwright, producer, and builder of theaters, Belasco (1853–1931), along with the Cohans and Foys, redefined the essence of Broadway and musical comedy before and after World War I. Belasco is famously quoted as saying, "Beauty? What has that got to do with the making of an actress?" He was often referred to as the "Bishop of Broadway" for his habit of wearing clerical garb as everyday clothing.

26. "Belasco's Suit on Trial," *Chicago Tribune*, June 4, 1896.

27. Delos Avery, "Presenting Mrs. Leslie Carter," *Chicago Tribune*, September 26, 1943. Quotation drawn from the work of William Winter (1836–1917), American dramatic critic and author who profiled the lives of Edwin Booth, Joseph Jefferson, Richard Mansfield, and other stage luminaries.

28. Delos Avery, "Presenting Mrs. Leslie Carter in a Stirring Drama," *Chicago Tribune*, September 26, 1943.

29. "Her Boy Dudley," *Chicago Mail*, February 9, 1891.

30. "Mrs. Carter's Success: Features that Distinguish Her Work in the Ugly Duckling," *Chicago Tribune*, February 15, 1891.

31. "As Mrs. Carter Tells It," *Chicago Tribune*, June 19, 1896.

32. "Belasco Wins the Suit," *Chicago Tribune*, June 24, 1896.

33. "Mrs. Leslie Carter, Star of Theater in Belasco Era, Dies in Retirement," *Hartford Courant*, November 14, 1937.

34. "Tiff, Prelude to Carter Wedding," *Chicago Tribune*, July 15, 1906. Charles Dillingham (1868–1934), a Hartford, Connecticut, native and noted producer, "rescued" a score of famed actors and actresses in the waning days of Vaudeville and pointed them in new career directions in Hollywood and on the stage; among them, Fred Astaire, Pert Kelton, W. C. Fields, and the Dolly Sisters.

35. "Mrs. Leslie Carter, Star of Theater in Belasco Era, Dies in Retirement," *Hartford Courant*, November 14, 1937.

36. *Chicago Tribune*, November 10, 1924.

37. "Mrs. Carter, Hussy of Nineties Revives Circle," *Los Angeles Times*, September 9, 1934. Caroline starred in a revival of *The Circle* that month.

38. Ibid.

CHAPTER 8. FOREVER OPEN, CLEAR, AND FREE

1. "Move to Block Victory of Ward," *Chicago Tribune*, October 27, 1909.

2. Richard Sears and Alvah C. Roebuck published their first mail-order catalog in 1887. In 1893 the firm relocated to Chicago to establish company headquarters and open a nationwide chain of stores we know today as Sears Roebuck and Company.

3. The Grange, founded as the Patrons of Husbandry by Minnesotan Oliver Kelley in 1867, was an advocacy and political lobby group that served the interests of the farm community. Each lodge was a "grange." In 1874, there were fourteen hundred Grange chapters active in Illinois.

4. By 1888, company sales reached $1.8 million.

5. In February 1865, Field, Palmer, and Leiter incorporated their firm with $600,000 in working capital. Marshall Field personally contributed $100,000. Potter Palmer, better known for his signature downtown hotel and his social ranking became a special partner.

6. Joseph D. Kearney and Thomas W. Merrill, "Private Rights in Public Lands: The Chicago Lakefront, Montgomery Ward, and the Public Dedication Doctrine," *Northwestern University Law Review* 105, no. 4 (2011), 1468.

7. Richard E. Schmidt was the architect of record. The twenty-one-and-a-half-foot gilded bronze figure held aloft a flaming torch and was conceived by J. Massey Rhine. It was given the name *Progress Lighting the Way for Commerce*, and received its unveiling on October 20, 1900.

8. Kearney and Merrill, "Private Rights in Public Lands: The Chicago Lakefront, Montgomery Ward, and the Public Dedication Doctrine," *Northwestern University Law Review* 105, no. 4 (2011), 1424–25. An act of the Illinois legislature on January 9, 1836, created the Board of Canal Commissioners to oversee the entire route of the Illinois-Michigan Canal and to select and sell town lots and subdivisions, with jurisdiction over the Fort Dearborn Addition encompassing Lake-Front Park, and to maintain it as a green space. The coming of the Illinois Central train depot in 1892 contributed to an exodus of residents and the demolition of the once stately Greek revival homes lining Park Row. In 1893 the Department of Public Works expanded the thoroughfare to a hundred feet wide and paved the roadway with asphalt. Much of the former space once occupied by homes became a pick-up and drop-off access area (a parking lot, if you will), for cabs and carriages.

9. Kearney and Merrill, "Private Rights in Public Lands: The Chicago Lakefront, Montgomery Ward, and the Public Dedication Doctrine," *Northwestern University Law Review* 105, no. 4 (2011), 1424–25.

10. Kearney and Merrill, "Private Rights in Public Lands," 1460.

11. *Chicago Tribune*, July 18, 1884.

12. Quoted in the *Tribune*, March 25, 1885, by an attorney seeking an injunction from the courts and the Chicago City Council to halt construction of the park. The team that eventually became the Cubs won the right to play their home games here but only on Mondays, Wednesdays, and Fridays.

13. Frederick Francis Cook, *Bygone Days in Chicago* (Chicago: A. C. McClurg and Company, 1910).

14. "Clears Lakefront," *Chicago Tribune*, November 9, 1897.

15. "Watchdog Given Contempt Order," *Chicago Tribune*, June 26, 1906. The Crerar Library, a great informational storehouse with one of the largest book collections in the United States, opened in 1920 at the northwest corner of Michigan Avenue and Randolph. The imposing fifteen-story library building designed by Holabird and Roche stood at this location until its demolition in 1981. The Crerar collection relocated to a new building on the University of Chicago campus in 1985.

16. Chicago philanthropist Max Adler bequeathed $750,000 to build the nation's first planetarium.

17. See George Packard, "Some Interesting Cases Decided by Justice Cartwright," *Illinois Law Review* 15 (November 1920), 248–51. Also John A. Lupton, "Illinois Supreme Court History: Montgomery Ward and the Chicago Lakefront," Illinois Supreme Court Historic Preservation Committee, March 2018. Justice Cartwright served on the Illinois Supreme Court bench from 1895 to 1924 and authored over seventeen hundred opinions.

18. US Army personnel, acting under the orders of Attorney General Francis Biddle, physically carried Avery out of Montgomery Ward headquarters April 27, 1944. Avery had refused to sign union contracts with the United Mail Order, Warehouse and Retail Employees Union. The photo of the obstinate company president being carted out of the building is one of the most enduring images from the home front during World War II.

CHAPTER 9. THE HAUNTING OF
THE SCHUTTLER HOUSE

1. John M. Van Osdel (1811–1891) was the first architect to permanently settle in Chicago, arriving in the city with his family on June 9, 1837.

2. Charles Dickens, *American Notes for General Circulation* (London: Chapman and Hall, 1842). Also: "Charles Dickens Didn't Enjoy Journey through Ohio," *Mansfield News Journal*, July 30, 2016.

3. *Chicagology*, "Peter Schuttler Wagon Works," chicagology.com/rebuilding /rebuilding038/.

4. "Army Wagons," *Chicago Tribune*, July 20, 1861. Medill was referring to a provisional state of the United States, proposed in 1849 by settlers from the Church of Jesus Christ of Latter-day Saints. The provisional Mormon state of Deseret existed for slightly over two years and was never officially recognized by the United States government. The name derives from the word for "honeybee" in the Book of Mormon.

5. Hotel magnate Potter Palmer and dry-goods merchant and philanthropist John V. Farwell were the only other Chicago business magnates that qualified during this period.

6. "City's Growth is Mansion's Doom," *Chicago Tribune*, November 15, 1912.

7. See the *Chicago Tribune*, October 16, 1881. The proposed transit line operated by the West Division Railway Company extended from Michigan Avenue to Halsted Street.

8. Quoted from Mary Dougherty, "Haunted West Side Mansion," *Chicago Inter-Ocean*, July 13, 1913. In this lengthy article, Ms. Dougherty lays out for the reader all the particulars concerning the history of paranormal activity from personal interviews she conducted with contemporary Chicagoans. Decades later, reporter Will Leonard discussed the Schuttler mansion and its infamous reputation in his *Chicago Tribune* feature story, "What's Happened to Haunted Houses?," April 7, 1957.

9. Mary Dougherty, "Haunted West Side Mansion," *Chicago Inter-Ocean*, July 13, 1913.

10. "Bullet in Back of Boy's Head Puzzles Police," *Chicago Tribune*, August 13, 1919.

11. *Chicago Tribune*, "Dies in Six-Story Plunge at C.A.A.," June 12, 1924.

12. *Chicago Tribune*, "Dies in Six-Story Plunge at C.A.A.," June 12, 1924.

13. *Chicago Tribune*, July 28, 1952.

CHAPTER 10. STARS AND BARS
AND THE SYMBOL OF A CITY

1. Not to be confused with John B. Rice, theater man and former mayor of Chicago, or John A. Rice (d. 1888), nationally known hotelier, hired as business manager of the Tremont House in May 1875. Rice acquired title to the hotel in 1879, and two other men (as the hotel lessees) became defendants in a civil suit filed by Ira and James Couch in 1883, in which they were accused of robbing Rice of his property and failing to provide a proper accounting of expenditures charged to his various accounts during the time he ran the hotel. Ira Couch managed the hotel at Lake Street and Dearborn from 1837 to 1858. Senator Stephen A. Douglas passed away in his Tremont House suite in 1861. The famous old lodging house fell to the wrecking ball on September 2, 1901. George Wellington "Cap" Streeter, the famous "squatter" who claimed ownership of a large swath of Lake Michigan shoreline at Oak Street (dubbed "the *Deestrict* of Michigan" by this famous eccentric), was the last tenant to vacate the premises.

2. "How the Chicago Municipal Flag Came To Be Chosen," *Chicago Tribune*, July 17, 1921.

3. Mike Royko, *Boss: Richard J. Daley of Chicago* (New York: E. P. Dutton, 1971), 83.

CHAPTER 11. AMERICA'S FIRST
AUTOMOBILE RACE

1. Herman H. Kohlsaat (1853–1924), a Galena farm boy born March 22, 1853, accumulated enormous wealth in Chicago beginning as a "cash boy" for the Carson Pirie Scott department store, before pooling his savings to open several downtown lunchrooms. Thrifty, aggressive, and persevering, Kohlsaat acquired controlling interest of the *Times-Herald* from James W. Scott, and the *Chicago Post* for $710,000 on April 20, 1895. He paid cash straight up. He added the *Chicago Record* in 1901 and the *Chicago Inter-Ocean* to his holdings in 1914 after the paper was thrown into receivership.

2. "Cut Off from the World," *Chicago Times-Herald*, November 27, 1895.

3. Ibid.

4. Elwood Haynes (1857–1925), an engineer and automotive pioneer, supervised construction of the first long-distance natural gas pipeline built in the United States. The pipeline connected Chicago with the Trenton Gas Field, a distance of 150 miles from the Windy City. In 1896 he organized the Haynes-Apperson Company with business partners Elmer and Edgar Apperson, to commercially produce automobiles.

5. The faster a tiller-operated machine drove the more dangerous and inefficient it became. Automobile designers borrowed the idea of circular directional control from the nautical industry. Practical and simpler to use than the tiller, which worked best with an uneven number of wheels, the steering wheel made its debut at the seventy-five-mile 1894 Paris-Rouen race—the *world's* first automobile race.

6. *Chicago Times-Herald*, November 28, 1895.

7. It was Duryea's good fortune that his accident occurred near a blacksmith's shop. The obliging smithy welded the steering shaft and sent him on his way to complete the race and claim the prize.

8. "The Duryea Motocycle: Description of the Vehicle That Won the Chicago Race," *Hartford Courant*, December 2, 1895.

9. *Chicago Times Herald*, November 29, 1895.

10. "General News," *Science Magazine* 2, no. 52 (December 27, 1895), 890. On November 2, only three contestants announced that they were road ready, thus forcing a postponement.

11. *Chicago Tribune*, September 20, 1899.

12. John Burress Burdett acquired the "Givens Castle," a famous South Side landmark in the South Side Beverly community from real estate developer Robert Cartwright Givens for the sum of $20,000 on February 11, 1909. The historic three-story gray stone turreted mansion is an architectural Chicago treasure. It is located at 103rd Street and Longwood Avenue, and truly resembles a castle.

13. "Auto Races Called Off," *Chicago Tribune*, August 23, 1905.

CHAPTER 12. THE *ROUSE SIMMONS*

1. "Bob Says Few Christmas Trees Here before 1890s," *Chicago Tribune*, December 20, 1959.

2. "Christmas Ship Lost on the Lake with 17 Aboard," *Chicago Tribune*, December 5, 1912.

3. Ibid.

4. Ibid.

5. "Arrive in Port Crusted with Ice," *Chicago Tribune*, December 8, 1912.

6. "Sells Wreck Trees Today," *Chicago Tribune*, December 11, 1912.

7. Ibid.

8. "Christmas Tree Trade Recalls a Fatal Voyage," *Chicago Tribune*, December 13, 1934.

9. "Finds Message in Bottle From Lost Rouse Simmons," *Chicago Tribune*, July 30, 1913.

10. "Lake's Widow Victim Bringing New Christmas Tree Ship," *Chicago Tribune*, November 23, 1913.

11. "Old Christmas Tree Boat Is Now a Freight Train," *Chicago Tribune*, December 1, 1919.

12. The Illinois Aero Club, with financial backing supplied by Harold F. Mc-Cormick, James Plew, F. L. Mudd, Grover Sexton, and James Stephens, sponsored the August 12–20, 1911, International Aviation Meet, an important chapter in the history of early civil aviation.

13. Delos Avery, "Why Chicago Missed Its Yule Trees in 1912," *Chicago Tribune*, December 24, 1944. Also: Kim Schneider, "The Legend of Northern Michigan's Christmas Tree Ship," mynorth.com, December 24, 2015.

CHAPTER 13. WRIGLEY FIELD BEFORE THE CUBS

1. James A. Gilmore (1876–1947) was a successful coal dealer and manufacturer. He grew up on Chicago's West Side and played amateur baseball with the Wyandottes team in vacant lots at Van Buren and Leavitt Streets.

2. "Gilmore Orders Fight to the Finish on Major Leagues," *Chicago Tribune*, March 9, 1914.

3. "Nearly 50,000 See Ballgames Here," *Chicago Tribune*, May 11, 1914.

4. "Half a Million in Cash on Deadline and Cubs Are His!" *Chicago Tribune*, January 4, 1936.

5. "Chicago Welcomes Feds Who Triumph Over Packers," *Chicago Tribune*, April 24, 1914.

6. Richard Lindberg, "The Chicago Whales and the Federal League of American Baseball 1914–1915," *Chicago History Magazine*, Spring 1981. Weeghman sponsored a contest asking fans to give his "Chi-Feds" a proper nickname. The winner, one D. J. Eichoff of 11451 Hood Avenue, explained that the "biggest commercial whales resided on the North Side," a blatantly fawning appeal to Charlie's vanity as a business titan residing north of Madison Street.

7. "In the Wake of the News," *Chicago Tribune*, August 5, 1959.

8. William Wrigley Jr. (1861–1932), confectionary magnate and a bulwark of the baseball world purchased Santa Catalina Island, located in the Pacific Ocean twenty miles west of Los Angeles with a vow to transform it into the greatest outdoor pleasure resort in the United States. The narrow strip of land, twenty miles long and one-and-a-half to nine miles wide, served as the Cubs spring-training headquarters from 1921 to 1951 (with the exception of the World War II years), but fell well short of fulfilling Wrigley's prophecy. In the 1970s the Wrigley heirs donated 88 percent of land to the Catalina Island Conservancy.

9. "Tennes Knew of Fixing," *Chicago Tribune*, September 26, 1920.

10. "Wrigley Offers Weeghman Aid in Difficulties," *Chicago Tribune*, August 12, 1920.

11. "Gum King Tells Key to Success," *Los Angeles Times*, May 7, 1928.

CHAPTER 14. THE LAST SUPPER . . . ALMOST

1. Founded in Chicago in 1905, the IWW maintained its national headquarters at 1001 West Madison Street. William D. Haywood, international secretary and treasurer, was among twenty-five IWW leaders arrested in Chicago on September 28, 1917, following a federal grand jury indictment charging the movement with plotting sabotage in "an attempt to take possession of the industries of the country."

2. *Chicago Daily Journal*, February 12, 1916.

3. "100 Poisoned; Chef Gone," *Baltimore Sun*, February 13, 1916.

4. "Chum of Cook, Soup Suspect Held by Police, *Chicago Tribune*, February 13, 1916.

5. *Los Angeles Times*, February 13, 1916.

6. "Crones Victims Missed Certain Death by a Slip," *Chicago Tribune*, February 23, 1916. Praised as one of the greatest police officers of his era, Herman F. Schuettler's exploits formed the basis for many true detective stories appearing in the pulp magazines and publications of the day.

7. "Verdigris in Soup Kettle," *Chicago Journal*, February 11, 1916.

8. "New York Police Mobilized for Hunt for Crones," *Chicago Tribune*, February 20, 1916.

9. "Chef Located: Letter Tells Poison Secret," *Chicago Tribune*, February 17, 1916.

10. *Chicago Tribune*, January 2, 1919.

11. "Ptomaines at Feast for New Archbishop," *Chicago Tribune*, February 11, 1916.

12. "Civic Booster Lost in Death of Mundelein," *Chicago Tribune*, October 3, 1939.

CHAPTER 15. THE LEANING TOWER WHY?

1. Contemptuous of the work of Thomas Edison through much of his professional life, inventor and physicist Nicola Tesla was found dead inside his Wyndham New Yorker Hotel room on January 7, 1943. He was eighty-six. In his lifetime Tesla held over three hundred patents, including the "Tesla coil" to amplify low voltages into massive voltages to light up bulbs without wire connections.

2. Inspired by the pioneering work of Tesla and Edison, Schuyler Skaats Wheeler (1860–1923) invented the desktop fan in 1883 with two unshielded blades powered by an electric motor.

3. Architect Alfred S. Alschuler (1876–1940), is the architect of record. The former Ilgfactory has gone the way of so many other vacated manufacturing properties across Chicagoland. Symbolic of the continuous erosion of the city's once vibrant manufacturing base, the plant is today a self-storage facility.

4. In his lifetime, Galileo conducted experiments from atop the Leaning Tower of Pisa to demonstrate that objects of different weight will fall to the ground at the same speed—"to the horror of all erudite men," or so said author H. G. Wells in his epic study of mankind, *The Outline of History*.

5. Mayor Nicholas Blase's forty-seven-year mayoral reign is a record in the United States. James J. Eagan of Florissant, Missouri (north of St. Louis), ranks second. Known as the "Jolly Green Giant" of Florissant, Eagan's tenure began in 1963, two years after Blase's.

CHAPTER 16. A WORLD'S FAIR OF RAILROADING

1. Hollis W. Field, "Chicago's New $12,000,000 R.R. Station Nears Completion," *Chicago Tribune*, September 25, 1910.

2. The staggering increase in transcontinental railroad traffic in the closing decades of the nineteenth century mandated the Northwestern and other passenger lines to enlarge depot and terminal facilities across the city. On October 6, 1906, President Marvin Hughitt of the Northwestern publicly announced a capital development plan to construct a $23.7 million terminal and train sheds on the south bank of the river between Lake Street (north) and Madison (south) and Canal (east) and Clinton (west). The structure displaced several blocks of decayed post-Chicago Fire saloons, shacks, and commercial buildings of the city's Iron District, including the Gault Hotel, once a premier destination for out-of-town visitors.

3. Major Lenox R. Lohr (1891–1968), attached to the Army Corps of Engineers after World War I, is an unsung hero of Chicago business, culture, and philanthropy. He took over management of the foundering Museum of Science and Industry in 1940, and infused the rather dreary and somnambulant space filled with dusty glass display cases and tired-out relics bearing stern warning signs "not to touch," with more interactive exhibits appealing to children.

4. "Railroad Fair Will Continue through September," *Chicago Tribune*, August 25, 1948.

5. Walt Disney (1901–1966), the son of Flora and Roy Disney, was born in a modest frame house on a corner lot at Tripp Avenue and Palmer Street (2156 Tripp Avenue) in Chicago's Hermosa neighborhood.

6. "The Chicagoland Fair," *Chicago Tribune*, June 16, 1957.

CHAPTER 17. THE WINDY CITY SONGBIRD

1. West Side Democratic leader Dennis J. Egan (1870–1924), served as a three-term alderman of the old Ninth Ward, three-term state legislator, bailiff of the municipal court (1920–1924), and Twentieth Ward committeeman, a position of enormous prestige and political influence in Chicago. He was a key member

of the inner circle of party slate makers and a lieutenant of George E. "Boss" Brennan, a national leader of the Democratic Party who maintained his office— and an afternoon pinochle game—on the fourth floor of the Sherman House until his death in August 1928.

2. "State Rests as More Witnesses Accuse Ruth Etting's Ex-Mate," *Los Angeles Times*, December 15, 1938.

3. "Women Find Chicago Always Worst or Best," *Chicago Tribune*, September 27, 1927.

4. John Blades, "Six with a Special Reason to Remember," *Chicago Tribune*, April 27, 1975.

5. Ibid. Vaudeville headliner Lou Clayton teamed with James Durante and Eddie Jackson to form a popular song and dance team that remained together for nearly twenty-five years. Clayton later managed Durante's career.

6. Civic leader, hotelier, restaurateur, and celebrated cabaret promoter Karl Eitel (1871–1954), cofounded the Bismarck Hotel and served as its chairman up until its death. Eitel and his five brothers emigrated from Stuttgart, Germany, in 1891 and launched a family business, Eitel Brothers Importers. They cashed in on the Chicago World's Fair two years later by converting two four-story hotels at Sixty-Third and Cottage Grove into temporary hotels to accommodate the expected crush of visitors to the great exposition. The Bismarck is the Hotel Allegro in the modern day, and the renovated Palace Theater reopened in 1999 as the Cadillac Palace Theater and is operated by Broadway in Chicago. Karl Eitel, his name is inscribed into the cornerstone of the building, was instrumental in the widening of LaSalle Street and the building of the LaSalle Street Bridge.

7. "Radio Star's Secret Husband Shot," *Chicago Tribune*, October 17, 1938.

8. James Simmons, "Star Calls Snyder Wastrel," *Chicago Herald-Examiner*, October 20, 1938.

9. *Chicago Herald-Examiner*, October 20, 1938.

10. *Chicago Herald-Examiner*, October 20, 1938.

11. *Chicago Herald-Examiner*, October 20, 1938.

12. *Chicago Herald-Examiner*, October 20, 1938.

13. *Los Angeles Times*, December 16, 1938.

14. John Blades, "The Thirties," *Chicago Tribune Magazine*, April 27, 1975.

15. "Audience Thunders Approval as Ruth Etting Sings Again, *Baltimore Sun*, March 28, 1947.

16. John Blades, "The Thirties," *Chicago Tribune Magazine*, April 27, 1975.

CHAPTER 18. HOW DALEY SAVED THE PARADE

1. The Saloon Building doubled as Chicago's first official city hall from 1837 to 1842.

2. "Green above the Red," *Chicago Tribune*, March 18, 1896.

3. Archbishop Feehan (1829–1902), born in the county of Tipperary, received ordination as a priest on November 1, 1852. The death of the Rt. Reverend Thomas Foley, administrator of Chicago for the Roman Catholic Church in 1880, led to Feehan's appointment as metropolitan of Chicago on September 10 of that year.

4. "South Side Irish Have a Go at Parading," *Chicago American*, March 18, 1956.

5. Every June, Old St. Patrick's hosts an annual celebration dubbed "The World's Largest Block Party," a summer concert, food fest, and fundraiser drawing thousands of people from across the region to the Near West Side.

6. See Thomas J. O'Gorman, *Beyond the Space of Fifty Years: Mayor Richard J. Daley and the Parade*, official program, March 12, 2005, 76.

7. "Doughty Irish Defy Cold to Honor St. Pat," *Chicago Tribune*, March 18, 1964.

8. "Steve Bailey: Portrait of a Plumber," *Chicago Tribune*, April 4, 1965.

9. "Chicago's St. Patrick's Day Dyer," *Chicago Sun-Times*, July 17, 2016.

CHAPTER 19. HE RAN FOR HIS LIFE

1. The Famous People, "Fifty-Five Inspiring Quotes by Joan of Arc for the Brave Hearts," https://quotes.thefamous people.com/joan-of-arc-1858.php.

2. Located at the southwest tip of Chicago, West Pullman is an amalgam of three "merged" communities—Kensington, Gano, and Pullman. Founded in 1891 by the West Pullman Land Association, European immigrants mostly from Hungary, Italy, Ireland, Poland, and Lithuania landed industrial jobs at International Harvester and the Carter White Lead Paint factory. As factories closed and jobs disappeared, "white flight" ensued following the arrival of African Americans into the community. By 1980, African Americans comprised 80 percent of the West Pullman population. The most recent census data reveals that the community is 93.4 percent black. From 2000 to 2015 the area lost 20 percent of its population base. The departed factories left behind a toxic waste dump and high levels of toxicity the community is still struggling to clean up.

3. Between 1910 and 1920, Gary, Indiana, grew from a town of 16,000 to 55,000. Its remarkable spike in population was due to the availability of mill jobs in flush times, concurrent with rising industrial output experienced all across America following the end of the 1892–1894 recession.

4. Hal Higdon, "The Tireless Candidate," *Chicago Scene Magazine*, February 1964.

5. "Runoff Battles Begin Rumbling on South Side," *Chicago Tribune*, March 8, 1931. This much can be said of the forgotten Healy. He was always punctual and rarely missed a city council meeting.

6. Hal Higdon, "The Tireless Candidate," *Chicago Scene Magazine*, February 1964.

7. Ibid.

8. Ibid.

9. "Jarecki and Lucas Winners," *Chicago Tribune*, April 13, 1938.

10. Dr. Noble J. Puffer completed a record seven terms of office and twenty-eight years as county school superintendent before retiring in August 1967.

11. Hal Higdon, "The Tireless Candidate," *Chicago Scene Magazine*, February 1964. Also, Scott Simon, *Unforgettable: A Son, a Mother and the Lessons of a Lifetime* (New York: Flatiron Books, 2015), 185–86. Also: John Schmidt, "The Constant Candidate," WBEZ (Chicago National Public Radio affiliate) Blogs, November 6, 2012.

12. *Forbes Magazine* Quotes: Thoughts on the Business of Life, https://www.forbes.com/quotes/2239/.

13. Hal Higdon, "The Tireless Candidate," *Chicago Scene Magazine*, February 1964.

14. Hal Higdon, "The Tireless Candidate," *Chicago Scene Magazine*, February 1964, and later in Higdon's *Bobby Kennedy and the Politics of the Sixties*, Kindle. Also: "Put a Chicago McArthur into Wisconsin Race," *Chicago Tribune*, March 1, 1952.

15. Hal Higdon, "The Tireless Candidate," *Chicago Scene Magazine*, February 1964.

16. "A Line O'Type or Two," *Chicago Tribune*, February 17, 1958.

17. Lar Daly campaign advertisement: in John Schmidt, "The Constant Candidate," WBEZ (Chicago National Public Radio affiliate) Blogs, November 6, 2012. https://www.wbez.org/shows/wbez-blogs/the-constant-candidate-lar-daly/dde63413-775e-4f2c-876d-3cbf7df66c1f.

18. Ibid. Daly's platform commentary is listed in this campaign flyer.

19. Harold E. Stassen (1908–2001), called the "Boy Wonder of Republican Politics" in his day, threw his hat in the ring for the presidential nomination nine times between 1948 and 1992.

20. See "Burditt, Illinois G.O.P. Candidate, Puts Mild Criticism between Himself, Nixon," *Chicago Tribune*, March 12, 1974.

21. Hal Higdon, "The Tireless Candidate," *Chicago Scene Magazine*, February 1964.

22. "Equal Time Rule Is Hit by Chief of N.A.B.," *Chicago Tribune*, March 16, 1959. The Federal Communications Commission issued an order on February 19, 1959, directing CBS to provide Daly with equal time. CBS refused to comply and on February 20, the FCC filed a petition for reconsideration. Because it was filed just four days before the February 24 primary election, there was not enough time to review the action, paving the way for Daly to appear on camera. District court judge Julius J. Hoffman later sustained the CBS motion to dismiss Daly's petition for compensatory damages of $146,075 and exemplary

damages of $25,267,187 for violation of Section 315(a). As a result of Daly's manipulations and other fakers encouraged by the FCC ruling, Congress passed a law to exempt news shows from the equal time provisions.

23. *Chicago Tribune*, "TV Officials Unhappily Give Lar Daly Free Time," February 14, 1959.

24. *Chicago Tribune*, "TV Officials Unhappily Give Lar Daly Free Time," February 14, 1959. Sterling "Red" Quinlan (1916–2007)—mentor to many young up-and-coming journalists and show business personalities, including comedian Bob Newhart, director William Friedkin, and news anchor Frank Reynolds—was general manager of the ABC Chicago affiliate WBKB (now WLS) through a dozen formative years extending from the early 1950s through the mid-1960s.

25. "Boo Lar Daly on Paar Show," *Chicago Tribune*, July 8, 1960. Author and radio personality Jack Paar (1918–2004), hosted the *Jack Paar Show* from 1957 to 1962, succeeding former Chicagoan Steve Allen.

26. Hal Higdon, "The Tireless Candidate," *Chicago Scene Magazine*, February 1964.

27. "Lar Daly Remembered for What Really Counted," *Chicago Tribune*, April 22, 1978.

CHAPTER 20. ALL IN A HARD DAY'S NIGHT

1. Mid-America radio powerhouse WLS (the call letters signified "World's Largest Store"—Sears Roebuck and Company) famous for its "National Barn Dance" country music program premiering in 1924, its daily farm reports, and a staple of hillbilly and religious music, converted to an all rock and roll format on May 2, 1960, supplanting WJJD as the main purveyor of the new musical art form in Chicago and the preferred venue for the teenaged listening audience that tuned into "personality radio" disc jockeys," such as Dick Biondi, Sam Holman, Mort Crowley, Gene Taylor, Bob Hale, Ed Grennan, and Jim Dunbar.

2. Elvis Presley, attired in a gold lamé suit, appeared in concert at the International Amphitheater for just one show on March 28, 1957, courtesy of his promoters Lee Gordon, Ben Reyes, and the zealous "Colonel" Tom Parker, a huckster of shrewd commercial instinct. Three hundred uniformed Chicago police officers provided security for the twelve thousand frenzied fans that had paid between $2.75 and $3.50 for a prized ticket. The Memphis rock and roll icon performed sixteen songs in just under forty-seven minutes before racing off-stage. "He fled not like a hound dog but like a jack rabbit," mused Louise Hutchinson in her *Chicago Daily News* review the next day. Presley collected $10,000 in performance royalties that night. It was his first and last Chicago appearance until October 14, 1976. He performed a third and final concert before a Chicago audience ranging in age from "grandmas to grandkids" at the

Chicago Stadium on May 1, 1977. Presley passed away at his Graceland mansion just three months later.

3. Opinionated and controversial newspaper columnist Jack Mabley (1916–2006) bridged eight decades of Chicago journalism, beginning with the *Chicago Daily News* on January 2, 1957. He moved on to the *Chicago American*, *Chicago Today*, and the *Chicago Tribune*, ending his long run with the suburban *Daily Herald* on July 4, 2004. He briefly served as president of the village board in suburban Glenview, Illinois, where it was rumored that his friend Richard Cain (née Scalzetti), former chief investigator for the Cook County sheriff's police during the administration of Richard B. Ogilvie (1962–1966), had personally trained guerilla fighters for covert CIA action in the failed Bay of Pigs invasion of Cuba on April 17, 1961. Mabley's close relationship with Richard Cain came under scrutiny after Cain was convicted of an armed robbery conspiracy to loot the Louis Zahn Drug Company warehouse in Melrose Park with organized crime operatives in October 1963. Mabley made no apologies for his friendship with the shady Richard Cain and remained loyal to him even after Cain's conviction and subsequent imprisonment. The two men exchanged frequent letters during Cain's period of incarceration.

4. "Winning Yeah-Nah Letters," *Chicago American*, September 5, 1964.

5. Ibid.

6. Author interview with Denise Janda, February 18, 2018.

7. *Chicago American*, September 4, 1964; *Chicago Tribune*, September 5, 1984.

8. Elvis Presley's concert promoters convened a press conference in the Saddle and Sirloin Room of the famous restaurant the day of his first Chicago appearance, March 28, 1957.

9. "Teens in a Tizzy—City Safe," *Chicago American*, September 6, 1964.

10. Ibid.

11. Richard Lindberg, *Chicagoly Magazine*, July 6, 2017. Also Jack Mabley, *Halas, Hef, the Beatles and Me* (Chicago: Contemporary Books, 1987), 85.

12. "Mabley's Report: Even Jack Couldn't Hear Jack Onstage," *Chicago American*, September 7, 1964.

13. Ibid.

CHAPTER 21. HUMANITY IN THE HEARTLAND

1. More than eighty thousand of these brick-and-stone dwellings, each with a low-pitched roof, an overhanging eave, an unfinished basement, and a side main entrance on a thirty-foot-wide lot, comprise the "Belt," exclusive of a number of older suburbs including LaGrange, Cicero, and Berwyn. Currently ten Chicago bungalow districts are listed on the National Register of Historic Places.

2. Author interview with Justice Anne McGlone Burke, June 13, 2018.

3. "Dyslexia Facts and Statistics," cited in www.austinlearningsolutions.com. Data sourced from the American Dyslexia Association and the Child Mind Institute. In 1887, German ophthalmologist Professor Rudolf Berlin (1833–1897) of the University of Rostock in Rostock, Mecklenburg-Vorpommern, coined the term *dyslexia*, from the Greek phrase meaning "difficulty with words."

4. Author interview with Justice Anne McGlone Burke, June 13, 2018.

5. Ibid.

6. Author interview with Justice Anne McGlone Burke, June 13, 2018. Three men, I. E. Brown, William Lewis, and Robert Weidensall founded a training camp near Lake Geneva in Williams Bay, Wisconsin, based upon the teaching ideals of George Williams. The camp movement became the university that in turn relocated to the Hyde Park community of Chicago in 1890. The main campus of George Williams College of Aurora University is today back in Williams Bay.

7. Albert Q. Maisel, "Bedlam 1946," *Life Magazine*, May 6, 1946. Psychiatric asylums (or "snake pits" as author Mary Jane Ward called them in her book of the same name), described in the controversial Maisel article have mostly disappeared from the American scene. The notion that individuals suffering mental illness and related conditions need to be housed in a central location or hospital—rather than the services coming to them—has over time, been repudiated by social workers and mental health care professionals.

8. Author interview with Justice Anne McGlone Burke, June 13, 2018.

9. Author interview with Justice Anne McGlone Burke, June 13, 2018.

10. Author interview with Justice Anne McGlone Burke, June 13, 2018.

11. Ulysses to Achilles in William Shakespeare, *Troilus and Cressida*, act 3, scene 3.

12. Freeberg earned his doctorate from Indiana University.

13. The Touch of Nature Environmental Center has since grown to over 3,100 acres.

14. Daniel J. Shannon, the son of Peter M. Shannon whose accounting firm conducted the annual audit of the city of Chicago funds for many years, succeeded William McFetridge in 1969 following McFetridge's death. In August of that year Shannon escorted eighty-four intellectually challenged Chicago children who were scheduled to participate in the Great Lakes Regional Olympics in Akron, Ohio.

15. "McFetridge Tells of Main Park Goals," *Chicago Tribune*, August 20, 1967.

16. "McFetridge Quits Unions," *Chicago Tribune*, August 9, 1967.

17. Author interview with Justice Anne McGlone Burke, June 13, 2018.

18. Author interview with Justice Anne McGlone Burke, June 13, 2018.

19. Author interview with Justice Anne McGlone Burke, June 13, 2018.

20. In 1946, former navy ensign and Yale man R. Sargent Shriver (then an assistant editor at *Newsweek Magazine)* accepted a job offer from Joseph Kennedy to work at the Merchandise Mart. Before marrying Eunice, he lived in the Ambassador East Hotel for a time, and in Karl Eitel's Bismarck Hotel, where powerful Democratic politicians often gathered. His business dealings with Kennedy began after Shriver was asked to read the letters and diaries of his late son, Joseph Jr., who had perished while flying a test plane over Belgium during World War II.

21. Rosemary Kennedy passed away at age eighty-six on January 7, 2005.

22. See: J. N. Oliver, "The Effects of Physical Conditioning Exercises and Activities on the Mental Characteristics of Educationally Sub-Normal Boys," *British Journal of Educational Psychology* 28 (June 1958), 155–65.

23. Author interview with Justice Anne McGlone Burke, June 13, 2018.

24. Lucinda Hahn, "Making History: How Anne Burke Met Eunice Kennedy Shriver and the Special Olympics Began," *Chicago Magazine*, November 2009.

25. Joseph Kennedy purchased the Merchandise Mart from the original owner, Marshall Field and Company, on July 21, 1945, for $15 million. Built over the air rights of the demolished Chicago and Northwestern Railway passenger terminal and opened on May 5, 1930, just east of Wolf Point where the commercial life of the city had begun in the early 1800s, the mart houses ninety-six acres of floor space and six-and-a-half miles of corridors serving wholesalers, retailers, and manufacturers. Until the completion of the Pentagon in Washington, the mart ranked as the world's largest office building. Marshall Field, represented by its president, Hughston M. McBain, liquidated the company's wholesale business in 1935–1937 freeing up nearly eight hundred thousand square feet of unneeded space. The sale was conditional on Kennedy's agreement to ensure that the building's principal business of retail marketing be maintained and upheld. "Chicago has a great commercial and industrial future. It is my hope that in years to come our success in in the Mart undertaking will be such as to make a real contribution to building a Greater Chicago and Midwest," vowed Kennedy, former ambassador to the Court of St. James. In 1947, Joseph Kennedy earmarked a quarter of all income derived from Merchandise Mart operations to fund the Joseph P. Kennedy Jr. Foundation, officially launched one year earlier.

26. Thomas C. Hynes won re-election four times as Cook County assessor (1978–1997). Another former Cook County assessor, James M. Houlihan (serving 1998–2010) headed the Illinois for Robert F. Kennedy campaign in 1968, prior to Senator Kennedy's assassination in Los Angeles in June of that year. He rendered great assistance to Chicago Special Olympics by bringing in Kennedy campaign volunteers to work in Soldier Field that day. North Side resident and park district attorney Neil F. Hartigan (son of former Forty-Ninth

Ward alderman David Hartigan) served as Illinois attorney general, lieutenant governor, and as a justice on the Illinois Appellate Court. In 1990, he lost the Illinois gubernatorial election to Jim Edgar.

27. "Sports for Retarded to Be Held July 20," *Chicago Tribune*, March 30, 1968.

28. "In the Wake of the News," *Chicago Tribune*, July 12, 1968.

29. Avery Brundage (1887–1975), a Chicago building contractor responsible for the construction of a number of lakefront luxury high-rise buildings beginning in the 1920s, served as the fifth president of the International Olympic Committee from 1952 to 1975.

30. Author interview with Justice Anne McGlone Burke, June 13, 2018.

31. "Brave in the Attempt," *Chicago Tribune*, July 19, 2008. The famous quote has been cited in numerous media accounts over the years.

32. "One-Thousand Retarded Kids Compete in Chicago Special Olympics," *Chicago Tribune*, July 21, 1968.

33. Francesca Gattuso, "How It All Began in Chicago 50 Years Ago," *Chicago Sun-Times*, July 8, 2018.

34. R. Sargent Shriver, speech at the Special Olympics Team Summit, Washington, DC, September 17, 1998.

35. Justice Anne McGlone Burke, keynote speech to the Paul Simon Public Policy Institute, Southern Illinois University, October 17, 2007.

BIBLIOGRAPHY

BOOKS

Abbott, Edith. *The Tenements of Chicago: 1908–1935*. New York: Arno Press and the New York Times, 1970.

Alford, Terry. *Fortune's Fool: The Life of John Wilkes Booth*. New York: Oxford University Press, 2015.

Andrews, Wayne. *Battle for Chicago*. New York: Harcourt, Brace and Company, 1946.

Asbury, Herbert. *Chicago: Gem of the Prairie*. New York: Alfred Knopf and Co., 1940.

Bales, Richard. *Great Chicago Fire and the Myth of Mrs. O'Leary's Cow*. Jefferson, NC: McFarland and Company, 2005.

Bourget, Paul Charles. *Outremer: Impressions of America*. London: T. Fisher Unwin Paternoster Square, 1895.

Casey, Robert J. *Chicago Medium Rare: When We Were Both Younger*. New York: Bobbs-Merrill Company, 1949.

Clinton, Craig. *Mrs. Leslie Carter: Biography of the First American Stage Star of the Twentieth Century*. Jefferson, NC: McFarland, 2006.

Cook, Frederick Francis. *Bygone Days in Chicago: Recollections of the Garden City in the Sixties*. Chicago: A. C. McClurg and Company, 1910.

Dale, Elizabeth. *Rule of Justice: Chicago vs. Zephyr Davis*. Columbus, OH: University of Ohio Press, 2001.

Debus, Allen G., ed. *World Who's Who in Science: A Biographical Dictionary of Notable Scientists from Antiquity to the Present* (1st ed.). Chicago, IL: A. N. Marquis, 1968.

Dedmon, Emmett. *Fabulous Chicago: A Great City's History and People*. New York: Random House, 1953.

Dickens, Charles. *American Notes for General Circulation*. London: Chapman and Hall, 1842.

Gale, Edwin O. *Reminiscences of Early Chicago and Vicinity*. Chicago and New York: Fleming H. Revell and Co., 1902.

Gilbert, Paul, and Charles Lee Bryson. *Chicago and Its Makers: A Narrative of Events from the Day of the First White Man to the Inception of the Second World's Fair*. Chicago: Felix Mendelsohn, 1929.

Grant, Bruce. *Fight for a City: The Story of the Union League Club and Its Times, 1880–1955*. Chicago: Rand McNally, 1955.

Grossman, James R., Ann Durkin Keating, and Janice L. Reiff, eds. *The Encyclopedia of Chicago*. Chicago and London: University of Chicago Press, 2004.

Haco, Dion. *The Assassinator of President Lincoln*. New York: T. R. Dawley, Publisher for the Millions, 1865.

Hamilton, Henry Raymond. *The Epic of Chicago*. Chicago: Willett, Clark and Co., 1932.

Hayes, Dorsha B. *Chicago: Crossroads of American Enterprise*. New York: Julian Messner, 1944.

Jacobs, Jane. *The Life and Death of Great American Cities*. New York: Random House, 1961.

Lewis, Lloyd. *Chicago: The History of Its Reputation*. New York: Harcourt Brace and Company, 1929.

Lindberg, Richard. *The Gambler King of Clark Street: Michael C. McDonald and the Rise of Chicago's Democratic Machine*. Carbondale, IL: Southern Illinois University Press, 2009.

———. *Quotable Chicago*. Chicago: Wild Onion Books, 1996.

Mabley, Jack. *Halas, Hef, the Beatles and Me*. Chicago: Contemporary Books, 1987.

Meeker, Arthur. *Chicago with Love*. New York: Alfred A. Knopf, 1955.

Niles City Staff. *Niles Centennial History 1899–1999*. Village of Niles, IL: 1999.

Pacyga, Dominic A. *Chicago: A Biography*. Chicago: University of Chicago Press, 2009.

———. *Slaughterhouse: Chicago's Union Stockyard and the World It Made*. Chicago: University of Chicago Press, 2015.

Rhodehamel, John, and Louise Taper, eds. *Right or Wrong, God Judge Me*. Urbana, IL: University of Illinois Press, 1997.

Royko, Mike. *Boss: Richard J. Daley of Chicago*. New York: E. P. Dutton, 1971.

Sautter, R. Craig, and Edward M. Burke. *Inside the Wigwam: Chicago Presidential Conventions 1860–1996*. Chicago: Wild Onion Books, 1996.

Sawislak, Karen. *Smoldering City: Chicagoans and the Great Fire 1871–1874*. Chicago and London: University of Chicago Press, 1995.

Sawyers, June Skinner. *Chicago Portraits: Biographies of 250 Famous Chicagoans*. Chicago, IL: Loyola University Press, 1991.

Simon, Scott. *Unforgettable: A Son, a Mother and the Lessons of a Lifetime*. New York: Flatiron Books, 2015.

Tyre, William H. *Chicago's Historic Prairie Avenue*. Charleston, SC: Arcadia Publishing, 2008.

Wells, H. G. *The Outline of History: The Whole Story of Man*. London: George Newnes, 1920.

Zorbaugh, Harvey Warren. *The Gold Coast and the Slum: A Sociological Study of Chicago's North Side*. Chicago: University of Chicago Press, 1929.

ARTICLES AND REPORTS

American Dyslexia Association and the Child Mind Institute. "Dyslexia Facts and Statistics." Cited in: https://www.austinlearningsolutions.com/blog/38 -dyslexia-facts-and-statistics.html.

Barrett, Rick. "Resurrecting the Lost Legacy of the Nation's First Policewoman." Unpublished. Edward Burke files.

Boorstein, Daniel J. "A. Montgomery Ward's Mail-Order Business." *Chicago History Magazine* (Spring-Summer 1973).

British Journal of Educational Psychology 28 (June 1958).

Chicagology. "Peter Schuttler Wagon Works." chicagology.com/rebuilding /rebuilding 038/.

Famous People. "Fifty-Five Inspiring Quotes by Joan of Arc for the Brave Hearts." https://quotes.thefamous people.com/joan-of-arc-1858.php.

Forbes Magazine Quotes. Thoughts on the Business of Life. https://www.forbes .com/quotes/2239/.

Fowler, Robert H. "The Tragedy at Ford's Theater." http://washingtonoddities .blogspot.com/2018/06/campbell-hospital-near-washington-dc-by.html.

"General News." *Science Magazine* 2, no. 52 (December 27, 1895).

Hahn, Lucinda. "Making History: How Anne Burke Met Eunice Kennedy Shriver and the Special Olympics Began." *Chicago Magazine* (November 2009).

Hall, James O., and Michael Maione. *To Make a Fortune: John Wilkes Booth Following the Money Trail*. Clinton, Maryland: Surratt Society, 2018. Booklet.

Higdon, Hal. "The Tireless Candidate." *Chicago Scene Magazine*, February 1964.

Holland, Evangeline. "Fascinating Women: Mrs. Leslie Carter." http://www. edwardianpromenade.com.

Kansas State Historical Society. "Kansapedia." www.kshs.org/kansapedia/joseph -mccoy/17219.

Kearney, Joseph D., and Thomas W. Merrill. "Private Rights in Public Lands: The Chicago Lakefront, Montgomery Ward, and the Public Dedication Doctrine." Northwestern University School of Law, 2011. Faculty Publication.

Lindberg, Richard. "The Chicago Whales and the Federal League of American Baseball 1914–1915." *Chicago History Magazine* (Spring 1981).

Lupton, John A. "Illinois Supreme Court History: Montgomery Ward and the Chicago Lakefront." Supreme Court Historic Preservation Committee (March 2018).

Lynch, Christopher. "Marching Forward." *The 56th Annual Chicago Saint Patrick's Day Parade Program Booklet* (March 12, 2011).

Maisel, Albert Q. "Bedlam 1946." *Life Magazine* (May 6, 1946).

O'Gorman, Thomas J. *Beyond the Space of Fifty Years: Mayor Richard J. Daley and the Parade.* Official program (March 12, 2005).

Packard, George. "Some Interesting Cases Decided by Justice Cartwright." *Illinois Law Review* 15 (November 1920).

Riis, Roger William. "The Man Who Made Standard Time." *Rotarian* (November 1950).

Schneider, Kim. "The Legend of Northern Michigan's Christmas Tree Ship." mynorth.com.

Sinclair, Upton. "What Life Means to Me." *Cosmopolitan Magazine* (October 31, 1906).

The Trial of the Alleged Assassins and Conspirators at Washington City, D.C., May and June 1865: For the Murder of President Abraham Lincoln; Full of Illustrative Engravings. Philadelphia: T. B. Peterson and Brothers, 1865. Indiana State Library and Internet Archive. http://www.archive.org/details /trialofallegedas00john.

Yale Quarterly Review (December 1895).

Zochert, Donald. "Heinrich Schliemann's Chicago Journal." *Chicago History Magazine* (Spring-Summer 1973).

PAPERS AND LEGAL DOCUMENTS

Belasco, David. Papers (1853–1931). Billy Rose Theater Division of the New York Public Library for the Performing Arts.

Patterson, Boyd Crummins. Papers. "The Story of Elisha Gray." Edited and prepared for publication by Assistant Professor Frank Merrill for the Historical Collection of Washington and Jefferson College Library, Washington, Pennsylvania.

United States v. American Bell Telephone Co., 128 US 315 (1888), argued October 9–10, 1888. Justia Legal Resources, justia.com.

NEWSPAPERS

Baltimore Sun
Chicago American
Chicago Daily Journal
Chicago Daily News
Chicago Globe

Chicago Herald and Examiner
Chicago Inter-Ocean
Chicago Mail
Chicago Sun-Times
Chicago Times
Chicago Times-Herald
Chicago Tribune
Hartford Courant
Los Angeles Times
Mansfield New Journal
New York Times
Niles Herald-Spectator
Niles Journal
Washington Post

INDEX

Page numbers in italics indicate illustrations.

Green Bay Packers, 37
Greenfield Village, 168
Gregory, Dudley S., 72
Grennan, Ed, 239n1
Griebel Corporation, 145
Gross, William, 22
Guilfoyle, Eleanor (Daley), 182
Gulf of Tonkin Resolution, 196

Haas, Frederick C., 121
Hale, Bob, 239n1
Hall, Mrs. Charles, 113
Hamburg Athletic Club, 182
Hamilton, Henry Raymond, 13
Hamline, John H., 97
Hammerstein, Oscar, 38
Hancock, John, 32
Hanecy, Elbridge, 97,99
Hanley's House of Happiness, 181
Harlem Race Track, 125
Harris, Daniel, 132
Harrison, Benjamin, 66
Harrison, Carter, I, 65, 180
Harrison, Carter, II, 98, 116, 132, 135, 144
Harrison, George, 187–98, 200
Harrison School, 54
Harris Theater, 100
Hartigan, David, 243n26
Hartigan, Neil F., 209, 242n26
Harvard College Observatory, 65
Havenor, Charles, 139
Havusiak, Chris, 163
Hawes, Kirk, 58, 224n11
Hayes, Nellie Mahoney, 19–20
Haymarket Riot, 56–57, 224n9
Haymie, James, 12
Haynes, Elwood, 121–22, 124
Haynes-Apperson Company, 231n4
Haywood, William D., 145, 234n1
Healy, John F., 187, 189, 237n5

Henderson, Reverend Mr., 58–59
Henrietta (Sister), 204
Henry, Clarence "Frogman," 201
Henshaw, H. H., 55
Herostratus, 7
Herrick, Genevieve Forbes, 171
Heydler, John, 142
Hickey, Rachel, 60
Higdon, Hal, 187
Highland Park Presbyterian Church, 45
Hight, Jennie, 7
Hilton, Conrad, 169
Hoffman, Julius, 238n22
Holabird and Roche, 229n15
Holloway, Charles, 119
Holly, Charles "Buddy," 179
Holman, Sam, 239n1
Holmes, Mary Ann, 217n5, 217n11, 218n17
Holum, Dianne, 210
Home for Destitute Crippled Children, 52
Home for the Friendless, 51
Hooley's Theater, 78
Hopkins, Miriam, 82
Horan, James J., 39
Horn, James, 22
Horn, Milton, 102
Hornung, Paul, 210
Hotel Allegro, 236n6
Hotz, Catherine, 109
Hotz, Christoph, 109–10
Hotz, Robert S., 109
Houlihan, James, 209, 242n26
House of the Good Shepherd, 52
Howe School for Boys, 112
Howland, George, 65
Hubbard, Gardiner, 49
Hubbard, George W., 56
Hubbard, Gurdon Saltonstall, 104–5

RICHARD C. LINDBERG is an award-winning author, journalist, and lecturer who has written and published nineteen earlier books about Chicago history, politics, criminal justice, sports, and ethnicity. The 2011 memoir of his Northwest Side boyhood, *Whiskey Breakfast: My Swedish Family, My American Life*, was named nonfiction book of the year by the Chicago Writers Association. His 2017 institutional history, *Northeastern Illinois University: The First 150 Years*, and a 2009 biography, *The Gambler King of Clark Street: Michael C. McDonald and the Rise of Chicago's Democratic Machine*, were honored for original research and scholarship by the Illinois State Historical Society. Lindberg is a past president of the Society of Midland Authors and the Illinois Academy of Criminology, and serves on the board of directors of the Illinois State Historical Society. He has appeared on *CBS News Nightwatch* and has been a commentator on numerous local and national television and radio stations such as A&E, the History Channel, Investigation Discovery, the Travel Channel, National Public Radio, PBS, and others. He resides in Chicago, his hometown, with his wife, Denise.